THE POLITICAL CAMPAIGN DESK REFERENCE

A Guide for campaign managers, professionals and candidates running for office

Second Edition

MICHAEL MCNAMARA

DENVER, COLORADO

The Political Campaign Desk Reference
A Guide For Campaign Managers, Professionals and Candidates Running for Office - 2nd Edition
All Rights Reserved.
Copyright © 2012 Michael McNamara
v2.0

Outskirts Press, Inc.
http://www.outskirtspress.com

ISBN: 978-1-4327-8732-5

Library of Congress Control Number: 2012904807

Outskirts Press and the "OP" logo are trademarks belonging to Outskirts Press, Inc.

PRINTED IN THE UNITED STATES OF AMERICA

Table of Contents

Acknowledgements

The Political Campaign Desk Reference was made possible with the help of many people. I want to thank Terry Grundy, professor at the University of Cincinnati, for encouraging me to finish my manuscript and using it in his classes on Urban Lobbying. Joe Statzer, one of my business partners, was invaluable in assisting with content. Thank you also to all of the candidates that I have assisted throughout the years. Most of all, thanks go to my wife, Lisa, for her editing skills and her English degree as well as her belief in me.

Introduction

Since I wrote the first edition of *The Political Campaign Desk Reference*, much has changed in the political world. I finished writing in May of 2008 as the Democrats and Republicans were solidifying who their choices for President were. The 2008 election employed more tactics and more money than any other Presidential campaign had previously.

The Internet and social media now play a greater role in campaigning than they ever have before. In fact, while the first edition of *The Political Campaign Desk Reference* was in production, the Internet surpassed newspapers as the primary method by which Americans receive their information. Many of the people who bought and read the first edition have asked me to expand my discussion of technology and its uses.

Technology also changed the way in which we communicate. I purchased my first "smart phone" the weekend before the first edition of *The Political Campaign Desk Reference* was released due to the outages caused by Hurricane Ike. I have replaced the "land line" phone in my home that I only used for my security system for a cellular device that now connects my security company to my house. It's more reliable and cheaper than the old land line. I carry around my phone, e-mail, apps, and everything I need to communicate in my front pocket, and many voters have followed suit. We access our social media sites, text, and e-mail on the go, anywhere our service provider allows us.

Although technology has changed, the fundamentals of campaigning have not. I have incorporated discussions that involve the Internet and technology as part of the tactical portion of this book, and my discussion of Internet tactics has broadened since the first edition. However, I still place the bulk of the focus on the rudiments of good strategy, message development, aesthetics (image), and delivery. The Internet provides campaigns with another effective means, and often cheaper means, of message delivery and information gathering.

One of the greatest strategists, and the most read strategist, in the history of the world taught that a general who calculates and plans before setting out on a military campaign will most likely succeed over a general who plans very little. Sun Tzu was a military consultant centuries before Jesus walked the earth, but military leaders and campaign consultants read his words today. Sun Tzu wrote *The Art of War* which has become the standard by which successful generals, consultants, captains of industry, politicians, educators, and many other professionals employ to get ahead and stay ahead.

This manual is designed to provide an overview of the most important components of a campaign from grassroots to fundraising. *The Political Campaign Desk Reference* will guide the reader through the basic steps of planning and running a successful campaign. It does not reveal all of the secrets and strategies that I have learned and employed throughout the years. There are elements to campaigning that only experience and battle can teach. Learning occurs in the field and not merely by reading books.

What this manual will do, however, is provide guidance to a candidate or campaign manager. I hope that the information in this book will give the reader an advantage over an unsuspecting opponent.

This book will not win campaigns, and it will not raise money. Only a candidate and a candidate's committee can do that. I strongly urge readers of *The Political Campaign Desk Reference* to employ the tactics and strategies outlined herein. And if your opponent also has a copy of this book, then you should hope that he will discard the information or only use his copy as a conversation piece. This manual provides the direction, but your campaign is the vehicle of success.

A first-time candidate facing strong opposition should always consider hiring an experienced campaign consultant or manager. That first campaign is what will lay the groundwork for a possible career in public service in elected positions of trust. In fact, even seasoned candidates who have been through many political battles would be wise to employ a professional, and they often do. A consultant will not perform all of the grunt work on a campaign, but he or she will be able to give it form. A skilled manager or consultant can employ the information in this book and create a plan and team that will be a formidable force in any election of any size.

The necessities to success are superiority in the four major resources of a campaign: time, information, money and people. The key to unlocking those resources and winning is careful planning, deliberate actions, well thought-out messaging and professionally executed delivery of the message. The details are truly important in planning, and a campaign should not be plotted out in a single evening. Care and time must be put into gathering and processing information.

It is important to point out that some campaigns are referenced in this book to illustrate a point. In the Appendix section, however, I use a fictitious candidate running for a fictitious elected seat in a fictitious county. The appendices help to demonstrate some examples of what various campaign materials will look like or to further assist the candidate or campaign manager reading *The Political Campaign Desk Reference*.

Looking back on my many experiences in politics, I remember my experience working with the White House Advance teams in 2002 and 2003 for their attention to detail. When people see the President or any Executive officer in whatever medium, they are seeing a production of near Hollywood magnitude. Even if the appearance seems impulsive, or it is a short stop, every detail has been worked out well in advance. Everything from the place where reporters can stand to take their pictures to the creases in the flag behind the President, every detail has been meticulously planned, executed and checked by another team member (if the advance team is doing their job properly).

Well run campaigns are the same way. Each detail should be methodically planned well in advance and then executed. There will always be moments when a campaign must adjust because of unforeseen circumstances. A good plan will allow for these adjustments and will be able to quickly adapt.

Luck is generally not a factor one should count on in winning a campaign, so I will not wish you luck. I will wish you well and urge you to work hard. The euphoria you will feel at the moment of victory makes the many months of effort working up to it worthwhile.

Happy campaigning!

Michael McNamara

Chapter 1

Getting Started

1.1   Strategy Vs. Tactics

One of the biggest mistakes that a campaign can make is thinking that putting a candidate's name on the ballot and throwing up some yard signs is a strategy for winning. Going through the process of placing the name on the ballot and distributing yard signs are merely tactics that should be part of a larger strategy, or winning plan.

A strategy for winning should be planned out far in advance of the campaign. This does not mean that a candidate cannot win without a plan, but if a candidate simply gets their name on the ballot and decides to make a few signs, they are at a disadvantage to an opponent who has methodically strategized their campaign months in advance.

Voters are more sophisticated than a candidate without a plan gives them credit. Especially in local races that do not occur in presidential or gubernatorial election years, often referred to as "off-year" elections, voters who go to the polls are usually more educated about the local issues and candidates. A candidate without a plan that includes a message, budget, timeline and tactical component will not stand much of a chance against a candidate who does have a plan.

The Political Campaign Desk Reference will use the terms "strategy" and "plan" almost interchangeably. Later in the book, specific tactics are discussed, but tactics are part of a plan. Tactics should never be confused with being the plan. Tactics are the methods by which the campaign plan is executed. The strategy is the plan for the use of the tactics, and this strategy should be well thought out. The tools in *The Political Campaign Desk Reference* are designed to develop a campaign plan for campaign managers and candidates running for office.

When a campaign consultant and prospective candidate first sit down to meet, the consultant should always ask what the candidate's strategy is. Because the candidate is seeking the advice of a consultant, there probably will not be much of a plan in place. The consultant will hear a few tactics from the candidate's perspective. It is the consultant's responsibility to take the vision and the ideas of the candidate and incorporate them into the larger plan. A good consultant will also be able to tell a candidate what tactics are not good ideas and show them how certain tactics will not fit into a specific plan.

If a campaign enters a race without a strategy, then it will merely engage in a few tactics with no guidance on how those tactics are making the goal of victory a reality. A campaign must plan if it wishes to win.

1.2   When Is It Too Early To Start?

Prospective candidates often ask the question "when is it too early to start?" A good counter question to prospective candidates is "when is it too early to start planning for college or a career or a major life change?" The answer is that it is never too early to start preparing for a run for office once the idea strikes. That does not mean to say that a candidate should hire a political consultant five years before an election, but there are a lot of things that a candidate can do in the early stages of a campaign that help to mold the plan.

In later chapters of *The Political Campaign Desk Reference*, the importance of a campaign database is discussed. Gathering other information is also important. Prospective candidates should be knowledgeable about a district and know the people they wish to represent. Candidates for office often have some stake in a jurisdiction other than residing there. Sometimes a candidate is a business owner, a parent of a child in the local school district, or a prospective candidate is active in local organizations. Other opportunities exist for prospective candidates to get involved long before a run such as joining one of the volunteer boards that a local government may have such as a zoning board or levy review committee.

It is never too early to begin working towards running for office. By getting involved in the community, a candidate learns important issues, makes invaluable connections to community leaders, builds a cadre of friends that can become supporters and demonstrates a vested interest in the community.

Not every candidate must do these things to win, but remember that voters in local, off-year elections tend to be savvier about local politics. Voter participation is lower in off-year elections. Voters who respond to more popular politicians and elections (presidential and gubernatorial), are less likely to come out on election day if local elections are not held in those years. Getting involved locally is important before running locally. But getting involved locally also means that a prospective candidate has started the journey of running for office.

Someone reading *The Political Campaign Desk Reference* might put the book down in disgust at this point because they are thinking of a specific instance in which they remember someone running for office who they feel attained the office simply because the candidate had a popular last name. Although a candidate who has a strong political pedigree (coming from a family active in politics) and a popular last name may have achieved victory in an election, one should not assume that this victory came without a strategy and years of preparation.

Hillary Clinton moved from Arkansas to New York and became a United States Senator within a very short time. Although her popularity and public background allowed her to make such a bold move, she did not gain this level of stature overnight. Her move also was most likely not made on a whim. Her victory was part of a process of careful planning, and her decades of experience and work were what paid off when she ran for United States Senate. The Clinton example is one that some may feel breaks the rule of careful planning, but it is actually an example that supports the rule and that it is never too soon to start preparing.

1.3   Questions Every Candidate Must Answer

There are probably as many reasons for running for office as there are candidates running for office. Sometimes a candidate is disgusted at the way the current administration is running the show. Perhaps a candidate runs for office for professional advancement. Some candidates have made an entire career out of public service and have never held a job in any other sector. Others may want to run because they honestly believe they can make a difference. Sometimes a candidate represents a movement. Whatever the reason a candidate chooses to run for office, there are a few questions that must first be answered.

1.   *Why am I running for office? (the "why" question)*

It seems basic enough, but if a candidate has made it public that he or she is running for office without thinking it through, this basic question can lead to embarrassing situations, and worse – lost votes. Few things are worse for a candidate than to be caught off guard by a basic question like this one when at a debate, in a public setting or going door-to-door and not knowing what to say. Every candidate needs to know the reason(s) for running for office.

In addition to having an answer for this question, it is important to have a well thought out answer that the candidate is confident in giving. It needs to be credible and sound as though some thought has been put into it. Delivery of the answer should be practiced to the point that the candidate can present his or her reason without much thought. Candidates should look forward to answering this question because it is the first one everyone will ask - including the press.

One may think that only a new candidate could make such a blunder as not preparing for this question. One of the best examples of how a seasoned candidate from a political family can make the mistake of not thoroughly preparing this question is the Presidential Election of 1980. Massachusetts Senator Edward "Ted" Kennedy had made the decision to run for President against incumbent James "Jimmy" Carter in the Democratic Primary. Carter was progressively unpopular, and Kennedy's campaign had gained steam. Just as Kennedy seemed perched on the cusp of becoming the popular Democratic candidate and snatching the nomination from Carter, Kennedy agreed to appear on a television interview. The interview was the opportunity that Kennedy had waited for to take center stage and steal the show. Unfortunately, he was ill prepared and failed to adequately answer some of the questions including the basic question of why he was running for President. Kennedy's popularity and seriousness as a candidate plummeted, and he lost the Primary to the widely unpopular Carter, who in turn lost to Ronald Reagan later in 1980.

The best answers to the "why" question include the message of the campaign, which is a topic that *The Political Campaign Desk Reference* will cover. For example, a candidate may be running for office in a mayoral race in which the current mayor has done a seemingly poor job or there are specific points of weakness that the incumbent will face. The challenger in the race should use these weaknesses in the answer along with the campaign message. Perhaps this challenger's slogan is "Time for a change", and the point of weakness of the incumbent is the fact that crime has increased under his watch. When asked why the challenger is running, he or she might say:

"I'm running because my neighbors and community leaders feel that we need change. Crime is increasing with no sign of getting better, and we need to keep our families and neighborhoods safe."

This candidate answered the question saying that "neighbors and community leaders" agree that change is needed and uses the promise of safety to appeal to the voters. An answer like the one used above would generally appeal to voters. This particular answer may flop if the proper research is not conducted beforehand to determine that crime truly is a major issue. Perhaps job loss is the biggest issue on the minds of voters. Researching the issues will be covered later in *The Political Campaign Desk Reference* as well. The point is simply to have an answer to the "why" question that is effective, practiced and natural. A good answer should contain the message of the campaign.

A winning campaign once used a slogan that answered the "why" question. The slogan on all of the signs, letterhead, stickers and literature said "…because our taxes are too high." This slogan was used by a challenger, and the incumbent lost by a very large margin. Although a slogan and answer to this initial question are not the only components that won that campaign, the reason for running for office was used effectively. The message was integrated into the larger plan.

2.   *For what office am I running, and what are the qualifications for, and duties of, the position?*

It is surprising how many candidates will jump into a race without a firm understanding of the duties of the job for which they are running. For countywide offices and legislative offices, state laws will often delineate the statutory duties of an office. For city or municipal seats, local laws, in addition to any state laws, may dictate the requirements and expectations of officeholders. It is important to gain a thorough understanding of the duties of the job prior to going public with an announcement of candidacy. This information is generally available through publications at any local board of elections or comparable agency. Most of the time, information on job requirements and duties is easily accessible on the Internet and may even be more current. The best resource may be the institutional knowledge from a person who has previously held the position being sought assuming that person is competent.

Also, it is important to understand any prerequisites for running for office. Some professional offices such as judge, prosecutor or sheriff may require professional training in order to be qualified to run. Furthermore, almost every office requires potential candidates to gather a certain number of signatures on a petition by a certain date for a candidate to be able to get on the ballot. If a board of elections or elections clerk requires 50 valid signatures in order to appear on the ballot, a candidate should gather three times the requirement or 150 signatures because it is rare for all signatures on a petition to be valid. Filing fees also often apply to run for office, and these fees are generally nominal and non-prohibitive. If a filing fee is cost prohibitive, there may be remedies available to potential candidates in order to waive the fee, but a candidate should seriously consider whether waging a campaign is a good idea if a nominal filing fee creates such a burden.

One important factor in seeking office is making sure the candidate meets residency requirements. Some races do not require a candidate to live within the jurisdiction of the office being sought. Most offices do require candidates to live within the jurisdiction. It is not advisable to run for an office if the candidate lives outside the jurisdiction or if the candidate recently moved to live within the district for the sole purpose of seeking office. A candidate must be able to answer questions as to qualifications for office as well as residency. Although moving into a district does not prevent a candidate's success, such as in the Hillary Clinton example, a candidate does not want to derail the campaign's message by not adequately handling inevitable charges of opportunism.

3.   *How much do I plan on spending, and how much am I willing to contribute myself?*

Determining how much a campaign will cost will be covered later in *The Political Campaign Desk Reference*. One key measure of determining the success of a campaign is how much a candidate will spend. There are many stories of candidates who win a race being outspent by many times by their opponent. Making decisions on such anecdotal information without knowing the other factors involved in the campaign in question is a common misstep in campaigns for the less experienced. There are many facets that go into a campaign that give certain candidates "political equity".

Political equity can be manifest in different ways such as the amount of name recognition a candidate has, high public satisfaction a candidate has (favorability), incumbency or other factors. For example, a candidate coming from a local family that is well known and has high favorability may already have a leg up on other candidates, which can cause the challengers to spend more money to make up the perceived difference. Therefore, each campaign is unique and requires decisions about money to be made irrespective of the success of the candidate in another campaign.

Once a general budget is determined for a race, the candidate must decide how hard he or she will work to raise the necessary funds. A candidate must also make a decision on whether to make up the difference if the fundraising goal is not met. Some candidates will take a mortgage or second mortgage out on their homes in order to finance a campaign for office. Taking personal risk in the form of mortgages adds to the stress of a campaign and can lead to candidates making bad emotional decisions if there is no campaign manager or consultant making spending decisions in a race. Personal wealth is a legitimate means of financing a campaign as well.

Fundraising methods and sources will be discussed in a later chapter, but the point is to know that every contested campaign, no matter the size, requires a significant financial commitment, and a candidate must make the decision before running if he or she is willing to do whatever it takes to fulfill that commitment. If not, building a campaign plan on an unrealistic budget is almost as bad as having no campaign plan at all.

4. *Is there anything in my background that can embarrass me or my family or fatally distract the campaign?*

All candidates are human.

That means that no matter who is running for office, no matter what their pedigree or their last name, no matter what school they went to or how much money they make or what church they go to, they have made mistakes and will make mistakes in the future. This is part of the human condition.

If a candidate employs a professional campaign consultant, it is important to disclose this information in confidence. A true professional will never reveal this candidate's indiscretions that were disclosed in confidence. It is not a professional consultant's place to judge a candidate, because the consultant is also human, and the consultant has also made mistakes and will make mistakes in the future. If a professional consultant finds the past indiscretions of a client too egregious to work past the initial meeting when this question should be discussed, then the consultant should treat the information the same way an attorney or priest would.

Once a candidate has conducted an honest self-evaluation, then the issues of a situation, vote or youthful indiscretion can be dealt with. Figuring out how to deal with a potential issue is much easier before it becomes a campaign issue than after. Dealing with the indiscretion can be worked into the campaign plan.

An opponent with an opposition research component to his campaign plan will most likely find out about any past votes or indiscretions. Voters understand that candidates are human and prone to mistakes and indiscretions. Something that campaigns throughout history have discovered is the ability for voters to forgive. One thing that voters will seldom forgive, however, is being lied to. Once voters feel as though they have been deceived, it is difficult, if not impossible, to regain trust or traction. An example of this rule is Congressman Anthony Weiner's handling of a personal indiscretion. He used social media on the Internet to send photos of himself to a female that was not his wife. Instead of leveling with the media and his constituents about what he did, he attempted to cover it up and suggested that someone "hacked" his account. The story hounded him every day until he resigned his position.

Would Congressman Weiner have survived, politically speaking, if he was honest about what he did? That will never be known, but once he was caught in his lie, his fate seemed sealed.

The best advice for a candidate is to be honest. Be honest on the self-evaluation. Be honest with the campaign consultant, and if the voters eventually find out, then be honest with the voters. It is easier to ask for forgiveness on one indiscretion rather than lie to voters and hope for forgiveness for two indiscretions.

The four basic questions in Chapter 1 are questions that should be answered before any formal announcement for office is made. If these questions are thought out and answered ahead of time, a candidate will be ahead of the game when the petitions for office are validated.

1.4 Strengths and Weaknesses

Before waging a campaign, a serious candidate should perform a self-evaluation as well as an assessment of any opponent. The easiest, and best, way to do this is by creating a chart for the candidate and a chart for each opponent. The chart is simple – write the name of the candidate at the top of a sheet of paper, draw a line down the middle of the paper and on one side, write "Strengths", and write "Weaknesses" on the other side. Create a new sheet for each potential opponent. It is usually helpful to do this with the inner circle of advisors identified for the team – a subject detailed in a later chapter.

In creating these charts in a meeting setting, using a marker and large pad of paper made for easels is most effective because the different sheets can be taped to the wall. The entire team can see the strengths and weaknesses of the candidates in the race.

In determining strengths and weaknesses, it is important to include experience, public voting record, fundraising capability, name recognition/identification (name ID), issues of the race, age, health, capabilities of each candidate, party affiliation, endorsements, individual supporters and every other factor that a team can think of regardless of how insignificant it is.

Sometimes a personal quality might show up in both the "Strengths" column as well as the "Weaknesses" column. For instance, youth and inexperience might be seen as a weakness. Waging a "time for a change" challenger campaign, those qualities could also be seen as strengths. Another example of something that can be both a strength and a weakness is a voting record. Officeholders who have been in office for a term or more have established a voting record. Raising taxes might put the voting record in the weaknesses column whereas heralding popular legislation may also put the voting record in the strengths column.

Candidate		Opponent	
Strengths	Weaknesses	Strengths	Weaknesses
Female	Single	Master's degree	Young
Incumbent	Female	Formerly held job	Lost to opponent
Raised $100,000	Only bachelor's degree	Married with children	Spent taxpayer money on stationary
Lowered office budget	No officeholder endorsements	Well-known name	Oversaw largest budget in office history
Improved computer system		Endorsed by Sheriff	Not much money

Assume that opponents will employ this same technique of listing strengths and weaknesses. If they are honestly evaluating their opponent's campaign, they will put similar details in both columns as well.

During this session of listing strengths and weaknesses, it is important to list any "baggage". Although the people who share in this knowledge must be trusted to keep it confidential, it is important to be open and honest with the "inner circle." A candidate must assume that if they have personal matters such as past convictions, marital indiscretions, experimentation with drugs or any other "indiscretion" that their opponent will find out and use it. Crafting a campaign plan without considering these factors because they are "private" or personally embarrassing could spell disaster or political death later on in the campaign. Everyone is human and makes mistakes in life. Making mistakes does not disqualify one for office, but not handling the issue responsibly with an electorate that wants politicians who are direct and honest could lead to political death. Remember the Congressman Weiner example.

Lists of strengths and weaknesses that the team creates should be kept for future reference – they will be used often during the planning stages of the campaign and should be referenced periodically throughout the campaign.

Only the individuals directly related to the strategy of the campaign should have access to these lists. If someone is a loose talker or is slightly untrustworthy, then that person should not be invited to participate in this process or be privy to its results. The security and confidentiality of campaign information is extremely important. Information "leaks" often occur on campaigns in which someone "in the know" begins talking to another person about the campaign. If the person who has confidential information wants to impress someone with their knowledge of the campaign, their closeness to a candidate, or for any other reason divulges confidential information, then the campaign has been compromised. Politics is built upon people who have many relationships and networks. It is hard to tell who knows whom and who may inadvertently let information leak to the opponent's campaign. A successful campaign must be vigilant about its security of information.

1.5   Gathering Political and Historic Data

A local board of elections or elections clerk will have valuable information needed to target voters, build a campaign database, budget and raise funds. The required items include:

- Requirements, forms and fees for running for office
- Election results for past elections
- Voter database for the district of the campaign
- Campaign finance reports

Requirements, forms and fees for running for office

Before running for office, candidates must acquire certain forms from the local elections office. Candidates must often obtain a prescribed number of signatures on petitions in order to qualify for the office being sought. There are also nominal filing fees that must accompany completed petitions. Every candidate plays by the same rules, and the forms required by the elections office are also public record. There are also timelines associated to the proper filing of forms. A candidate should always be familiar with deadlines for filing the required petitions and paying the required fees.

Once a filing deadline has passed, it is easy to find out who the official candidates are in a race. At this point, a campaign should acquire copies of the petitions and forms that any opponents have filed. A candidate may be able to gauge important information from these forms such as who is supporting the opponent and when and where the petitions were circulated. Sometimes a campaign may find an issue that will result in a challenge to an opponent's petition. Different elections offices require varying levels of information, but obtaining opposition forms is a good start to the opposition research file.

Election results for past elections

In order to target areas to focus resources, it is important to retrieve precinct-by-precinct results for past campaigns for the same office being sought. For instance, a city council campaign will want the results by precinct for the last two city council elections. A county commission candidate will want precinct-by-precinct results for the last two county commission races. If a challenger is running against an incumbent, then the challenger will want results of his opponent's last race.

Studying the results from past elections will help a candidate become familiar with their jurisdiction. Results will indicate which precincts turn voters out to the polls as well as precincts that have barely any turnout. By studying these results, a candidate will know which areas have the strongest turnout and where to spend time and resources on a campaign.

In a race in which a candidate is challenging an incumbent, it is important to examine results from the incumbent's past election(s). It is important for the incumbent to do this as well in order to find areas of strength as well as weakness. Targeting techniques will be discussed later in *The Political Campaign Desk Reference*, but knowing what to ask for and why in the "footwork" phase of the campaign is important.

Voter database for the district of the campaign

The voter database is a wealth of information. It is important to ask for as much information for each voter as the elections official can provide. A proper elections office should be able to provide the database in an electronic format that is easily convertible to off-the-shelf database or spreadsheet software. Information that an elections office might provide for voters includes:

- Voter history (when a voter voted and his/her party)
- Date of birth (or year if full dates are unavailable)
- Address
- School district
- Congressional district
- Legislative district(s)
- Judicial district(s)
- Phone (not all elections offices acquire these)
- e-mail (not all elections officials acquire these)

For city council races, candidates should only acquire voter information for the city. The same rule applies for county seats or school districts or judicial districts. Sometimes a race crosses county lines and the elections official in multiple counties should be contacted for the appropriate voter information.

The voter database is only valuable if it has the voter history for each voter in the jurisdiction for the office being sought. A campaign needs to be able to determine when the voters voted and for what party they are voting in primary races or races where data for party affiliation is available. With the voter database, a campaign will be able to determine who the most devoted voters are and who the inconsistent voters are as well as those who may never consider voting for a candidate based on party affiliation. Furthermore, a campaign can target voters based on age if date of birth is included.

Campaign finance reports

Campaign finance reports are a wealth of information for candidates and campaign managers. In a race against an incumbent or someone who has run for office before, a campaign should obtain the historic finance reports of its opponent. From these, one can determine who has supported the opponent in the past, how much the opponent can potentially raise and the source of funds for past campaigns (self-funding versus fund raising) and if the campaign has any debt. But campaign finance reports have so much more information.

Campaign finance reports can also provide valuable leads on who may potentially give to any campaign. For this reason, a campaign will want to retrieve as many reports as possible for people in the area of the race. In a partisan race, a campaign can save a lot of time, effort and money by not retrieving the finance reports of the opposing party, except for the reports of the opponent. Campaign finance reports usually contain information about donors including the amount of giving, the date of giving and the donor's address. Some jurisdictions have rules about the use of campaign finance reports for prospecting potential donors. It is important to know the rules and abide by them.

Campaign finance reports may also be a source of campaign issues.

For instance, if a significant portion of a candidate's finances come from out-of-state donors, then an opponent may want to question why that is. If a significant portion of a candidate's finances can be traced to donors who work in a certain industry, a valid question to ask during a campaign is what interest that industry has in that candidate. Whatever the reason, a well run campaign will obtain appropriate campaign finance reports.

1.6   Identify Issues

In a race that gains high voter attention, either because the press will cover it, a candidate will create urgency among the electorate, or because it is an important race to individuals in the jurisdiction where one is running, it is important to know the right issues. Gauging the issues can be accomplished in a number of ways depending on the budget, size of race and means available:

- Polling by a firm
- Automated phone calls
- Direct mail solicitation
- Monitoring the local press and public documents
- Direction from the campaign team
- Discussions with local elected officials
- Door-to-door
- Monitoring blogs and social media

Polling by a firm

There are many firms that will assist a campaign in polling the local electorate. Polls can be helpful because they can gauge the name identification and popularity of a candidate and any opponent(s), voter satisfaction in current officeholders, and prioritize general issues (crime, taxes, traffic, environment etc.). A downside to polls is that they can be expensive. A poll for a countywide race that has extensive questioning can cost thousands of dollars. The sample size, or number of respondents, of the poll also affects its cost. The larger the sample, however, the more accurate the results will be.

A good poll will have crosstabs that will allow the reader to view how voters in a region responded to questions or how women responded versus men. Crosstabs can indicate if a candidate is strong with women or if an opponent is weak with the elderly. Crosstabs cross reference answers to campaign questions with answers to demographic questions. Not only will a good poll indicate what issues are priorities for voters, but it will also gauge which messages are strongest and with whom certain messages will resonate.

Another valuable resource in a poll by a firm is an option that prompts voters to provide responses to a question about issues in their own words. These responses, that should be recorded word-for-word, are referred to appropriately as "verbatims". By reading through the verbatims, a campaign can identify common themes that voters have in their responses. Many voters are articulate and can formulate a thought in just a few words that can sum up an important issue. It is through these verbatims that candidates may develop sound bites for their speeches, press releases or press conferences. Words commonly repeated by respondents to describe the current state of affairs, such as "violence", "poverty" or other commonly repeated word can easily become the buzz words in the campaign because they are words and ideas already present in the thoughts and minds of voters.

Using thoughts directly from the verbatims can be particularly effective. Some candidates are seen as identifying with voters and knowing exactly what to say and how to say it. Candidates who become familiar with the verbatim responses, in correlation with the data from the poll, can develop some very powerful messages. If used properly, many voters will identify with the candidate on a more intimate level intellectually because the candidate is using the same language as the voters.

If a budget is too tight for a proper poll, other methods of determining issues exist. Also, it may be wise to learn more about any opponents before conducting a poll. Chapter 3 talks about opposition research and testing messages, and an initial poll may be the tool a campaign uses to test a message as well as information about an opponent.

Automated phone calls

Many people moan about receiving automated phone calls from a machine. The fact remains that automated phone calls with voice response or touch-tone response technology can be very helpful in determining everything discussed under "Polling by a firm" with the exception of verbatim responses. Advantages of an automated phone poll include the ability to reach a much larger sample size and obtain more respondents at a lower cost.

Automated phone calls generally require respondents to provide "yes" or "no" answers. Anything more complicated should be handled by a poll from a live operator.

Phone polls can be more versatile in terms of identifying voters that take sides on any number of particular issues from abortion and character to 2nd Amendment and taxes. This sort of polling can develop into "micro targeting", and that is a subject that will be discussed in a future chapter. "Targeting" refers to how a campaign chooses exactly who will receive a campaign message.

Direct mail solicitation

Some candidates have used the tactic of mailing likely voters directly and including a survey for them to return. It is generally more difficult to gain participation through this method, but by using these means, a candidate sends a response vehicle to a prospective voter and receives a survey back with checked boxes and, hopefully, handwritten responses to questions that can be used in a similar way as the verbatim responses from a live phone poll.

This method is generally more expensive than automated phone calls on a per-contact basis but less expensive than a live poll if the mailing list is targeted to voters who rarely miss an election. Direct mail respondents are voters targeted by the campaign who want to have an impact and voice because they took the time to read the materials sent to them, respond in a written format, and send it back with their own postage. These respondents can become a wealth of volunteers, potential donors and votes later in the campaign.

Monitoring local press and public documents

By leafing through past issues of the newspaper, it can become easy to determine the issues that have gained the attention of the local reporter or publisher. By knowing the issues important to the press, it is easy to determine the issues to which they will respond. In the information age when news web sites are constantly updated, it is easy to gauge what makes editors respond. These issues, however, may not be the same issues most important to voters, but they are issues that allow a candidate an opportunity to gain media attention. Media attention is important in a well-executed race.

Other resources to assist in determining the issues of a race include public documents. Minutes from council meetings, school board and commission meetings or legislative sessions can provide a wealth of information on the hot button issues of the day. Particularly helpful are any public comment sections of the minutes in which local residents addressed the council, commission or legislature. These community activists that took time to speak publicly on an issue potentially represent the voices of many others (similar to verbatim responses from surveys or polling). Much of this information can be accessed on the Internet in some jurisdictions.

Monitoring media and public meetings is generally a very inexpensive way of gauging the issues. It can be very accurate, but this method does not provide the same benefits of polls and surveys.

Direction from the campaign team

The campaign team, an important group of people that will be discussed in detail in Chapter 2, can be an invaluable source of information on important issues if the right people are on board. A diverse and educated team, if comprised of close friends from various professions and regions in the jurisdiction of the office sought, can help guide the discussions on issues. The campaign team should never be the sole source of issue identification, but a roundtable discussion during the planning stages of a campaign can identify issues not previously discovered or bring up issues that may require further thought and research. Furthermore, it is a good idea to have an expert on the team for issues important to voters.

It is always good to have employers in the inner circle for guidance on issues about jobs and small business. If a candidate lives in an agrarian area, then having a farmer on board can be helpful with agriculture issues. Education leaders are also valuable to have on board not just for their issue expertise but for their popularity.

Discussions with local elected officials

One thing a responsible candidate for office should do is seek out meetings with appropriate elected officials and even appointed government employees to learn as much as possible about the issues of the region. Elected officials are an excellent resource since they are the ones dealing with issues on the front lines daily. Elected officials should be willing to meet with constituents to discuss the issues or, at the very least, have a knowledgeable government employee provide information. In seeking information from elected officials, it is not necessary for a potential candidate to discuss plans for running for office if an announcement has not been made. Strategically, there is no reason to alert potential opponent(s) to one's intentions.

Even if a candidate has already announced, seeking meetings with elected officials will be beneficial. Although an elected official may be supporting an opponent, he or she will probably still meet with a candidate in order to gather their own information. It is more important to be a good listener in such meetings rather than a talker. If a candidate is easily disarmed by small talk, too many meetings with other officials could be undesirable. The goal is to gather information - not provide it.

A secondary effect of meeting with local elected officials is that it may engage them in a way that will be helpful in the future. It is also important to add local political party chairmen into the mix of people to know. Although knowing both major political party chairmen is a good idea, it is not a good idea to be too friendly with the chairman of the opposite party.

Door-to-door

A well-run campaign will have a strong door-to-door component. Since this operation will be discussed to a greater extent in a future chapter, it will suffice to say that a great amount of issue information can be gathered as a candidate knocks on the doors of likely voters. If a candidate walking door-to-door is a good listener and note-taker, then the campaign will benefit from the information gathered.

Monitoring blogs and social media

Some social media sites have developed a critical mass of members that it is useful for someone on a campaign team to monitor what people are saying on their personalized sites. This type of monitoring can have a similar effect to reading the verbatim responses from polls or monitoring letters to the editor in papers.

Many newspapers allow anonymous comments at the end of stories that are posted on their Internet sites. These comments reflect what some of the people in a jurisdiction may feel. It is important to weigh these comments against others collected by the methods described above, but they provide another avenue of gauging how voters feel.

It should go without saying that any information gathered should be recorded while it is still fresh. A candidate should never be deceptive but should not feel compelled to reveal any intentions that are still private.

1.7   Developing the database

One of the most valuable, and essential, assets of a campaign is a good database. Campaigns will have different databases with which it will work in order to target voters, build mailing lists, prospect donors or make phone calls. The campaign database includes information on every person with which the candidate or member of any of the campaign's team come in contact. The database will include information on each person including name, address, phone number, fax number, e-mail address, dates and amounts of any contributions, where the person might stand on any issues, if the person is a volunteer, if the person wants a yard sign, what social media sites that person uses and any other important detail that allows the campaign to make effective use of each person in the database.

First-time candidates must begin to build their own databases, and knowing everything possible about each person entered into the database will increase the ability to target each person for effective use as a volunteer, financial donor or information resource. If an incumbent has never created a database, then there is a lot of ground to make up. Even if a potential candidate does not plan to run for office for a few years, it is never too early to start a database.

Components of a campaign's database may include the finance reports of other candidates (discussed earlier in this chapter), any databases that other officeholders or former candidates may be willing to share, any friends or family of the candidate, and any friends or family of any member of the campaign team and add them all to the database. Each entry in the database should have a flag or field that describes the source of the record.

Once this initial database is created, each unique person in that database should receive a letter from the campaign in the mail. The letter should include a response vehicle, usually an envelope that contains a flap with fields for the respondent to answer, that is self-addressed to the campaign. As individuals respond favorably, they should be flagged in the campaign database indicating their answers, level of support and any other valuable information.

Once the list has been mailed, and ample time has been given for a response, those who did not respond should receive a phone call from the campaign requesting their support. Each time someone comes in contact with the campaign in some way, that person should be added to the campaign database. Anyone who attends a campaign function should be added. As the database develops, the management team should use it to begin executing the campaign plan.

It is important to note that the campaign database is different from the voter database. The campaign database is the listing of the campaign's human resources – the people that have an interest in the campaign. The voter database is the listing of voters in the jurisdiction of the race. The voter database is the resource that the campaign will use to target and deliver its message.

1.8   Media contacts

Contact with the media is essential in a successful campaign. In the early phases of a race, the campaign should contact each newspaper, television station and radio station in the area and obtain a press contact. This person should be a reporter, assignment editor, news director or someone that in some way has influence on what political stories will be covered. Information for each contact should include name, address, phone, fax and e-mail address. In the early stages of a campaign, whoever contacts each media outlet should not feel compelled to reveal the reason for gathering the information. Reporters are naturally curious, and it is their job to sniff out a story. This information is important for when a candidate wishes to make an announcement of candidacy. If one reporter gets advanced notice of a potential candidacy, he may "scoop" the other media outlets by reporting it first. If that happens, by the time an official announcement is made, it may be old news and less likely to be covered by the other outlets.

Campaigns should have a single person dedicated to speaking with the media. This person is the gatekeeper for information as well as access to the candidate from the media. The candidate will also work and speak with the media, but the designated media contact on the campaign is important. This person, be it the campaign manager, the press secretary or other designated spokesman, makes certain that the information supplied to the media is complete, accurate and consistent. Someone who does not have all of the information on a campaign and decides to talk to the press may say things that are inconsistent, inaccurate or incomplete to the press. The press contact is also briefed as to what information is appropriate to share. Campaigns would never knowingly supply strategic or tactical information to the opponent.

Ensuring that the press does not transmit such information is critical. Every member of the campaign should understand who the media contact is and that any reporter who approaches anyone on the campaign should be directed to that person.

In relating with the media, it is important for candidates to keep their cards close to their vests. This does not mean one should be secretive, but a reporter is trained to ask questions, and as long as someone is answering, reporters will continue asking. Media should be treated with the same respect that anyone related to the campaign would receive, but knowing when not to reveal too much is as important as having that contact when the campaign needs to release information.

1.9   Local Elected Officials and Community Leaders

As the campaign begins to take shape and the information gathering process is in high gear, an important list of contacts every candidate for office should have is a comprehensive list of local elected officials and civic leaders. These are the people that the candidate should begin contacting to gauge their level of interest in the campaign, whether or not they already support an opponent and if they would be willing to support someone.

These leaders are also an excellent source of information. Calling them or meeting with them as a courtesy to their office demonstrates that a candidate is serious about the race. Even if a leader supports an opponent or is neutral in the campaign, he will probably let the people they talk to know that they met with a candidate and then give them his impressions.

The local elections office should be able to provide a full listing of local elected officials. The list should be complete including every level of government including congressmen, state legislators, county commissioners, county elected officials, city council members and mayors, township trustees and school board members, fiscal officers and clerks. If the position is elected, a candidate should know who occupies that seat.

The database of local elected officials should be built without regard to party affiliation –no one should be left out because of it. However, party affiliation should be noted if available.

This chapter probably raised more questions than it answered. It is designed to do that. In order to adequately prepare for a race, a candidate or manager should have a lot of questions. What this chapter does is help guide thoughts so that the right questions are being asked, and the organization can begin taking form. Each subsequent chapter in this book relies on information gathered from the suggestions in this chapter. Laying a strong groundwork now can save immensely later in the campaign. It is never too early to begin preparing.

Chapter 2

Building the Team

The campaign team consists of a number of components: the core team, the management team, volunteers, financial supporters, campaign committee, coalitions and endorsing groups and individuals. Another component not discussed at length but requires mentioning is the candidate's family. The family of the candidate is as important to the campaign as any of the other components. The candidate's family should be involved in the campaign as far as public appearances. Family members should volunteer on the campaign, and they should be knowledgeable about what is happening on the campaign.

The candidate's family, including the candidate's spouse, should not be involved in the management of the campaign especially if the campaign has hired a political consultant to manage the race. Many times a candidate will make the mistake of allowing a spouse to have management control of the campaign. This situation creates an atmosphere in which the core team may not be honest in giving advice as they would with an objective campaign manager. Or this situation could lead to a loss of campaign morale and energy because the spouse is running a show that he or she may have little or no knowledge about. Other times, the family being involved in management decisions can lead to bad decisions being made by someone too emotionally involved with the campaign. If a consultant has been hired, a family member involved in campaign management may inadvertently undermine the authority of the consultant and derail the campaign plan.

A properly run campaign will integrate family participation. The family is important because a candidate will require the support and input from the family throughout the campaign. Input from the candidate's family should occur directly with the campaign manager just as any member of the core team or management staff would do. A campaign manager exists in order to mange the campaign, and a spouse or other family member who does not understand the management dynamic can create a situation in which decisions are being made without the knowledge or consent of the professionals. There are instances of campaigns that have won when the candidate's family is involved in big decisions. Consider these examples the exception and not the rule.

What an experienced consultant will do, while building the campaign plan, is understand the family of the candidate. The consultant should understand the direction and vision that the family has regarding the campaign and use that information to shape the plan. Integrating the family into the campaign plan intelligently will allow for a more melodious campaign and a more satisfied family. It is important to remember a golden rule when dealing with a candidate's family: if the candidate's family is not happy, then the candidate is not happy. By extension, the campaign team is also unhappy.

2.1   Four commodities of a campaign

Simply put, there are four commodities in a campaign that cannot be replaced. They are finite and must be managed effectively. These commodities are Time, Information, Money and People (TIMP). A proper organization will be able to effectively manage these four components.

Time, the first component, can be a campaign's worst enemy. Every day of the campaign means one less day left until Election Day. That is one less day to raise money, one less day to meet voters, one less day to deliver message. If a deadline is missed, there is no going back. On the other hand, time can also be a campaign's best friend. A necessary component of a campaign plan is a timeline. A timeline will dictate when the campaign will execute certain tactics. A timeline contains deadlines for filing, fundraising, events, message delivery and all other activities of a campaign. A message takes time to penetrate with voters, and that must be considered in the timeline. Time management is as important as money, information and human management on a campaign.

Information includes all of the intelligence gathered by the campaign as well as the message that the campaign delivers to voters. Every campaign has an array of issues from which it can choose to address. Information management allows a campaign to effectively identify those issues. Proper information management helps a campaign target voters. Without information management, fundraisers are ineffective. Information is the bedrock from which a campaign is built.

If information is the bedrock for the campaign, money is the resource that builds the campaign. Effective use of money can allow a campaign that is being outspent by an opponent to become competitive. Money management is addressed in the budget of the campaign plan. Although this resource fluctuates in a race, a campaign plan is built around a target budget that is realistic.

People execute the campaign plan. From volunteers to vendors to the candidate, effective management of human resources is essential to a winning campaign. Chapter One focused on the commodity of information. Chapter Two turns its attention to people. Future chapters will discuss money and time. All components must be integrated into the strategy for an effective, winning campaign.

2.2   Core Team

The Core Team, also referred to as the "inner circle", "kitchen cabinet" and other similar names refers to the very close group of supporters, ideally about six people, that act as a focus group for decisions, sound bites, speeches, direct mail or television spots. They help to guide the campaign direction by going to meetings, developing the lists of strengths and weaknesses, identifying issues, tapping their own networks of people for volunteers and donors, putting their name to campaign materials when necessary, acting as surrogate speakers at community events, working with the campaign manager to identify areas needing attention, and providing feedback to ideas.

The core team should consist of the candidate, campaign manager and a few friends who have been successful in business, civic associations or running for office themselves. An ideal core team will have a local elected official, a successful member of the business community, and a member of a local board of directors for a charity or foundation. Someone of equal caliber or level of success meets the requirements. The point is to surround oneself with people who are friends that have a personal interest in seeing their friend, the candidate, win the campaign. These members of the core team also have experienced a level of success in the community as well and have proven that their advice carries weight. Along with their level of success comes a network of people who can help on the campaign either as volunteers, donors, or both.

The core team should be kept apprised of all campaign functions. Meetings or conference calls should be scheduled regularly so that everyone can plan to attend. The campaign manager also needs to know that he can approach any member of this team at any time for assistance and vice versa. A good core team can make the difference between winning or losing or having an effective campaign or ineffective campaign.

The core team should not be exceedingly large. If too many people have input, then decisions become harder to make. Too many participants cause longer meetings and less activity. The key is to identify the handful of close friends that meet the criteria of success and community involvement and engage them in the race.

2.3   Management Team

Depending on the size of the race and the budget, a management team can consist of one person or many people. Members of the team may be paid or volunteer, but these will be the people that will make sure that the "trains run on time," the candidate is scheduled properly, the bills get paid, the campaign stays within budget, goals are met, voters are targeted, and the message is delivered effectively.

Campaign Manager

Campaign organizations begin with the Campaign Manager. The campaign manager does just what the title describes. A good campaign manager will develop a strong staff and volunteers that will work together to make everything on the campaign function like clockwork. In smaller campaigns, a good campaign manager can be a student at a local university, a retired worker, a homemaker or someone who has extra time and good organization skills. The larger the campaign, the greater the need is for a campaign manager with experience and one that can devote a good amount of time to the campaign.

If hiring a campaign manager full time, it is important to check references on other employers and on campaigns that the prospective manager has worked. The political business is a business that runs on reputation, and the most important qualities a campaign should seek are competence, loyalty, honesty and work ethic. The prospective campaign manager does not have to be the nicest or best looking individual in a group of applicants, but the one hired needs to produce good results and be completely loyal to the candidate.

If a prospective manager has lost races, then it is important to understand what caused the loss. Sometimes factors that a campaign manager could not control are what caused a candidate to lose (candidate baggage, inability to raise needed funds, etc.). Perhaps the prospective manager is willing to take on campaigns that no one thinks can be won. It is also important to evaluate if the prospective manager has learned from past losses.

The bottom line when it comes to campaign management is that a candidate should never self-manage the campaign, and a family member can be equally devastating. An exception to this rule would be if a campaign's manager is a family member, such as a brother, who is skilled. The important component for the candidate, and the candidate's family, to understand is that the campaign manager is the person through whom all decisions are made. Input can be given to the campaign manager, but a family relationship between the manager and the rest of the campaign must take a back seat to the concept of making objective decisions. A good manager should be someone who can be objective, has ample time, and utilizes good organizational skills.

Examples of siblings, or other family members, running campaigns exist throughout politics. Robert Kennedy ran some of the campaigns of his brother, John. Bay Buchanan managed campaigns of her brother

Patrick who had run for President. Family involvement is important, but objective decision making takes precedence.

Other members of the management team for larger campaigns would include political director, communications director, scheduler, treasurer, finance director and volunteer coordinator. In congressional, statewide or large urban races, a policy consultant may join the team.

Political Director

The Political Director (PD) is an important cog in the machine in races at the county level or larger depending on the size of the jurisdiction and the diversity of the constituents. The political director's duties are almost as varied and complex as the campaign manager's. The political director will work closely with the campaign manager to implement strategy and execute tasks. While directing campaign staff in the execution of events, sign posting, volunteer activities and other activities, a good director also builds a rapport with important community leaders, allies to the campaign, volunteers and other people with whom the campaign comes in contact. Essentially, the political director can act as the "glue" for a larger organization.

A political director should be able to evaluate how to fit each person touched by the campaign into the team. Does a person at an event become a contributor, volunteer, advisor, or campaign informant on community events and other field intelligence? The political director must evaluate whether a person he meets should take the campaign manager's time or even the candidate's time. In a political campaign, one of the most valuable resources the campaign has is time. Directing every person who has contact with the campaign to the candidate is not an effective use of the candidate's time and distracts the candidate from other tasks such as raising money, attending events, and staying on the campaign trail.

The qualities of the political director must include loyalty, diplomacy, tactfulness and initiative. The political director will be the face of the campaign with people when the candidate cannot be there. A political director must be a self-starter who can look at the playing field of the campaign, identify the important groups to meet and ally with and then bring them into the campaign fold. If the political director meets people who will be good volunteers, he should plug them in with the volunteer coordinator. As one of the chief intelligence gatherers in the campaign, the political director keeps a finger on the pulse of the people in the district. People who can give money, or tap the resources of other people, should be directed to the finance director.

Communications Director

The Communications Director is the person responsible for maintaining good relationships with the press and how the campaign image is projected through the web site and other media. The duties of a communications director range from meeting with each member of the media to develop a strong rapport and issuing press releases to working with the web designer and attending events to videotape the candidate and any opponents. Since the communications director works with pushing the image and message of the campaign, this person should work with the campaign manager in order to develop TV scripts, direct mail and other campaign communications. The communications director makes sure that all messages from the campaign are consistent and somehow develop the message of the campaign.

In order to ensure efficient delivery of campaign communications, the communications director should have, or quickly develop, a comprehensive list of all local media including large newspapers, community newspapers, television stations, radio stations and any other media outlet as well as the AP wire. Smart campaigns that want to appeal to voters who receive their information from the Internet will seek out local bloggers as well. This list should include a reporter, editor or news director's name, phone number, fax number and e-mail address. Most media outlets prefer to receive e-mail notifications from campaigns, but it is important to use all means available to push campaign information to the press. An e-mailed press release may get more notice if it is also faxed. Most importantly, the communications director is responsible for making certain that each press contact is called when a release is sent out in order to confirm receipt of the release. This lets the campaign know that the release was received and viewed by the press thereby improving the chances of the item getting "play".

Some members of the campaign staff will answer directly to the communications director. Some of these positions may include the web designer, media monitor, direct mail graphic designer, social media coordinator and press secretary.

A communications director works with the other members of the management team to determine the worthiness of an item for a press conference. In addition to the press, a communications director should build relationships with known bloggers or recruit web bloggers themselves. With the advent of the Internet, the way in which people receive information has changed, and an effective campaign will take advantage of all means necessary. Any allied bloggers should also receive press releases. Furthermore, the communications director should also maintain and nurture a campaign e-mail list for regular updates.

The communications director is also responsible for monitoring the news media and recording television news and political ads, clipping papers and recording radio programming or ads pertinent to the campaign. Internet, blog mentions and social media monitoring also fall under the communications director umbrella. All records from the media should be kept in a well-organized file or cabinet. Electronic records, if possible, are preferable.

Scheduler

The Scheduler closely works with the campaign manager to direct the candidate's time. Most candidates for office have jobs or businesses of their own and require time to conduct business. When the candidate is available, the campaign team should be working to gain exposure for the candidate by either attending breakfasts or lunches with civic organizations, attending new business openings or ribbon cuttings, or going to community festivals, parades and events. When the candidate is not meeting voters, then the scheduler should focus efforts towards fundraising phone calls or appearing at a campaign event such as a coffee, fundraiser, rally or volunteer appreciation get-together.

An effective scheduler also works closely with the volunteer coordinator to make sure that someone is with the candidate at events or to drive the candidate. The scheduler must also be a pleasant person due to the amount of contact with supporters this person has. From scheduling and confirming events to gathering event information, the scheduler may have as much contact with voters and potential supporters as the candidate.

Finance Director

The Finance Director works directly with the candidate and scheduler to carve out time for raising money. The finance director maintains the donor portion of the campaign database and keeps the candidate disciplined to make calls. The finance director will make follow-up phone calls to potential donors that the candidate contacted and will generally be responsible for retrieving checks or making sure they are mailed in. The finance director will track all pledges and donations as well as the responses of potential donors who have not yet committed to the campaign. The finance director will work with the campaign management team to schedule and execute fundraising events as well as decide who is invited to each event. Each person who comes in contact with the campaign is a potential donor, and the finance director should add those people to the list for the candidate to call.

The finance director will work closely with the campaign treasurer to make certain all reporting requirements are satisfied. In addition, the finance director will assist the treasurer in meeting deadlines for reports. The finance director is the source of much of the information required by the treasurer, and the finance director will also often be the one to deliver donations to the treasurer for deposit.

Volunteer Coordinator

The volunteer coordinator works with the campaign manager, political director and scheduler to determine how to manage volunteers and coordinate their activities. The volunteer coordinator will access the campaign database to recruit campaign workers to be with the candidate when out in public. The volunteer coordinator will ensure that campaign events are properly staffed with workers, coordinate envelope stuffing for mailings, coordinate phone banks and make sure that volunteers are out representing the campaign at events where the candidate cannot attend. The volunteer coordinator also ensures that campaign workers have the proper wardrobe and campaign materials to hand out if needed. The volunteer coordinator also makes sure volunteers are adequately trained for each assignment, have directions or maps to their destinations, and are properly taken care of if food or beverage needs arise.

The volunteer coordinator may also work with the communications director in order to assist the social media portion of the campaign, find bloggers, recruit letter writers or find a crowd of "extras" for a press conference. The volunteer coordinator has to be effective at managing human resources.

Policy Advisor

For larger campaigns that require the campaign management team to focus on campaign activities and communications, a campaign may enlist the help of a Policy Advisor to assist on issues development, issue research and message development. The policy advisor works closely with the core team and campaign manager to develop message and determine what issues are strongest for the candidate. As the chief policy officer of the campaign, the policy advisor must understand the finer points of issues and be capable of briefing the candidate. The policy advisor will work closely with the communications director on campaign communications.

Treasurer

In all races, without exception, a treasurer is required. The treasurer is often a volunteer, but the treasurer is one of the key positions that operate the campaign machinery. The treasurer is responsible for maintaining the campaign account, writing checks, depositing money, and filing finance reports. Furthermore, the treasurer reports to the candidate and campaign manager on all activities and keeps them informed of the account balance. The treasurer works with the finance director to properly report in-kind donations, and to make sure that all reportable items are properly disclosed. Reimbursements go through the treasurer. The treasurer, in short, must become an expert on campaign finance rules, laws and procedures. A bad treasurer can sink a campaign. Since being treasurer is a back office function, the position is a thankless job. Good treasurers are seldom recognized for their efforts to the same degree that other members of management are.

In many instances, the name of the treasurer appears in the legal disclaimer of campaign materials. The disclaimer is printed on campaign materials and lets voters know whose campaign paid for the item they are seeing or holding. A campaign treasurer should be a person with an excellent reputation. A campaign with a treasurer whose name will distract from the campaign's message should be avoided.

Candidate's Family

The saying "blood is thicker than water" means that a family relationship would trump any other type of relationship such as friendship or business. In a campaign in which the candidate has an interested or active spouse or child, the campaign manager and candidate must decide early on how the family will be involved. The campaign manager must be the person through whom the members of the family will take direction – not the candidate. If family members are asking for direction and taking it from the candidate, then when they have problems, or suggestions about the campaign, they will go to the candidate.

By not establishing the chain of command early on, a campaign manager can quickly lose control of a campaign. For instance, an excellent campaign staffer might not work well with the candidate's spouse. If the spouse works directly with the candidate and not the campaign manager, then the campaign manager might wake up one day missing one of the most important members of the staff along with some important information. Conversely, if the campaign manager has to eliminate a weak link from the campaign, but the staffer who is being let go has a friendship with a spouse who does not understand the management dynamic then the campaign manager now has a subordinate who can effectively undermine decisions.

Everyone on the campaign must understand and respect the chain of command on the campaign. The candidate and the candidate's family must respect the decisions made by the campaign manager. If these components do not occur, and the campaign manager does not have control over the management of the campaign, then the likelihood of success is diminished as well as the morale of the team and the efficiency of the political machine.

2.4   Volunteers

Volunteers are an incredible resource for a campaign. They can create momentum and project an image of strength and support at public events. Volunteers will work tirelessly for candidates they believe in whether it is on the phones, stuffing mail, or placing yard signs. The most important thing that a campaign must do with volunteers to make sure they feel useful is engage them on the campaign. Volunteers need jobs to do, or they will lose interest in the campaign.

Volunteers can help out with tasks that the management team may not be able to do. Volunteers can write letters to the editors of papers, proofread campaign communications, recruit other volunteers or perform any number of tasks on a campaign. With the Internet playing such a prominent role in campaigns, they can monitor sites, comment on blogs, assist with social media, or update the news file. Many volunteers are even happy to run errands, pick up checks from donors, or even help keep the campaign office clean. As long as a volunteer knows that he or she is performing a necessary task and contributing in some way, then the campaign will keep them on board when tasks become more important. If the volunteer coordinator fails to properly engage a volunteer, thank the volunteer, or feed the volunteer when appropriate, then losing volunteers becomes easier than recruiting them. In addition, each volunteer should have a small supply of literature to keep in their vehicles for their friends, family, and neighbors along with a campaign t-shirt that they can slip on if the opportunity arises at an event they attend.

Some volunteers have proficiencies in one area but not in another.

If a volunteer does not want to make phone calls but wants to place signs, go door-to-door or attend an event, then that volunteer should be plugged in where they are willing to work. Sometimes a volunteer, once he is satisfied with doing one or two of the higher profile jobs, will be happy to stuff mail or make phone calls. A volunteer should never be turned away because they have thoughts about where their own strengths are. An effective campaign will eventually be able to train people in areas that the volunteer may have been initially hesitant.

Also, it is important not to burn out volunteers. For campaigns with a small handful of volunteers, they will begin to recognize that they are the only ones showing up at events. This type of overuse can lead to resentment and a loss of a few excellent workers. Good managers always attempt to keep a large group of volunteers ready to work, and managers should give volunteers breaks from time to time. Volunteers can become recruiters for the campaign as they bring their friends and family into the office or to an event. The more volunteers on the campaign, the less burden each one carries.

2.5   Financial Supporters

Some people are unable to give their time to a campaign but are able to give money. A place exists for everyone who wants to be involved in a campaign. Financial supporters make it possible for the campaign to produce television and radio ads or send out direct mail. Financial supporters are important because they appear on the campaign finance report, and every campaign should count on the opponent obtaining a copy of its report. It is important to have a large number of contributors as well as contributors at all levels of giving. A candidate with a small number of high dollar donors may have an issue explaining that those donors do not have undue influence. Likewise, many low-dollar donors can create an impression of mass support.

Some financial supporters will also be on the campaign committee while others may be willing to hold a fundraiser in which they access their own network of friends, associates, coworkers and family. Some people will give $1.00 while others may contribute the maximum amount allowable by law.

"Small dollar" donors on a campaign are just as important as larger donors. Small donors can many times become as powerful on a campaign as large donors when they come out in numbers. Success stories include Howard Dean's campaign for President in 2004, Barack Obama's 2008 campaign and Ron Paul's 2008 campaign. These candidates were able to raise massive amounts of money in a short amount of time from a large volume of small donations. Furthermore, small donations are a sign that a campaign has bedrock support from people who do not regularly give to campaigns. It is more impressive for a campaign to raise $1 million from 10,000 people than a campaign to raise $1 million from 100 people. Campaign plans should incorporate donors of all categories small and large.

Donors are also people. This means that they need to be thanked when they contribute. A short, handwritten note from the candidate goes a long way in keeping a donor happy. They must be appreciated if the campaign wants to see any future donations.

2.6   Campaign Committee

Not to be confused with the core team or the management team, the campaign committee is a list of influential community leaders who will allow the use of their names as supporters of the campaign. The campaign committee may include members of the core team as well. Chapter One discussed the importance of making contact with local elected officials. It is important to evaluate the appropriateness of each person asked to be on a campaign committee. A good campaign committee will demonstrate support from different regions of a jurisdiction as well as individuals from different professions along with any elected officeholders recruited. Having a doctor, esquire, or other professional credentials next to a name enhances the prominence of the campaign committee. All elected officeholders should be referred to as "Honorable". Their respective constituents will recognize the name.

The campaign committee will appear on the campaign web site as well as the letterhead. Some direct mail, emails or print advertisement may also use the campaign committee or specific members of the committee. For instance, a campaign may include the mayors of two local towns. When direct mailing voters in Town A, the campaign will use the mayor of Town A but not Town B and vice versa.

A campaign committee is often a "living" body meaning that it can grow over time. Once a committee has been formed, a campaign should utilize it to its greatest advantage. Some may just be willing to allow use of their names and not wish to give support any other way. Others will contribute time, money and effort. Each person has a spot on the campaign if only to allow the use of his or her name. The committee is only as effective as the campaign makes it. Unless the campaign tells the voters who its committee members are in its communications, then the campaign is not effectively using its committee.

2.7   Coalitions

Coalitions are important to developing a groundswell of support within a large group with a relatively small amount of effort. Many different groups build coalitions that will work en masse on behalf of a candidate that they believe in. Furthermore, it is important to reach out to coalitions because they want to vote for someone they understand is sympathetic with them or will, at least, listen to them. Unions, Christian conservatives, gun owners, Tea Parties, and African American organizations are some examples of groups that seek out candidates that will work with them. Coalitions become even more responsive to those who proactively seek them out.

Building coalitions can lead to procuring a large amount of volunteers with just a little effort. Building coalitions also instantly increases name recognition within a group and can enhance the momentum of the campaign.

Some coalitions may be undesirable. A campaign would rarely want to work with groups that support the legalization of drugs or promote extreme controversial views. Sometimes it is difficult to decide if a group is a good ally or an undesirable ally based on the subject matter. A candidate who personally believes in the legalization of marijuana may not wish to have the support of pro-legalization groups although they would seem like natural allies. The decision about with whom a campaign builds coalitions should be a carefully considered process. Although a candidate may personally believe one way on a particular issue, the people that candidate seeks to represent may largely disagree. A campaign is under no obligation to broadcast its candidate's views on issues not pertinent to the office sought. Therefore it is sometimes wise to downplay a personal issue so that other issues rise to the forefront of the campaign.

It is important to identify the various coalitions in an area and determine which ones are most likely to both agree with the positions of the campaign and be desirable allies. Coalition support may even come with an endorsement from a like-minded organization or prominent individual or multiple organizations and prominent leaders. Leaders from coalitions with a campaign should appear on a campaign committee such as the President of a local NAACP if the campaign is aligned with that organization.

Coalitions form around issues such as the environment, pro-life and pro-choice, law enforcement, government spending, community values and many others. If a coalition has formed a Political Action Committee, or PAC, then support may also come in the form of a donation.

2.8   Endorsements

Many groups endorse in political races. Some groups are part of a coalition being courted by the campaign. For instance, the local Fraternal Order of Police (FOP) that endorses may be part of a law enforcement coalition that includes multiple FOP organizations. Having law enforcement on the side of a campaign is generally desirable. A good campaign plan will include money, time and effort being invested in endorsements, and subsequently, coalition building.

Groups that traditionally endorse include newspapers, local political parties, Right-to-Life, National Rifle Association, unions, environmental groups, Anti-Tax Political Action Committees (PACs), and other similar organizations.

Political Action Committees are political entities chartered with a local Board of Elections, elections clerk or the Secretary of State's office. Some Political Action Committees have large memberships and have a significant fundraising capability. Not only can a PAC endorse, it can contribute money to a campaign. For a list of PACs that may be available for solicitation, a campaign should check the local elections office as well as the Secretary of State's office. Many Secretaries of State have the PAC information on the Internet.

Endorsements can be selectively used on campaign literature, web sites and ads. In sending out a pro-law enforcement direct mail piece to voters, an endorsement from the FOP would be good to print on that piece. Consequently, leaving off an endorsement from trial attorneys would be a wise decision. A good campaign will make certain that any organization that endorses its candidate will have the endorsement prominently displayed on its web site. Voters of a local Right to Life organization are much more likely to visit the web site of their organization than the web site of a campaign, so it is important for them to view the endorsement when they view the organization's site.

Similar to the campaign committee, endorsements are only as effective as the campaign makes them. If endorsements are not communicated to voters by the campaign, then the value of the endorsement shrinks. Gaining an endorsement is just a tactic in the overall strategy of a campaign.

Building a strong campaign team will relieve a lot of stress during the campaign. A team that can take initiative, build good relationships, plan ahead, and execute plans properly will reduce the amount of "campaign emergencies". Every campaign that has worthy opposition will encounter situations that require immediate action, but a good team can adapt easily to such challenges.

Everyone has a place in a campaign. Take someone's help as far as they will allow. If a campaign fails to ask for help, then it likely will not receive it. Campaign team members must feel as though they are contributing, feel appreciated, and never go home hungry or thirsty. If volunteers are treated well, it is surprising how effective they can be.

Coalitions and endorsements should be sought in a wise manner. Once a bond with a group or individual is formed, a campaign should exploit it fully. The groups and individuals who do endorse or support candidates wish to be used in a campaign because it promotes their issues as well as their candidates, and the attention elevates their recognition and status with the general public.

The names of prominent committee members and the endorsements that organizations may bestow upon a campaign are only as effective as the campaign makes them. If a campaign works hard to receive an endorsement, then it should broadcast it once it is earned. And all people involved with a campaign should always understand that they are appreciated. Without an acknowledgement of their value, a campaign may unknowingly lose supporters.

Chapter 3

Message and Strategy

3.1 Ethics and Message

Chapter One briefly discussed the importance of being truthful with voters. Voters can be forgiving with a mistake or past indiscretion, but they are less likely to forgive a cover-up of a current indiscretion or a direct lie from the candidate.

In the heat of a campaign, a candidate or his team may find it tempting to stretch the truth, lie, or even violate the law. Although doing the right thing should be incentive in itself to dictate the actions of a campaign, the potential cost of violating ethics standards should be an even better deterrent. However, some campaigns still succumb to the enticement of making a short-term gain at the expense of a little honor.

Violating ethics may take the form of intentionally distorting an opponent's message. A campaign may bank on the idea that, by misleading voters about the opponent, they can force the opponent to spend valuable campaign resources to repudiate the charge. The campaign responsible for this breach may do so because the candidate or members of the team have taken a "win at all costs" attitude. The short term gains that may be made could possibly be negated by an authority that oversees truthfulness in campaigns or even by the next election. It is also possible that permanent damage can occur to the candidate's reputation and future possibilities of success.

Some campaigns will be guilty of inadvertently engaging in unethical practices. Perhaps proper research was not conducted on a topic. Perhaps a campaign heard a rumor and used it in the campaign as truth. Sometimes a campaign team member might have a penchant for embellishing a story before sending it to the candidate. Instances such as these can be just as damaging to a candidate as if the campaign knowingly engaged in the deception. A professional campaign will always check facts and be able to back up what it broadcasts before the message goes out. Some campaigns will footnote specific public documents in campaign communications on the Internet, direct mail, and television. Footnoting is an excellent method of protecting the campaign from a possibly destructive mistake. Furthermore, footnoting can enhance the power of campaign communications by lending a greater level of legitimacy to the communications.

Another form of unethical campaign practice is infiltration of an opposing campaign. Receiving the intellectual property of another campaign is not a practice campaigns should embrace. Some states have laws against campaign infiltration. For instance, a volunteer may show up at an opposing campaign's event pretending to be an objective observer or even a supporter of the campaign holding the event. Over time, the campaign may begin to trust this "volunteer" while the "volunteer" passes whatever information is gathered onto the campaign that he wishes to win. Some campaigns may engage a disgruntled staff member to provide privileged information. Any practice that attempts to infiltrate an opposing campaign, to gather information through deception, or to gather information through illegal methods is unethical and possibly subject to prosecution. Furthermore, if caught in the act, the revelation of such a practice can compromise the integrity and electability of the candidate who benefited from such unethical practices.

Whatever the reason for violating ethical standards or truthfulness, it is wrong. It may seem as though such advice is elementary. However, such violations occur every year in races big and small throughout the country. Although a campaign with good intentions should never engage in unethical practices, a campaign plan should consider that the opposing campaign may be unethical. Being prepared to deal with an unethical opponent would include knowing who the local or state campaign authorities are, how to file a complaint, and what to expect when a complaint is filed.

3.2   Opposition Research

Many first-time candidates shy away from discussion of "opposition research". They often feel that it is just another way of saying "digging up dirt on the opponent". Although that interpretation is one way of looking at opposition research, a well-prepared campaign conducts research that examines opponents through a thorough study of public records. Opposition research may reveal facts that seem unsavory about an opponent, but the goal of opposition research is to know who it is a campaign is running against, how they think, why they do what they do, how they may have voted in the past, what their record of success, failure and support is and their fitness for the job. An excellent reason to conduct opposition research is to find out if an opponent has filed required reports with authorities such as campaign finance reports, ethics disclosures, or other form that may be overlooked. Finding a violation such as a failure to file a report required by law can be a fatal blow. Whether or not a campaign publicly discloses any of the research gathered is a matter of strategy and personal choice. It would be a mistake not to spend some time to be forearmed.

Various resources are available to begin a thorough research operation. The first thing a candidate should look at is any record of voting that an opponent has. If an opponent is or was a city councilman, township trustee, legislator, or held another elected position, a public record exists of his or her decisions. The first step is to contact the clerk or secretary of the body upon which this opponent served. It is most helpful to receive information in electronic format whenever possible. If a list of votes for a candidate can be produced in a word processing document or spreadsheet document, it becomes easier to search for key words, sort by date or sort by other criteria.

Once a complete record of the decisions made by an opponent has been compiled, highlighting controversial votes on issues, issues in which taxes or fees were raised and issues in which the opponent may have had special approval for travel expenses to distant locations or any other expenses which may have been reimbursed or granted is important. Careful accounting of an opponent's attendance should be noted. Some candidates have lost their elections because they took many trips out of state for "seminars" or "development" with little or nothing to show for it. Other incumbents have lost their elected positions because they failed to appear at many of their scheduled meetings. Voters, most of whom are employed, can easily become offended if their hard-earned money is being spent on what they perceive as personal junkets or if the person they hired in the last election fails to make it to work regularly.

Once key legislation or controversial issues are identified, a list of the dates of those issues should be made. This list of dates can be taken to a local library that has microfilmed copies of the local newspaper or news source that may have covered the decisions. Some web sites also archive news to make it available over the Internet. A search of the dates of the decisions in question, as well as the issues of the publication leading up to the decision and immediately following, may reveal useful headlines or stories. Online archiving, however, is usually available for a fee, so spending some money on opposition research should be expected. When high profile issues arise, media hype tends to begin before the meeting in which the decision is made, and it will last a few days after. A check of the opinion pages for editorials about decisions an opponent may have made as well as letters to the editor about the opponent may produce usable material. A printout of all pertinent articles should be made with notations detailing where they were originally published and the date of the publication. These headlines and quotes will become useful in future campaign communications should the campaign feel it necessary to hold its opponent accountable.

Other information a campaign should seek includes any criminal history available in public record format. A quick search of the local clerk of courts records can reveal any past indiscretions, altercations, liens, bad business ventures or anything that may be filed in the courts in the area. A point should be made to check court records in surrounding jurisdictions and areas in which an opponent has business dealings. Bankruptcy information may be found in a federal court, but there should be indications of that bankruptcy beginning in lower courts because creditors will often file actions or liens against bad debts before the creditor pursues bankruptcy. Voters have a difficult time putting someone in charge of their tax dollars that has demonstrated a failure in their own lives to manage their own finances.

Candidates who are not felons but continually accumulate speeding or traffic tickets generally make easy targets. A quick request for information from the local police station for records relating to an opponent might yield some surprising results.

Searching for property records of an opponent through the local auditor, recorder or clerk's office will help in the opposition research phase. By searching property records, one may be able to determine if an opponent has received a personal benefit by holding a position or stands to receive a personal benefit if elected. By regularly checking mortgage records filed with the proper authority, a campaign may be able to determine if an opponent has decided to leverage some of his or her personal assets in order to wage their campaign. It is important to find out where an opponent owns property, with whom they may own that property, and how much property is owned.

Another easy but essential piece of information is a voter history of any opponent. A quick trip to the Board of Elections or clerk will yield a history of voting frequency, if this opponent votes Republican or Democrat, how consistent the opponent is, or if elections are frequently missed. A voter history will also have an opponent's voting address, and a campaign should verify that the opponent actually lives at that address. Some voters have been known to register at an address where they do not live in order to maintain eligibility to run in an election.

If the opponent currently holds an elected office, he or she may be required to file an ethics report or a disclosure form of some sort that will list assets, gifts, investments, sources of income, and business relationships. It is important to request this disclosure from the proper authority and check it against information gathered from other research.

Human intelligence can be just as valuable as the public record documents detailed in this section. Human intelligence means talking with people who know the opponent. Conversations with past acquaintances, business associates, school friends and even family members can provide insight into the opponent and of possible shortcomings. It is important to weigh the value and validity of each person with whom the campaign speaks. Some people will be more credible than others, and some informants may try to provide a campaign with misleading information or red herrings. Good notes are important, but all human intelligence must be verified. Sometimes the best human intelligence can come from a past opponent who has an opposition research file of their own.

With the availability of information on the Internet, one of the quickest and easiest means to gather information on a person is by conducting some searches on the World Wide Web. Internet searches can yield information about positions an opponent may have taken on issues in the past, undesirable organizations that may have endorsed, or any number of details about an opponent that may eventually be useful. A thorough search should be conducted by someone who has extensive knowledge of finding information on the Internet.

An opposition research checklist is provided at the end of this chapter to assist in the gathering of information. This checklist should in no way be considered a complete list. It is provided as a reference for some of the most basic and easily accessible information. Once opposition research is finished, or as new information is added, a campaign should go back to the "strengths vs. weaknesses" charts created in Chapter 1 in order to make all information current. Good opposition research will yield both strengths and weaknesses of an opponent.

One resource may also include seeking out organizations opposed to a specific candidate. If an organization or PAC is opposed to a candidate, it may be because they have gathered their own information that they are willing to share. It costs nothing to ask for such information, and the results could be fruitful.

A campaign should include thorough research on its own candidate as well. While conducting opposition research, a campaign should perform the same tasks to research its own candidate. Conducting research on one's own candidate will most likely yield information that any opponent will also accumulate. It is extremely important to understand the information an opponent will have to use in the campaign.

3.3   Determining the Message

The most important part of an effective political campaign is developing a message that is both relevant and will resonate with voters.

Based on the information gathered in Chapter One, the campaign's core team should be able to form the message.

Chapter One discussed the gathering of issue information. Part of this information gathering requires understanding the mood of the electorate. If the people who are voting are generally positive and up-beat about how things are going, then the message will be different if voters feel that government is on the wrong track. Determining the issues foremost on the minds of voters will also determine the direction a campaign's message will take.

Once the campaign has completed the information gathering in Chapter One, built the team as described in Chapter 2 and conducted the important opposition research discussed earlier in this chapter, there will be enough information to begin formulating the theme and message for a campaign.

The overall message of a campaign is determined by four factors:

1. Issues important to voters
2. Priorities of the voters (an issue may be important to a voter, but a campaign must evaluate the priority of that issue among voters)
3. Strengths of the candidate
4. Weaknesses of the opponent

The campaign team should evaluate the issues important in a race and determine which ones are most important to voters thereby prioritizing the issues. For instance, being pro-life may be very important to voters in a certain district, but if their concern is currently focused on economic problems, then the "life" issue may not be one upon which they make their decision. Once the strongest issues have been prioritized, the campaign team must evaluate the issues in which the candidate has strengths. Once the list is narrowed to the issues people care about and the candidate is strong, they should then be compared to the opponent's weaknesses.

A campaign that follows this process will usually find only one or two issues that are important to the voters in which the candidate is strong and the opponent is weak. A smart campaign will also reverse the process from the opponent's point of view to find the issues important to voters in which the opponent is strong and the candidate is weak. Knowing the issues that the opponent must emphasize is as important as understanding the issues one's own candidate must use.

The way in which a campaign uses its message will depend upon the type of campaign. Whether the race is a reelection campaign, challenging campaign to a current incumbent, a field race in which more than one candidate will be elected or an open seat in which the current officeholder is not seeking reelection, the campaign will use its message information differently. Different scenarios require different approaches to the message.

An incumbent facing reelection

If a campaign is one of incumbency, then it should reflect any successes in office. A common theme for incumbents who had specific benchmarks from their campaigns that they met is "Promises Made. Promises Kept." It is also important to know where an opponent will try to attack in terms of issues. If the opponent uses the theme of "Failure in Office", then the incumbent's theme needs to counter that sentiment. "Experience That Matters", "Working For Us" or "Leadership That Works" are also common themes for incumbent campaigns. A general campaign theme of "Keep Jane Smith Working for Us" works well if voters have a generally positive mood about the leadership. If an office has won awards, and the candidate is running for reelection as mayor, the theme "Jane Smith – Your Award Winning Mayor" will help the rest of the message resonate.

In cases where the electorate is unhappy, or voters feel the government is on the wrong track, the campaign should work directly with the issues on the forefront of people's thoughts. If crime is the biggest issue, a message that reflects a tough record on crime would help serve the campaign. An ill prepared campaign for an incumbent will allow itself to be constantly on the defensive. Knowing the issues people care about and knowing one's own strengths and initiatives in those areas ahead of time will allow a campaign to promote a winning message before a challenger has a chance to define where the incumbent is on the issues.

This is where the lists of strengths and weaknesses discussed in Chapter One become important. By promoting strengths and knowing the weaknesses an opponent may attack, a campaign will be prepared to talk about strengths and a successful record before the attacks begin. Knowing an opponent's weaknesses will allow the campaign to respond with a message of "John Doe wants to attack Jane Smith on crime, but Jane Smith has been working to make our streets and families safer while John Doe has a poor record of his own when it comes to the law." Then the campaign lists the successes of Jane Smith's administration.

When the campaign is one of incumbency:

- Play to strengths
- Know the opponent's weaknesses
- Know the issues voters care about
- Tailor the message to fit the incumbent's strengths into the issues voters care about

It is also important to know which areas of the jurisdiction have different demographics. For instance, some areas may have lower income residents, higher priced homes, seniors, young families, or empty nesters. Knowing each area and being able to tailor a message that fits and appeals to each can be more effective than using a general blanket message. It is important not to contradict oneself among various areas in a jurisdiction.

Once a campaign has a message that voters are listening to and like, it is important to repeat it often. Consistent repetition is paramount to communicating a message effectively. Tactics on grassroots and media, which allow the campaign to broadcast the message, are discussed in later chapters.

Challenger of an incumbent facing reelection

Based on the opposition research conducted earlier in this chapter, as well as the general background information gathered during

Chapter One, building a case against the incumbent becomes the task. Voters generally need a reason if they are going to vote against an incumbent. If there is no apparent reason to vote against the incumbent, then it is the job of a challenger's campaign to educate the electorate as to why the incumbent does not deserve reelection.

Common themes in the challenger campaign include some variation of "It's time for a change". As a general rule, the "time for a change" theme does not resonate unless the reason or reasons for change become apparent. Voters will not elect a change for change's sake. Therefore it is important to study the top issues foremost on the minds of the voters and cross-reference those against the list of the opponent's weaknesses. Regardless of the issues that are foremost on voters minds, if an opponent has done something dishonest or illegal in office, those points of weakness should be used. Using the transgressions of an opponent to go on the attack is more effective if the challenger campaign can present itself as the better alternative. General dissatisfaction with an opponent among the electorate is not necessarily enough to win an election.

One of multiple seats in a field race

In a race for city council in which the top four vote-getters win a seat, or a township trustee race in which the top two candidates win a seat, the goal now becomes one of gaining more attention than the other campaigns. Some campaigns find this job easier while others see it as more difficult. For instance, it can be difficult to set a candidate apart when the top issue among the electorate is job creation, and everyone has the same pro-job message. A field race can easily become a political shouting match in which each candidate is trying to be the loudest one in the crowd on the same issue.

If a candidate is in a race in which everyone is trying to "out conservative" the others or "out patriot" the others, it is wise to find a way to take the common theme and make it work in a way that separates the candidate from the group. Making a candidate out to be the sensible choice, the consensus builder, or the only one with a plan, can make the difference in a shouting match if this approach distinguishes the candidate from the field. "Jane Smith, the consensus builder with a plan" can become a theme that differentiates a winning campaign from everyone else. Keep it simple.

Open seat in which the incumbent is not running

A race in which there is a single open seat can be similar to the field race if multiple candidates are seeking the position. However, if only one opponent is seeking that position, then the race for an open seat is a heads-up match with similar characteristics of a challenger campaign.

Perhaps the opponent is someone who is the hand-picked successor of the former officeholder. If that is the case, then the weaknesses of the predecessor may become the weaknesses of the opponent. A candidate would not wish to be the hand-picked successor if the officeholder doing the picking is seen as unpopular, dishonest or unfavorable.

An advantage in winning in an open seat race without an incumbent is to be able to define the issues and the candidates in the race before anyone else does. That is not to say that the first person who announces for a seat is effective in defining the issues or candidates. For instance, a candidate might voice an intention to run for a seat four or six years before the current officeholder is term-limited, thereby making the candidate a presumptive successor. However, if that candidate who hastily announced early on is not able to begin performing the preliminary work discussed in the first three chapters of *The Political Campaign Desk Reference*, then the campaign may easily be overtaken by a newcomer to the race who is more successful in delivering an effective message to the voters. Being first is not the same as being effective. Furthermore, announcing early allows any potential opponents to perform effective opposition research.

In a field race in which one seat is available, a candidate cannot be satisfied with being one of the top vote getters – being "number one" is the only option. Multiple candidates for a single office create a situation in which unlikely candidates can win a campaign. Open seats with multiple candidates seeking that seat require aggressive grassroots campaigns, or "ground wars," in addition to the traditional message delivery. Due to the competition for endorsements, campaigns should endeavor to secure these endorsements early.

A winning campaign in a field race will determine its message on a number of factors including geography, the purpose of other candidates seeking the post, the messages being delivered by the other candidates and the particular strengths and weaknesses of the opponents.

An example of a tough race for Congress occurred in 2005. A Congressman left his position mid term in order to take another position. A special election occurred which allowed for approximately 6 weeks of campaigning to replace him. Eleven candidates filed to run for the vacated post. The person who won was a candidate who many presumed had no chance. Three of the presumptive front-runners campaigned vociferously, and maligned each other's records, while the candidate who won ran an aggressive grassroots campaign and did not engage in campaigning "against" any of the other candidates. On Election Day, the three candidates who spent most of the money in the special election had driven each other's favorability down to the point that the fourth candidate, who stayed out of the fray, stuck to her message, and maintained a strong ground war narrowly won by less than 1,000 votes.

The challenge that campaigns face is finding the right message, the right tactics and identifying the right people to target. The effective campaign is able to use the four resources of time, information, money and people (TIMP) to make it all work. The four types of campaigns described above build their messages in different ways, and sometimes a campaign can actually benefit by the presence of other campaigns in the same race. The fundamental need to determine the right message, however, does not change even when the approach to the campaign does.

3.4   Defining the Issues

So far, *The Political Campaign Desk Reference* has focused on gathering information, conducting research and examining strengths and weaknesses. Once a campaign gathers its information, defines the type of race it has, and determines how many opponents it will have, as well as its blanket message ("time for change", "your award winning incumbent" etc.) it is time to define the issues.

Defining issues is different from identifying issues. A campaign defines an issue in a campaign once it identifies the issue that it must define. Identifying issues occurred during the information gathering portion of the campaign. By the time a campaign team is ready to define an issue, it should have an abundance of information at its fingertips. The art of defining the issue is explaining to voters why it is important, how the campaign addresses it, and how the opponent does not measure up. Traditional campaigning communicates all of this information in either a two-sided direct mail piece or 30 second television spot. The Internet allows for more flexibility, but keeping the message simple and brief is still necessary.

If high taxes are the issue in a race, and the incumbent has a record of either raising taxes or doing nothing to lower them, then the campaign message for Challenger Bob Smith can easily become "Smith – Because taxes are too high." The campaign should have numerous opportunities through press releases, press conferences, campaign rallies, and other means to point out why taxes are too high, how they can be lowered, what Bob Smith will do to correct it and where the incumbent failed. Furthermore, the campaign will be able to define why taxes are too high in its direct mail, telephone, door-to-door or television advertising. Regardless of what the message is, a campaign must take certain steps to define the message:

- Present the message in a way voters understand (keep it simple)
- Appeal to the hearts of voters first, and grab their attention
- Back up initial emotional appeals with evidence
- Tell a story of how the opponent fails to address issue
- Explain how the candidate is the answer to the problem

Because of all of the elements and steps involved in defining the message, a well run campaign will not introduce too many issues into a campaign. One or two good issues are generally enough. Some campaigns feel it might be a good idea to constantly introduce new issues in a campaign or that the opponent has so many weaknesses that all of them should be exposed. A campaign that engages in such a "shot gun" strategy, trying to hit the target with as many little jabs as possible, may not be able to accomplish victory as smoothly, easily, or inexpensively as a "sniper" strategy that calculates how it will define its one or two messages.

Expense of campaign communications is also another concern for a campaign. With each issue that a campaign wishes to address, it has to spend money to educate the voters. If a campaign budget is $20,000, it does not make sense to communicate six different messages when one or two will do. If voters are not swayed by the two key issues in a campaign, introducing a handful of new ones will only serve to confuse them. In order for a message to resonate, it must be repeated, not obfuscated by other issues. A common theme in *The Political Campaign Desk Reference* is "keep it simple." Keep it simple.

A campaign message of "Because taxes are too high" can become increasingly effective, as well as repeated, if the opponent has a record of voting for increases, misusing money, overseeing failed projects, or has poor attendance at meetings. The single message of high taxes is repeated every time the campaign issues a new TV spot, direct mail piece, press release, e-mail or phone message. If the opponent has raised taxes, the campaign can issue material talking about how high taxes are while the opponent raised them. If the opponent also oversaw failed projects, then the next message issued by the campaign repeats the high tax message by describing how taxes remain high while the opponent fails to complete projects or stay within budget. Each successive repeat of the issue can have different information backing it up, but the theme must be a common thread through the campaign.

Effectively defining a message requires the issue to resonate with voters, be easily understandable, and consistent throughout the campaign.

3.5   Targeting

Chapter One discussed obtaining both a voter registration database with voter history as well as election results from previous campaigns. This section will explore various methods of targeting individual voters as well as targeting precincts, wards and other jurisdictions. Targeting refers to how the campaign chooses who specifically will receive campaign communications.

Targeting Individuals

Effective campaigning relies heavily on the ability of a campaign to target its message to likely voters and to deliver a message that will resonate with each targeted voter. By using the voter database, a campaign manager can begin the process of eliminating those voters not likely to vote in the election. The purpose of targeting individuals is to maximize the effectiveness of each dollar spent on the campaign. By eliminating those registered voters that are unlikely to vote because of an inconsistent voting history, a history in which they only vote in presidential elections, a campaign can more effectively deliver messages to those likely to vote in an off-year election. Also, by eliminating die-hard members of a rival party, a campaign can further target directly to voters who are more likely to be receptive to the message of a campaign.

When looking at a voter database, the first people it is wise to eliminate are inactive voters – voters who have not voted in four years or more. These voters may have moved, died, decided not to vote, or are unable to vote. By spending money on voters who are inactive, a campaign takes money away from the pot that can be effectively used on active voters more likely to participate in the election.

In any race, the database should eliminate all voters outside the jurisdiction of the office being sought. For instance, an elections office may provide a database for the entire county, but the race is for city council. All voters that cannot participate in the election should be eliminated from the database. Although this suggestion seems like an obvious move, there have been races in which a campaign relied on someone else's database for their targeted list, and a significant amount of mail and phone calls were delivered to voters outside the district. A campaign should always rely on its own information because it controls every aspect of the database and knows that it came directly from the source. Relying on someone else's targeted list is a gamble and always runs the chance of being outdated.

A list can further be targeted by eliminating multiple voters in a single household. By sending a direct mail piece to a family or a single household, a campaign eliminates unnecessary duplication. Some candidates with larger budgets will send literature to every voter in a household because they feel this method will have a greater reach. Those candidates may be right, but when a campaign is on a budget, sending a single piece of literature to a household is nearly as effective as mailing individually to everyone at the address, and it will save significantly.

If a budget forces a campaign into a situation where it is required to target only those most likely to vote, then the campaign should eliminate everyone who has not voted consistently in a similar election. For instance, a candidate may be running for city council in an off-year election. By eliminating all voters who have never voted in an off-year election, then the campaign has eliminated a significant amount of voters who have never shown interest in a city council race. Sometimes, the database needs to be narrowed even more. In cases such as this, a campaign can assign a value to each voter. If a voter in a database has only voted once in the last three off-year elections, then that voter receives a value of 1. If the voter voted twice, then the value is 2, and a voter who voted in all of the last three elections might receive a value of 3. A low-budget campaign may decide only to send mail to voters with a strength score of 2 or 3.

Once the campaign has narrowed its database as much as comfort allows, another method of further targeting is to identify as many of the remaining voters as possible. One relatively inexpensive way to identify voters is to call each of those voters with a survey of questions very similar to the survey discussed in Chapter 2 in the section "Developing the Database". These questions can be used to determine which voters are planning on voting, which ones have made a decision already in the race and which voters will be receptive to which messages. This method of targeting can be referred to as "microtargeting".

It can be an effective means for candidates to get the most out of each dollar spent on the campaign.

For voters who did not have published phone numbers or did not respond to the telephone survey, a direct mail survey can be sent to them in order to help microtarget the remainder of the list. The process of microtargeting can yield potential donors and volunteers as well.

Targeting Precincts, Wards and Other Jurisdictions

When looking at a database, it is sometimes important to target only specific geographic areas. For instance, perhaps a candidate is challenging a township trustee who voted to put a strip mall near a specific neighborhood. Perhaps this idea was an unpopular decision among the residents in precincts surrounding the new shopping center but popular with precincts in the same township that are not as near the strip mall. A campaign may wish to send a specific mailer reminding the residents near the shopping center of the opponent's vote while ex-cluding residents with whom the shopping center is popular. In order to do that, a campaign will specifically target the precincts near the shopping center for this mailing.

Targeting specific jurisdictions is important in larger races because each local area faces different issues. There may also be some pre-cincts that have very low voter turnout based on results of past cam-paigns, and a campaign may wish to remove those precincts. The voter database from the elections office should also signify in what precinct a voter lives as well as the state legislative district, congressional dis-trict, judicial district and school district.

Another reason to target precincts is to have the candidate in a race travel door-to-door in the precincts of the highest turnout. If the size of the race or time availability of a candidate does not allow for door-to-door in every precinct, then targeting should occur for the precincts with the highest turnout. In addition, precincts that historically leaned heavily towards candidates with similar values or message as one's own campaign should be targeted precincts. Such precincts may be more likely to be "low hanging fruit" in terms of support, yard sign locations, and volunteers.

As the campaign conducts literature drops, or lit drops, precincts that are "swing" precincts should be targeted. Swing precincts are precincts in which voters will sometimes vote one way and sometimes vote another. For instance, a swing precinct is a precinct in which both Republicans and Democrats have the ability to do well or a tax levy that fails on one ballot might pass on another. Finding swing precincts can be accomplished by comparing election results for local candidates and statewide or national candidates for an election or over the course of multiple elections.

Simply put, swing precincts represent areas that can be swayed one way or another based on the aggressiveness and message of a campaign.

If a candidate is against a highly unpopular school tax levy, it may be wise to target voters by school district and deliver the campaign's message regarding the levy only to them. This same concept can be applied to any number of political subdivisions if appropriate.

Targeting is a means to maximize message delivery to likely voters while saving valuable resources. A campaign can better utilize money and time resources by using information resources effectively. Voters that can be identified as less likely to vote or less likely to support a candidate can be eliminated thereby making it more possible to focus on votes a candidate can obtain.

3.6   Testing the Message

There are different methods to test messages with voters. A campaign will generally want to test its message with a smaller audience before fully investing in the message. For small campaigns, testing the message may be limited to running it by the kitchen cabinet. Different means of testing a message may include telephone surveys, focus groups, direct mail or any other method that will yield feedback from a representative group of people. A campaign is seeking messages that "move" voters, which means a voter once hearing a message will move from an opponent's camp to becoming undecided or from undecided into a candidate's camp.

If a campaign has not yet conducted an initial poll, or baseline poll, to gauge the race, working the message into the poll would be a good expenditure. By giving voters a message and asking "would you be more likely or less likely to vote for Jane Smith..." then the poll can measure their responses. A poll is a good method by which one can test any messages against an opponent.

A focus group is a small gathering of different people who will listen to a message or read about a message and provide feedback. It is important to do this without prompting the participants with information about what a campaign wishes to hear. Typically, a campaign would want a third party to conduct this type of focus group. The elements of focus groups ask participants how they feel about certain messages and gauge their reaction to the messages. Understanding what a representative sample of voters likes and dislikes about a message helps the campaign to craft an even stronger, more resonate message.

3.7   Building Name Identification and "Favorability"

In addition to crafting a message that works, a candidate must be seen and heard. In order to have confidence in voting for a candidate, voters need to know, and have trust in, the candidate. Future chapters will discuss methods to increase name recognition or name identification. A candidate must understand that in order for a message to have the maximum effect, voters need to know the person broadcasting the message. Throughout the race, a campaign manager will need to place primary importance on the candidate's exposure to voters through any means necessary prior to spending the bulk of the budget on communicating the message.

Along with the importance of name identification, voter perception of a candidate is vital. It is a challenge for a campaign when a candidate enters the race with a negative message. Negative messages drive the favorability of the opponent down, but they also have a detrimental effect on the person delivering the negative message. Therefore, a well-planned campaign will begin with a positive introduction prior to leveling attacks at the opponent.

Crafting the right message that meets a candidate's principles and resonates with voters is a complex process. Smaller campaigns may wage races with an untested message that may, or may not, be well thought out. There are ways for even small campaigns, or campaigns on a budget, to craft a solid message and test it before substantially investing in it. By taking the steps outlined in these first three chapters, a campaign will move on toward the planning stages confident that it has a good campaign message that will not only be heard but resonate and move voters.

Opposition Research Checklist

The following list is not a comprehensive list of items that a campaign can research, but it is a listing of the most common sources that tend to yield important information. It is important for a campaign to conduct the same research on its own candidate that it conducts on its opponent.

Item Sought	Where to get it	What campaign is looking for
Public voting history	County Board of Elections or Elections Clerk	When candidate registered, registration address, consistency of voting history, history of changing parties
Employment files (if current or former government employee)	Human Resources of current or past employers	Derogatory information, infractions, safety violations, complaints, supervisor comments, work history, performance reports
Campaign finance reports	County Board of Elections, Elections Clerk or Secretary of State	How much candidate is capable of raising, undesirable contributors, undesirable expenditures, employee giving, family on payroll, contributors who get special treatment through office
Official voting record (if the candidate is an elected officeholder)	Clerk of board or body upon which candidate served	Any legislation or projects that candidate has proposed, any votes that affect a person's employment, votes affecting contributors, friends, family or business partners

Official meeting minutes (if the candidate is an elected officeholder)	Clerk of board or body upon which candidate served	attendance at meetings, silly statements, conflicts
Video of official meetings (if the candidate is an elected officeholder)	Clerk of board or body upon which candidate served	Physical evidence of statements, conflicts attendance (empty seat during important votes), record of controversial vote
Newspaper clippings	Library microfilm archives and/or Internet	Headlines that put candidate in poor light, quotes that can be used against candidate, third-party reporting of controversial votes or situations, evidence of improprieties recorded in press
Ethics disclosure reports (for officeholders or public employees required to file them)	State ethics commission, Secretary of State or other controlling authority	Improper reporting, incomplete reporting; business relationships, large spikes in income, investments, gifts
Criminal history	County clerk of courts, municipal clerk, local police or sheriff department	Any criminal history, tickets or infractions against the law including large numbers of parking tickets or anything that can demonstrate a scofflaw attitude
Property records	County auditor, assessor, recorder or clerk	Properties that candidate owns, how much land, if land candidate owns is in areas where candidate made decisions, mortgages on land or dwellings
Civil History	County or municipal clerk	Liens or judgments against candidate
Previous opponent(s)	Past elections records at board of elections or elections secretary	Past opponents may have an opposition research file to share or vital information

Chapter 4

The Campaign Plan

4.1 Why Bother Planning?

As discussed in the Introduction to *The Political Campaign Desk Reference*, the ancient general Sun Tsu asserts that planning is essential to winning. Some wars are won before any troops take the field because one general has planned whereas another has not.

The campaign plan is where the campaign manager lays out how the resources of time, information, money and people are to be utilized. The campaign plan details when and how the message will be broadcast, how much will be spent doing it and the tactics involved.

A campaign in which the candidate thinks that putting his name on the ballot and putting up some yard signs is mistaking tactics with strategy. A campaign plan lays out the tactics while also developing a deeper team understanding of the message and how it fits into the timeline and budget.

A campaign plan also develops how various team members will function within the campaign, and the plan will provide focus.

If there are two competing campaigns in a race, the campaign with a plan is more likely to succeed than the campaign without.

4.2 Budgeting

The most important aspect of formulating a budget is to prioritize where the campaign's dollars are going to go. Figuring out where the campaign will get the largest return on its investment requires discipline. Return is measured by votes and not money. Candidates for office often spend far more money to seek an office than the office salary pays. Political campaigns are not about seeing how little a campaign can spend. A candidate trying to relate a campaign budget to how much an elected job pays is not viewing the campaign from an objective point of view.

A township trustee race may pay $10,000 a year, but a motivated candidate who wishes to be able to affect policy will not limit a campaign budget to how much an office pays. If the candidate limits expenses to the annual salary of an office, then is the candidate looking to affect policy, or is the candidate merely looking for a job?

A campaign budget should never rely on the potential future earnings of an elected office. The campaign budget relies on how much money a campaign can raise and how much a candidate is willing to contribute to win an election - nothing more. A campaign is completely irrespective of the office being sought as far as expenses are concerned. If a candidate is counting on a win in order to finance the campaign, then the likelihood that rational budget decisions will be made is reduced. A campaign is separate from an elected office.

Future sections of *The Political Campaign Desk Reference* discuss the advantages and disadvantages of various types of message delivery a campaign can use. In formulating a budget, a campaign must answer the following questions:

- How much is needed to run an effective media campaign?
- How much can the campaign raise from donors?
- How much is the candidate willing to contribute?

Once a campaign team has an idea about how much it will be able to spend on the race, it must prioritize. If the campaign cannot raise much money, and the candidate is not willing to contribute much to the campaign, then efforts will primarily be focused on grassroots. If the campaign will have more money to spend beyond a grassroots effort, then a media campaign or "air war" can be discussed. Most aspects of an air war also have a production cost associated in addition to air time or postage. Components of an air war can include television, radio, telemarketing, direct mail and the Internet. Components of a ground war include signs, door-to-door, lit drops, handbills, t-shirts and volunteer needs.

A campaign will budget starting from the ground and working up. This means that the components of the ground war should be quantified in the budget first. The financial costs associated with a spirited grassroots campaign are far less than an air war, but the human resources needed to be effective are far greater. Once the ground war has been budgeted, the campaign now focuses attention on remaining money for the air war.

For smaller campaigns, an air war will consist primarily of direct mail. A smaller campaign such as a township or municipal election generally does not require the wide appeal and reach of television. Multiple targeted direct mail pieces can be delivered to select households in order to communicate the campaign message. Many campaigns of this size will place the remainder of their budgets, after accounting for a ground war, into direct mail.

An inexpensive air war can be waged through social media and the Internet. Regardless of the budget, a campaign should plan on using the Internet. Many services on the Internet are free for a campaign to set up, such as an account on a social media site, and others are nominally expensive such as setting up a web site with a template from an Internet Service Provider.

For larger budgets, an air war can expand to telephones, radio, and into television. A larger budget also allows for expanded Internet exposure. Factors that should be considered before placing money in various media include how much saturation can be attained, if the message will be diluted, if voters are exposed to this medium, what media opponents are using, and other factors.

Each item in the budget requires its own line:

1. Web Site
2. Internet/Social Media ads
3. Yard signs
4. Road signs
5. T-shirts
6. Handbills
7. Web site
8. Direct mail

9. Design for direct mail
10. Telephone marketing
11. Radio time
12. Radio production
13. Television time
14. Television production
15. Professional assistance

Some campaigns will have more line items and others will have fewer. All costs associated with a campaign should be placed in the budget so that the management team can get a good snapshot of the race.

4.3   Tactics

There are numerous methods of message delivery in a campaign. Some are more effective than others. Once a campaign knows how much it will have to spend, and it has an idea of how much it will spend in each area, it can then map out the various tactics. This chapter touches the surface of the myriad methods involved in a campaign in order to provide an idea of how to prioritize the tactics in the budget. Chapters seven and eight will discuss how to utilize these tactics in greater detail.

Trinkets

Candidates will often want to spend money on trinkets to give out at festivals and parades. Trinkets include cups, nail files, fans, water bottles, rulers, change purses, pencils and any number of items. Most often these items will be thrown away. Sometimes they end up in the possession of a child or in a drawer of clutter. Trinkets cannot vote, and they seldom raise candidate awareness. They appeal to candidates because they are tangible items with the candidate's name, and the candidate feels that something is being accomplished as these trinkets are distributed. Unfortunately trinkets are not he most cost effective method of message delivery.

The important thing to remember about races is that they are marketing campaigns, and producing items that will be thrown away or will sit in a drawer somewhere for months after an election are not wise investments. Vendors that peddle trinkets are usually very persuasive and create a sense of urgency in a candidate to make a purchase of trinkets immediately. Trinket peddlers also produce a large volume of items that have a very low unit price. Campaign budgets should focus on expenditures that help raise candidate name recognition and deliver the campaign message. Advertising such as direct mail, television, radio and road signs can contribute to the overall success of the campaign. In order to win, candidates must be seen and heard, and trinkets are less effective than most other methods.

Signs

In campaigns that require name identification and awareness, signs are typically a good expenditure. The more aware voters are of the candidate, the greater the likelihood that they will pay attention to a message when they receive one in he mail, over television, on the radio, through the Internet, or any other medium. A candidate for office must compete against thousands of other messages that the average person is bombarded with on a daily basis. Companies spend millions of dollars marketing products trying to reach people on the same level that a candidate does, but a candidate works on a shoestring budget. A campaign is not only competing for attention against other candidates, campaigns are competing against every other message that voters receive from advertisements to municipal road signs to the music on the radio.

Prices vary based on quantity and size of signs. If the campaign is for a city council race of a small town, a campaign may want to budget for only 500 small signs whereas countywide or Congressional races will have larger sign budgets. Some media vendors want campaigns to avoid signs so that more money can be spent on media. Signs are an important, cost effective means of raising name identification of a candidate, and the signs are sustainable through a campaign. People will pass them many times and gain awareness over time of the candidate's campaign. Signs are not, however, effective in message delivery, and for this reason are frowned upon by some media consultants.

There are many different varieties of signs, and size does matter in a sign campaign. A campaign can invest $50 and produce a large 4' x 8' sign that has high visibility from far away. For the same price, a campaign may also be able to produce 25 small yard signs that are not very visible until a driver or pedestrian is right on top of the sign. The goal in a sign campaign is to be seen. Campaigns should consider spending money on large signs in high traffic areas rather than small signs in low traffic areas. Small signs are good for neighborhoods, but larger signs are excellent for thoroughfares.

Handbills

In an aggressive door-to-door campaign, handbills are essential in communicating who the candidate is and the reasons for running for office. The quantity of handbills that should be budgeted is based on the number of houses that the candidate will visit and leave the literature, how many pieces will be needed for literature drops and how many pieces are needed for community events and civic meetings. Also, handbills are good for distribution at the polls on Election Day.

Handbills can be full color or black and white for lower budget campaigns. However, visual impact is important in a campaign, and if a voter sees an attractive, full color, visually driven piece of literature on a table next to black-and-white copies from an opposing campaign, the literature with greater impact will receive more attention.

T-shirts

As with signs, volunteers in t-shirts can raise awareness of a campaign. Remember that a campaign is competing against other campaigns, manufacturers, retailers, other advertisers and even municipal signs for peoples' attention. Many of those people are voters. Whenever a campaign has a chance of introducing its brand at a low cost to voters, it should capitalize on the opportunity.

T-shirts are helpful for volunteers to wear as mobile billboards at community events and meetings. When traveling door-to-door, volunteers should also be wearing campaign t-shirts. The cost of shirts should be kept low, but the campaign should have enough for all volunteers. Also, volunteers working polling locations on behalf of a candidate should wear campaign t-shirts. The budget should include enough t-shirts for all activities that require them.

Television

Some races make it impractical for a campaign to purchase television time. Television has production costs. Also, the message on television must be repeated many times across many hours over many days in order to have an impact on the voters a candidate is attempting to reach. Unless a candidate is able to saturate the airwaves effectively with a message, it may be better to focus on less expensive message delivery tools such as Internet, direct mail, telephones or even radio.

If a campaign has enough for television, the amount budgeted will be dependent upon whether the campaign is purchasing broadcast network affiliate time or specific cable channels. The duration of the spot is also a consideration. Some spots can be fifteen seconds long while most are thirty seconds long. Also, the longevity of the spot is a consideration. The dates over which the spot will play will factor into how much is spent on television. Other barriers to the effectiveness of television may include missing voters who watch satellite over cable or voters who skip commercials with a DVR.

Unless a significant dollar amount can be spent on television, this medium should not be considered. Other air war activities such as telephones, the Internet or direct mail may be more appropriate expenditures for a smaller dollar amount.

Direct Mail

Direct mail is probably the most effective means of communicating a campaign message for a lower budget campaign. Whereas television reaches a broad audience that includes voters and non voters, direct mail allows a campaign to target a specific voter. Through direct mail, a campaign can speak directly to any voter it targets with a tailored message. And direct mail is generally less expensive than other media, so multiple messages can be delivered to a specific voter over time, and the likelihood is high that the targeted voter will see most, if not all, of the direct mail messages. Campaigns of any size will invest a large portion of its budget into direct mail. In small campaigns, the remainder of the budget, after the ground war is planned, is often placed in direct mail.

Telemarketing

Telephone messages can be effective, but they also can be detrimental. Too many phone messages left on voicemail can seem intrusive. Therefore it is wise not to spend a large portion of a budget on telemarketing. The advantage to phones is that they are inexpensive, and specific households can be targeted by phone. Phones can also be an effective, inexpensive means of gathering information and micro-targeting through automated polling.

Internet

Every campaign should have an Internet component. At the very least, a free account on a social networking site provides some sort of presence of the campaign on the Internet. Most campaigns, large and small, will pay the nominal fee to a service provider to set up a web site and use a web template in which the campaign can easily drop in information. Other low-cost methods of using the Internet can include posting videos to social network sites, blast e-mails to supporters and blogs. Higher cost methods of using the Internet involve ads and paying to appear at the top of the list on search engines for key words.

In prioritizing the budget, begin with the ground war and work up to the air war. Signs and handbills are important for candidate recognition and door-to-door message delivery. Direct mail is effective in the air war followed by television, telemarketing, and radio. Every campaign should have an Internet component, and it is generally wise to expend enough to start a web site in addition to having a presence on social networking sites. Every element in a budget requires its own line item. A budget can only include expenditures for how much it knows it will have to spend. Budgeting beyond what a campaign will have places the campaign in debt, and operating in debt is not advisable.

4.4   Building the Timeline

The timeline is the part of the campaign plan that describes when tactics will be implemented on the campaign. It is wise to begin the timeline at Election Day and work backwards. The reason a campaign builds a timeline in reverse is that most money is spent in the last week or two of a campaign. If a campaign were to work a timeline from six months out from Election Day and try to distribute where money is spent during those six months, it is likely that the campaign will have little to no money left by the time the campaign heats up in the final two weeks when most voters have just started paying attention.

Therefore, a campaign must exercise discipline in wisely timed message delivery. Once a timeline is set, every effort should be made to stick to the plan. Of course, a campaign plan is a living document and subject to frequent corrections, but the general timeline should not need much change. Election Day is a constant that will not change.

The bulk of electronic media, Internet ads, radio, and television will play during the final week of the campaign. For campaigns with larger budgets, electronic media may begin as early as a month before Election Day and build in frequency until the day before the election. It is generally considered wasteful to spend too much money on media after early morning on Election Day although some campaigns feel that they still reach viewers, listeners, and Internet users after those hours. In most campaigns, the media purchase is heaviest on the day before an election as well as the week leading up to the election.

Direct mail should be targeted to land two to three days after it is mailed at the post office. Because direct mail is usually sent as bulk mail, it is important to allow those extra days for delivery whereas first class is more dependable in being delivered the day following its mailing. The final piece should be scheduled to land in mailboxes the Friday before Election Day. If the campaign has multiple mail pieces, they should be sent approximately three to four days apart from each other so that they do not get delivered at the same time. Therefore, a campaign timeline should include both the mailing date of direct mail, the anticipated delivery date of that mail as well as design and production time.

Telemarketing is very important in that it is more effective the closer to the election that it is used. Unfortunately, it becomes diluted in its effectiveness if multiple candidates are utilizing it. A campaign will generally schedule a telephone message to be delivered the day before the election as well as one to two messages the week prior to the election. Multiple calls should never be made on the same day. It is not wise to exceed three or four telephone calls on a campaign.

Handbills are needed for poll workers on the day of the election, and the campaign should order enough for the poll workers it will have. Working backwards from Election Day, the campaign will also plan to distribute handbills through literature drops to doorsteps. The candidate should personally walk targeted precincts throughout the campaign with the most important precincts being walked the weeks leading up to the campaign. More handbills will be used at community events and civic meetings. The campaign should decide in advance how much total printed material will be used for these grassroots activities and order at one time. A single order of handbills will be more cost effective than multiple orders. Of course, if the content on the literature changes, (the campaign may receive new endorsements) then the campaign will need to reorder new handbills.

Although poll workers are mostly used on Election Day, the planning, recruitment and training must begin sooner than that. Sometimes states allow for early voting at polls for a few weeks leading up to Election Day. It can be wise to have poll workers at the board of elections or designated voting place prior to election day if voters are voting.

A campaign timeline should reflect when these activities begin so that the campaign manager can follow up with the assigned person to check on progress. A campaign must arrange the materials that poll workers will use. Once a campaign determines that poll workers will use signs, literature or other materials, it must distribute these materials to the poll workers and provide adequate training so that each voter is greeted or contacted by the poll worker in the manner that the campaign wishes. Each component of handling this operation must be added to the timeline.

Almost every jurisdiction allows for absentee or mail voting beginning roughly a month out from the campaign. The handling of absentees and how to court absentee and mail voters will be dealt with in a later chapter of *The Political Campaign Desk Reference*, but the campaign timeline should reflect each day that absentee and mail ballots are being sent out from the elections office. Early voting also affects when the campaign might begin its broadcast media campaign.

Community events are usually fixed dates that are not subject to campaign needs. Therefore, any community event in which the campaign plans on participating should be placed on the timeline so that campaign rallies, fundraisers and other events can be scheduled around them. During the final weeks of the campaign, the highest profile events should be targeted over lesser profile events. Grassroots efforts begin to increase during the final two months of the campaign, and volunteers should see evidence of their contributions by the final two weeks. Everyone gets a break after Election Day. By the time the polls close, all campaign resources should be depleted including time, information, money and people. That does not mean that people should not be well taken care of because the candidate will need those volunteers for the next race.

Each member of the management team should have a copy of the portion of the campaign timeline that affects him or her, and it is the duty of the campaign manager to oversee the implementation of the timeline. Every aspect of the campaign timeline must run like clockwork. If an event is being held on a certain date, and invitations are mailed three to four weeks in advance, and an RSVP deadline is included, a complete timeline should include each step. Each member of the campaign team has the duty to add pertinent information to the timeline including the candidate, scheduler, campaign manager, political director and volunteer coordinator. Only one person in the campaign should oversee the timeline. Whenever changes are made to the timeline, all members of the management team, including the candidate, should receive the revised timeline.

4.5   Assigning Responsibilities and Duties

A campaign plan, like any other project management plan, will have duties assigned to certain people. Whenever a campaign activity appears on the timeline, a name or names should appear next to it so that the campaign knows who is responsible for making the event successful.

The duties in the campaign should be assigned according to the TIMP resources. Smaller campaigns will have fewer people to whom duties are assigned while larger campaigns will have a more complex management structure. Time is a resource that should be managed by the campaign manager, the candidate and the scheduler. The campaign manager is responsible for prioritizing when and where the candidate is going as well as the campaign timeline. In addition, the campaign manager is responsible for managing the other coordinators in the campaign.

The candidate generally has two jobs during a campaign: making money and meeting people. The candidate should be scheduled for door-to-door heavily during the final two months of a campaign. If the candidate has more than 30 minutes available between events during times appropriate for door to door, then the best use of time would be for the candidate to be knocking on doors in targeted neighborhoods. If the candidate cannot make it out to a neighborhood, then the candidate should be making calls to donors to raise funds for message delivery. The campaign manager should work directly with the scheduler to manage the candidate's time.

The execution of the air war falls on the shoulders of the campaign manager. When it comes to media, a campaign will generally hire a third party firm to handle production and buying of time. In the event a third party is involved, the campaign manager is still responsible for ensuring that all benchmarks are being met and that the timeline is being followed. The campaign manager must follow up with the vendors associated with the campaign to hold them to task.

The ground war generally falls under the responsibilities of the political director with the help of the volunteer coordinator. Everything from assisting in the candidate's door-to-door and scheduling events to literature drops and poll workers, the ground war is the foundation of a campaign.

The poll worker operation should be entrusted to a member of management, such as the political director or volunteer coordinator, because of the importance of the operation. The polls on Election Day are the last opportunity a campaign has to appeal to voters. The timeline involved requires a diligent person who can recruit, train, assign and supply volunteers for the job. Poll workers and volunteers are human resources, but their activities are part of the political machine. A campaign plan should involve both the volunteer coordinator and the political director in the guidance of volunteers.

Absentee and mail ballot operations should be conducted by the volunteer coordinator. The timeline should reflect when the mail ballot operation begins. The mail operation is dependent upon the local elections office. Campaign volunteers respond to the ballots being sent out from the board of elections by sending out campaign literature to the same list of recipients. Since timing is important, each day the local elections office sends out mail ballots, volunteers should be mailing literature to the corresponding voters. This is not an operation that can be "batched" or backed up. The timeline should reflect each day that mail ballots are distributed.

The campaign manager is the sole arbiter of how duties are distributed among the campaign team. Each duty in the campaign should be listed in a chart with a corresponding team member assigned to it. Also, a roster of team members should be kept with a listing of each member's duties.

4.6   Laying It All Out

Once a campaign has developed a budget, conducted research, built a team, created a timeline and assigned duties, the campaign plan is complete. The campaign manager should be able to take a tabbed binder and open it to the section dealing with everything that was discussed in the first four chapters of *The Political Campaign Desk Reference*. If the campaign manager wishes to access the timeline, then the tab for "timeline" is immediately available. The same concept applies for the budget, timeline, opposition research, election results, finance reports, listings of officeholders, media lists and all the other information gathered early in the campaign. Project management software is also available that can take the place of a physical binder.

The campaign plan should have the following components available in an organized format:

1. Abstract on campaign message
2. Description of issues in campaign
3. Charts of strengths and weaknesses of candidate as well as any opponents
4. Historical and political data on the jurisdiction of the office being sought
5. Media contacts
6. Listing of local elected officials at all levels with contact information
7. Campaign team with contact information
8. Campaign committee with contact information
9. Opposition research
10. Budget
11. Timeline
12. Assignment of duties

The campaign plan is a living document. Team members may change over time. The timeline may be adjusted during the campaign. The budget may fluctuate. A campaign must be able to adapt to changes in the environment. However, a campaign without a plan is going to be considerably weaker than a campaign that has a plan. The campaign plan provides a structure for the decisions in the campaign. A study of failed campaigns would probably demonstrate that losing campaigns often have undeveloped campaign plans if they have any plans at all.

The campaign plan will also have a finance plan. The finance plan is how the campaign will raise the money necessary for the campaign. The next chapter discusses fundraising and building the finance plan. Once the finance plan has been completed, it should be added to the overall campaign plan.

Because the campaign plan contains an enormous amount of sensitive information, only the campaign manager and candidate should have unfettered access to all portions of it. Parts of the plan are accessible to other team members, but it could be devastating if a copy of the campaign plan found its way to an opponent's camp.

Chapter 5

Fundraising

5.1 Why Do People Give?

Anyone who has ever tried to work with a candidate on fundraising will testify that the process is like pulling teeth. Candidates hate asking people for money. Some candidates will hide from the campaign manager or finance director in order to avoid the time consuming and dreadful task of sitting at a phone and dialing for dollars. It is one of the most disliked tasks on a campaign, but it is one of the most necessary tasks unless a candidate wishes to fund the entire campaign out of his or her own bank account.

Perhaps one of the reasons that candidates do not like the process of fundraising is because they do not understand why someone would part with their hard-earned, disposable income in order to support someone's campaign for elected office. The candidate may be thinking, *Why would Mrs. Smith care about my race*, or *What will Mr. Jones expect for his contribution*, or *Can't I just send a letter?* Although some candidates find it difficult to wrap themselves around the idea that someone will contribute money to their effort, there are a number of reasons a donor may give to a campaign.

Sometimes the donor has a personal relationship with the candidate, and that is the reason he gives. One of the best reasons to donate is simply because someone wants their friend to succeed. That personal relationship is irreplaceable. A friend of the candidate may be the largest donor in terms of money, but that same dedication may also translate into that donor also being the campaign's best volunteer. A candidate should never underestimate the relationships that they have built throughout the years. Furthermore, a candidate should never overlook a friend when it comes to requesting donations. How would Mrs. Smith or Mr. Jones feel if their best friend ran for office and did not bother asking them for help?

Often, people support a candidate because they share beliefs. One of the most remarkable movements in modern times is that of the Tea Party. As the Tea Party movement gained steam, Tea Party candidates began running for office. Supporters of this movement would send contributions, large and small, to those candidates who shared their beliefs and values. Members of a coalition that endorses a candidate are an excellent prospect for donations.

There are donors out there who will give to candidate simply because they are asked. This is an important point because a candidate must learn how to get over the hump of not wanting to ask for money. If a candidate does not ask, he will not receive. Sometimes people who are involved in the community feel that it is part of their duty to send a contribution to a candidate they like, but they will not do it unless the candidate asks for the donation.

Some donors will give because they are angry at the current administration. Perhaps they disagree with the politics of the current officeholder, or they feel that they have been wronged. Anger is a powerful emotion, and it can translate into campaign dollars if a candidate knows how to identify those angry prospects.

There are possibly as many reasons to give to candidates as there are donors. Everyone is different, and some donors may give for multiple reasons. The bottom line is that a candidate must be willing to commit some time to fundraising if he does not want to commit his own bank account. Once a candidate begins fundraising, he may be surprised at how easy it is and how much people are willing to give. However, a candidate will never find out what potential is out there if the candidate refuses to ask.

5.2 Opening the Candidate's "Black Book"

When the candidate begins fundraising, the first people that should be considered for giving are friends, family, business acquaintances, and anyone who may have benefited by being associated with the candidate. There are many people who profit from each person's existence: the candidate's doctor, car salesman, insurance salesman, realtor, dentist, plumber, car mechanic, landscaping professional, or anyone else to whom the candidate has hired over the years. These potential contributors are referred to as "low hanging fruit" because they should be easily reachable donors. These prospects are also the ones who will most likely be friends of the candidate throughout his or her political career.

Before contacting the people in the candidate's "black book", a campaign manager or finance director should sit down with the candidate and make a comprehensive list of all relevant people who can give. In the Information Age, a candidate can probably download their entire contact list from their phone that they synch with their computer or e-mail account. The list should include name, address, all available phone numbers, fax, e-mail address, and the level at which they are capable of giving. Plugging this information into an easily sorted and updated spreadsheet will be helpful throughout the campaign.

Most candidates, especially first time candidates, underestimate the power of their own list. They often are hesitant to list someone because they do not want to ask them for money for their campaign. Sometimes a candidate will feel as though fundraising is begging for money. The important aspect of making this list is that these people are not giving charity as much as they are making an investment in good government by supporting the campaign. When it comes to fundraising and making the list, the candidate should look at the campaign the same way as raising money for a church or other organization.

This "black book" list should be created early in the campaign. A good database is one of the most important assets a candidate can have, and it must be vigilantly updated. The more thorough the job of research and database building that is done in the beginning will increase the chances for success later on. The candidate should personally approach the people with whom he or she has preexisting relationships rather than having a campaign team member do it.

5.3   Making the "Ask"

Asking for money from friends, family and potential donors is not as hard as many people think. It requires getting past a level of discomfort most people have when it comes to the subject of money. In addition to the barriers discussed earlier in this chapter, candidates find a plethora of reasons to avoid asking for money. Some candidates do not like the idea of asking for money because they feel it is a form of begging and is beneath them. Other candidates fail to be effective at fundraising because asking for money requires effort, and making that effort worthwhile is difficult. Others do not like the idea of rejection and feel that they would rather pay for their campaign out of resources personally available to them. If a candidate looks at fundraising and finds it impossible for any of these reasons, perhaps running for office should be reconsidered.

The most successful candidates are ones that make fundraising calls positive contacts. The calls for money do not have to be unpleasant. They can include some amount of small talk in order to ease into the "ask." More successful fundraising calls may have a candidate listening to the concerns of a prospective donor so that a campaign staff member can follow up on those concerns. The components of a successful call include:

- Introduction
- Brief small talk
- Overview of why candidate is calling including why the candidate needs money to run
- Assigning a reason as to why the person the candidate is calling has a stake in the race
- Making the ask for financial support

Another good way to ask for money is for the candidate to have a specific campaign need that he can tell the donor about. Perhaps a candidate needs $10,000 for a direct mail piece. He can call a donor capable of giving $5,000 towards the direct mail piece and ask specifically for funding of that mailing. A printer's proof of the piece can be e-mailed to the prospective donor so that the donor knows how his money is being spent. Once a prospective donor can see exactly where their investment is going, it is easier for them to part with their money.

A sample dialogue of how a successful campaign call can go appears at the end of *The Political Campaign Desk Reference* in Appendix L. It is a campaign's responsibility to be aware of any restrictions local, state or federal law places on fundraising activities. The campaign treasurer and finance director must work together to ensure all laws are followed. The treasurer and finance director must become experts in campaign finance law. Also, prior to the phone call, the amount that the prospective donor can contribute should be researched and known. This can be gauged by viewing what they contributed to other candidates, what they do for a living or how close they are to the candidate.

It is always a good idea to ask for more than what the prospective donor may be able to give. When donors are asked for money, they can be flattered by the fact that they are viewed as able to give at such a level. Sometimes they will make an extra consideration and contribute what is asked. At the very least, a candidate can reduce the request when the donor expresses an inability to give at a suggested level. On the other hand, if a campaign asks a donor for $1,000 when the donor is capable and willing to give $5,000, then the campaign just made a mistake that cost $4,000.

Once a donor gives to a campaign, he has made an investment towards the success of that candidate. That means that the donor may be willing to give again. Donors should be given multiple chances to give to the campaign through multiple channels. That donor who was capable of giving $5,000 but only gave the $1,000 asked of him may decide to give more at another point in the campaign because the candidate was persistent. Sometimes donors give again because a campaign's momentum is high. If a campaign looks like it will win, then donors are more likely to give. Another reason donors give is that they like a winner. A campaign must look like a winner to donors.

In situations involving fundraising events, the campaign staff must work closely with the donor to make sure all invitations and printed materials comply with applicable election laws. It should remain the host's responsibility to secure venue, guests/donors and pay for the event. The campaign benefits by the benevolence of the donor's network and is involved only to make sure everything complies with law, that the event runs smoothly and money is collected.

5.4   Identifying Potential Donors

Once the candidate has compiled the list of all friends, family, associates, colleagues, and others who may be willing to invest in the campaign, and the low-hanging fruit has been picked, the campaign should pursue other avenues of prospective donors. The candidate should expand the universe of potential donors to include anyone locally who has given to other candidates in the past. This identification requires gathering the finance reports from these past candidates and officeholders. Such compilation should occur with the permission of the person whose reports are sought. Local election boards and clerks are excellent sources for this information. Some secretary of state web sites contain information for statewide officeholders and legislators.

The campaign will have more success in partisan races by sticking with donors to candidates of the same party. Some areas prohibit the use of other lists for prospecting purposes so understanding the local rules for use of other candidate finance reports is important.

Another way of obtaining the lists from other candidates is to simply ask that candidate for their list. Many candidates will be reluctant to share their list because it took them a long time and a great deal of effort to build their own database. However, if the campaign team worked the way it should have from the beginning in Chapter One, the campaign should have some officeholders in the campaign committee who have a vested interest in the success of the candidate. These officeholders will be more likely to provide their lists, or partial lists, upon request.

Campaigns should also pursue the mailing lists and membership lists of all coalition groups that have endorsed the candidate. These prospective donors already have a relationship with the campaign because their organization does. Letting these lists go is a wasted opportunity for a campaign.

5.5   Refining the Database

Once the campaign has compiled the various lists of friends, colleagues, coalition lists, and historical donors, the next step is to enter these individuals into a database or spreadsheet that is compatible with a word processing program in order to personalize letters. When sending a letter to a prospective donor, never address it "Dear Fellow Republican/Democrat" or "Dear Township/County Resident". If a direct mail piece looks like bulk mail, then it will more likely than not be treated like bulk mail and placed in the trash. However, if Robert Jackson receives a letter with the salutation "Dear Bob", the likelihood that the letter will be read is increased significantly as is the prospect of a response.

A campaign team can use volunteers to help fill in missing fields in a database. For instance, if the campaign database does not have a home address for a prospective donor, a volunteer can look it up in the voter database. If a phone number field is missing, a volunteer can look up that information. If an e-mail address is missing, the volunteers should check social media sites to see if the prospective donor has their address listed. A complete database is a valuable database.

As the campaign progresses, the campaign should track donations in its database. By tracking donations, the candidate can see how much a donor has already given before asking that donor for more money. A campaign can also identify the large donors as well as the donors who give smaller amounts. Donors who give smaller amounts may also be willing to volunteer on a campaign. Various team members on a campaign should be in constant communication with each other in order to share relevant information. A volunteer coordinator's job becomes easier when the finance director shares the list of small dollar donors. If more volunteers are recruited for the campaign, and the campaign's momentum increases as a result, then donations can go up. A good database helps various aspects of a campaign excel.

As soon as the database is compiled and duplicate records have been removed, the campaign is now ready to mail a letter to the prospective donors. The "prospecting" process is discussed in the next section.

5.6 Prospecting New Donors

There are two components that are necessary in all campaign communications that are going to prospective or current donors and supporters. These components are applicable to mailed communications as well as e-mail communications. These components include:

- Personalization
- An opportunity for a response

The personalized communication is a letter or e-mail specifically addressed to each person on the list. As stated earlier in this chapter, a salutation of "Dear Bob" to Robert Jackson is considerably more effective than "Dear Knox County Resident". In addition to the personalization, the initial communication to the prospective supporter should be brief, contain relevant information about the candidate, and should speak to the message of the campaign. A seasoned campaign manager with good writing skills will be able to draft a prospect letter quickly. For first-time campaigners, this first prospect letter should go through many drafts to comply with the components: brevity, relevance, and message of the campaign. An example of a prospect letter can be found in Appendix B.

The prospect letter can come from the candidate, or it can come from a known, respected community member writing on the candidate's behalf. For instance, if Jane Carpenter is running for State Representative, a letter from the current State Representative asking for support on behalf of Jane Carpenter may be more effective than a letter from Jane herself.

A mailed letter should also be signed in blue ink. The purpose of signing in blue ink is to let the recipient know that the signature was written instead of printed from a printer. That level of personalization leads the recipient to believe that he or she is part of an exclusive group that received the letter. That exclusivity leads to a greater level of attention from the prospective donor. The more attention the prospective donor gives the letter, the more likely they are to go from prospective donor to campaign supporter.

Candidates cannot sign thousands of letters themselves. A campaign staff can sign on behalf of the candidate if the candidate permits. This proxy signature is recommended for large mailings exceeding one or two hundred letters. The candidate's time on a campaign is scarce, so whenever the team can make the best possible use of the candidate's time, the more money the campaign will raise.

If e-mail is the communication of choice, the e-mail should also be personalized. There are a number of software programs that allow e-mails to be personalized on the market and can be found at most computer software stores. Some web-based services allow campaigns to personalize e-mails while also using attractive looking templates. Whatever method the campaign uses, prospective donors should be identified by name.

The second component required in all communications is an opportunity for the prospect to respond. In mailings, the response vehicle is a self-addressed envelope to the campaign. Ideally, this self-addressed envelope will have an extended flap upon which the prospect can write their personal information and mark appropriate boxes indicating their level and scope of support. An example of a good return envelope is in Appendix C.

For e-mail communications, a link should be placed at the bottom of the communication that gives the prospective donor an opportunity to donate, volunteer or lend their support with the ease of a click. A campaign should never make it difficult for someone to give it money. The easier it is to give money, the more likely someone will donate to the campaign. Many campaigns will place links throughout an e-mail to the donation site so that it would be virtually impossible for a reader to miss the link.

Another method of prospecting new donors is to identify potential donors of a coalition. For instance, a candidate may have a pro-business platform that the campaign team feels will resonate with small business owners. A quick search of vendor license applications from the county or state government may yield a large number of small business owners in target zip codes.

Once these small business owners are identified, the campaign may invite them to a "gateway" event or an event that draws them into the campaign. The event should not be a fundraiser, nor should it cost the prospective donors anything to attend. Most of the small business owners on the list have probably never given to a political campaign in the past, and they may not even see the advantage of supporting one candidate over another. They are employers trying to succeed. The elements of a gateway event that will be most likely to engage them include: holding the event at a time that does not take them away from their business, it does not cost anything, and the event has a reason for them to attend.

If the campaign holds an early morning breakfast before regular operating hours for businesses, provides breakfast with no strings attached, and allows business owners to have access to current officeholders, then a large number of business owners may attend. After the event, the campaign should begin engaging these business owners by sending them information about the campaign and pro-business platform of the candidate. Once a relationship has been established, and small business owners understand the importance of helping the candidate, the candidate should then make the initial call to ask for a donation. Prospective donors who show less interest can still be engaged by the campaign, but only the most interested should be engaged by the candidate. At the very least, the less interested business owners may still be part of a small business coalition for the campaign.

The campaign team should be creative when it comes to prospecting potential donors. Engaging those who have given to other candidates or charities in the past are the best prospects. These individuals have demonstrated that they will part with their money for the right reason. Prospecting new donors that have never given before is more difficult, but it can be rewarding. Regardless of how the campaign team creates its prospective donor list, the candidate is the best fundraiser of the campaign, and the most serious prospective donors should be placed on the list for the candidate to call.

5.7   PACs

Political Action Committees (PACs) are a good potential source of donor money. Choosing the right PACs is as important as the initial communication to the PAC. For instance, there are PACs on each side of many issues. A campaign does not want to market itself to a pro-abortion PAC such as NARAL and take money from NARAL if the campaign has a pro-life message. It also does not want to court gun control groups if the campaign is also courting pro-2nd Amendment organizations such as the NRA. Working both sides of an issue, wittingly or unwittingly, can be just as defeating as taking money from the wrong group.

A listing of local PACs can be obtained from the local elections board or clerk. A listing of statewide PACs can be obtained from most secretary of state offices or websites.

The best way to approach a PAC is to be introduced by a current officeholder with a relationship with the PAC. Once an introduction has been made, and the campaign has had an opportunity to listen to the PAC president, board or administrator, quick follow-up is important. Always assume any opponent may be contacting the same PACs. A campaign does not want to lose potential support because it was "out of sight, out of mind."

Many PACs seek out candidates. They have web sites, provide questionnaires, and promote their endorsement process. When filling out PAC questionnaires, the campaign manager should always be involved. Candidates may feel as though they can fill out a questionnaire without assistance. If the candidate misses key points, the effectiveness of a questionnaire can be impacted. Two sets of eyes are better than one when filling out questionnaires. A double-check also makes certain that the candidate does not contradict his own campaign's message. A campaign does not want to lose support or money because of a simple error on a question.

The campaign should invest in 2-pocket folders. Place a campaign lapel sticker on the front cover of the folder. On the inside, place a business card on the pocket with the appropriate slots. Inside the left pocket should be an introductory letter personalized to the PAC. Pertinent press releases or news clippings of the campaign should be placed in the right-side pocket along with one or two pieces of campaign literature. The press releases and clippings should relate to the issues in which the PAC is interested. If those are not available, then clippings and releases demonstrating the strength and activity of the campaign can also be effective. After all, a PAC wants to back a winner.

The packet should be sent within 24-48 hours after the initial meeting. Once a few business days have passed, the PAC contact should be called to follow-up, confirm receipt of the packet and to listen to any thoughts the PAC has. Because a campaign has made an effort and demonstrated that the PAC support is important to them, the PAC knows that it will have someone that will listen to them in office. If a campaign was introduced to the PAC, the person who made the introduction should also make a follow-up phone call or send a letter geared towards energizing the PAC towards the campaign.

Once the lines of communication are working, it is reasonable to invite the PAC to campaign fundraisers.

5.8   Fundraising Events

Most of the critical fundraising will be done over the phone and through prospecting and PAC contributions. There are people who will expect an invitation to a fundraising event before they send money. Fundraising events should be targeted and cost the campaign very little. At best, the campaign will hold the fundraiser at the home of a supporter, and the host will cover the costs of the event. If this is the case, the host must be made aware up front of any expectations. If expectations are not clearly communicated and put into writing in some form (an e-mail confirmation and detailing of expectations should suffice), then the campaign might find itself saddled with the costs of a fundraiser, which will reduce the amount of usable money raised.

In order to hold a strong fundraising event that requires little from the campaign, the first course of action should be to recruit a host committee for the event. A host committee is a group of people listed on the invitation who are responsible for inviting paying guests to the event. Expectations of the host committee should be clearly laid out at the onset of planning. Benchmarks for the host committee should also be established so that the campaign can track the success of the event. Good communication should be maintained with the host committee so that any members who have the proclivity to procrastinate will have the required motivation to work.

Once a host committee is formed, the campaign must decide how large the event will be, how many people can attend and how many will be invited. If the campaign wishes to have an event for 50 people, then the host committee might be 10 people who are required to bring 5 paying guests to the event at the predetermined amount. It could also be a 5 person host committee with a 10 person commitment. The host committee should be prepared to make up the difference of the amount raised if they fail to bring in the goal. For instance, if the expectation of a host committee member is to sell five tickets for $100 each, then any member who sells less than five tickets will buy their unsold tickets. If the host committee members agree to that stipulation, then the campaign has a guaranteed minimum level of funds from the event.

Some candidates will set a reasonable dollar amount for a ticket and invite hundreds of people to be on the host committee. The candidate should still make the personal contact so that the expectation is clear that a ticket must be purchased to appear on the host committee. Although the invitation that is mailed may have 300 members of the host committee, if they all gave $250, then the campaign raised $75,000 with one event, and the invitation looks impressive. A prospective donor who receives an invitation with so many host committee members may feel as though this is the event to attend, and the event is now earning even more money. Host committees make the work of the candidate and campaign easier on multiple levels.

Fundraising etiquette suggests that drinks and hors d' oeuvres be complimentary with admission to an event. A campaign does not want to alienate a supporter for the lack of common sense hospitality. There are many ways to keep costs on such items low, but the idea of having a host is to have someone cover the costs.

Additional invitations to an event can also be distributed or mailed out. These invitations can go to the prospects in the database built in the earlier sections in this chapter. A good host committee will consist of names that might compel a potential donor to attend the event who otherwise may not attend. For instance, if the local sheriff, state representative or county commissioner is on a host committee, there may be people who will attend who do not know the candidate but want to have exposure to the dignitary on the host committee.

If a prominent member of a local country club or member of a local church is the host for the event, consider inviting the entire membership of that country club or church. This holds true for any other organization of which a host is a member. It is a form of prospecting that may not provide a high rate of return, but the campaign will most likely obtain new supporters it otherwise would not have had. Sometimes the directories of these organizations are difficult to acquire, but the returns can be great.

A fundraising event should be as high-dollar an event as possible in order to make it worth the amount of effort expended. There are a lot of things the campaign needs to work on, and an event that does not yield much funding would be a net loss for the campaign in terms of its other resources of time and people. Make sure that the event host and host committee of the event understand the need to raise the expected level of funds. The campaign manager or the finance director can call a meeting of the host committee prior to the event to drive home the need to raise the expected donations.

At times, a campaign may hold low-dollar events. These events are usually cookouts and have a ticket price less than $50. This type of event will raise a small amount of money, but it is geared towards the more grassroots oriented people in the campaign. These people will most likely comprise the volunteer base. Having a low-dollar event serves as a mechanism by which they can feel financially vested in a campaign. A good event of this type will serve as an energizing event. Low-dollar events are good because they also provide those who cannot afford the expensive events access to campaign functions and an opportunity to meet the candidate.

5.9   Making Large Donors Work For the Campaign

Some candidates rejoice when they are able to get a large donation from a target donor. The difficulty with calling donors who are capable of large contributions is getting a few minutes of their time. Once a candidate has a few minutes of a large donor's time, do they ask for a contribution, or do they ask for something more? What else could they ask for?

Donors capable of large gifts usually have friends who are capable of equally large gifts. Sometimes these friends of the donor have never given to a campaign before and simply need a friend, such as the donor on the phone, to tell them whom to give to and how much. A large donor can be much more than just a single, large contribution. A large donor can be a gateway to a handful of large donations, and these new donors can become friends of the candidate.

When a candidate is finally able to gain access to a donor capable of a large gift, the ask needs to become more ambitious. The candidate has a short time to make a connection with the large donor, explain why the campaign is important and then go in for the "ask." If a candidate has an opportunity, he should request that a large donor open their own black book and hold a fundraiser on the campaign's behalf.

Using a tactic discussed earlier, a large donor may be more willing to accommodate such a request if he believes the event will make a difference, the candidate will probably win, and there is a specific project that requires funding. For a group of large donors, the campaign may use the need to fund a direct mail piece to cause the need and the specific ask. If the donors are capable of substantial gifts, perhaps the campaign could focus the topic of the event on the need to fund a television campaign. Once the donors are in a room, the "gateway" donor should run the show. He should introduce the candidate who will then provide a brief overview of the campaign. Once the candidate is finished, the group should view the television spot that requires funding for air time. If the donors made the effort to attend the meeting because their friend asked, the event will most likely be successful. The event is short and inexpensive.

What happens if the "gateway" donor wants to help but does not have the time to put together an event for his friends to attend? The candidate should ask if the donor can circulate the television spot or direct mail piece that requires funding to his friends on e-mail. If the gateway donor will make the ask of his friends, even through e-mail, it could be effective in raising large amounts of money with little effort.

Many presidential campaigns will use the concept of the gateway donor to raise money. Donors capable of raising $25,000 from their friends may be labeled a donor of a certain level. The same could go for gateway donors of graduating levels. Some gateway donors do not even put their own money into the race. They do the work for the campaign to raise money, and that makes the gateway donor more valuable to the campaign than if he had given a $5,000, or $10,000, gift himself.

Once the money is raised, the campaign now has a relationship with a cadre of new donors that it did not have before the initial contact with the gateway donor. Some of these new donors could become gateway donors themselves with future events. A candidate should try to maximize his or her own time. This means being smart with how they engage donors.

5.10 Myths About Fundraising

Some candidates jump into the role of fundraiser with the wrong idea. There are a few myths that a candidate should be aware of before making mistakes on the phone:

Myth #1- You can always count on rich people to give. Just because someone has money and has given in the past does not mean that they will give to the candidate. An effective fundraising list will have as much information about a prospective donor as possible. What are the issues important to the donor? To whom has he given in the past? What are the donor's interests? Making a connection on a personal level is important in talking to donors. Being able to articulate why they should give to the campaign with a reason that resonates is also important. Just because a prospective donor has money does not mean they want to give it to a candidate.

Myth #2 – People will always give if you simply ask. Although it is true that a candidate should not count on a donation unless he or she asks, a donation should not be expected simply because a prospective donor is asked. Sometimes prospective donors need to see action or a message from the campaign that they feel strongly about. Other prospective donors may want to believe the candidate is going to win. Campaigns asking for money need to be ready to supply reasons for donors to give.

Myth #3 – Solicitations can be "one size fits all." A message that resonates with small business owners may not be the same message that will resonate with law enforcement. A campaign should understand each message that it sends out should be targeted. Perhaps veterans receive one appeal for donations while pro-life activists receive another. The more tailored a solicitation can be to specific donors, the greater the chance for success.

Myth #4 – Past donors and supporters of the candidate will always give again. The job of the candidate is one of constant gardening. Donors need to feel that their money was well spent. They need to be thanked. Donors need to feel that they are appreciated or that the candidate still believes what they claimed in past campaigns. Never take a donor for granted. Thank all donors, large and small. Keep donors engaged, and ask donors for their thoughts on issues important to them. Keeping a donor can be a bigger challenge than finding them at times.

A candidate should not have any preconceived notions about donors. Each donor is a unique individual, and each donor wants to feel as though they are personally important to the candidate. The job of the candidate, and officeholder, is one of constant cultivation. A garden that is neglected will be overrun with weeds and die. The same goes for a donor list. The moment someone makes their first contribution is the moment a "thank you" note should be sent back.

5.11   Online Fundraising

When it comes to online fundraising, some candidates feel that putting up a web page with a "Donate" button is enough. The only thing that setting up online donations does for a campaign is make it easy for donors to contribute online. Potential donors must be driven to the site and then given a reason to donate to the campaign. Setting up a donation page on the web is simply opening the door. Potential donors must be identified and ushered through that door just as they are with other fundraising methods.

In addition to the "Black Book" fundraising prospects identified earlier in this chapter, a campaign should harvest as much contact information from all of the candidate's social networking accounts. Anyone who follows a candidate, or befriends a candidate, on a social network site is someone who is interested in the campaign. If that person is interested in the campaign, then that person may become a donor. A campaign team should periodically harvest information of social network contacts.

If a candidate has a social media presence, then the campaign has opportunities to broadcast the donation through updates, "tweets" or other methods. Web sites can promote social media, and social media can promote the candidate's web site. Using the Internet in this way is a great fundraising method.

When someone receives an e-mail from a campaign, the e-mail should be personalized. Personalized communications receive a greater response than do "Dear Voter/Supporter" letters. If a voter opens an e-mail addressed directly to him, then he will be more likely to respond with the requested donation. There are web services that allow campaigns to upload their databases to create personalized e-mails. Some campaigns may have a computer whiz on staff who can write a script that will personalize an e-mail from a database. However a campaign does it, personalizing communications increases results.

In the age of smart phones, e-mails with large attachments or multiple graphics can slow down the download time. A prospective donor who might have given while they were using their smart phone may lose interest if there is a long wait time for downloads. As with all campaign communications, keep it simple. E-mails should be personalized, simple and easy to open. Furthermore, the donation site to which the e-mail links should be friendly to mobile devices and free of too many graphics.

The Internet provides so many opportunities to spruce up communications, but the fundamentals will always remain the same. Voters, donors, volunteers and all of the people who have some sort of contact with the campaign like things simple. Complicated communications are not helpful when a less complicated message or method could have achieved what the campaign wanted. Use the Internet, but do not feel as though all of the bells and whistles have to be activated especially if those features slow down the process of downloading or donating.

5.12 Direct Mail Fundraising

Direct Mail fundraising is similar to online fundraising in that the campaign is communicating a message directly to a targeted donor. The communication is personalized, and there is a response vehicle for the prospective donor to use in order to respond.

Not all prospective donors respond the same way to e-mail solicitations, and not all prospective donors respond the same way to direct mail solicitations. Some donors disregard solicitation e-mails as spam and respond to mail, whereas some prospective donors throw away the solicitations they receive in their mailbox and respond solely to e-mail or other solicitation methods. Direct mail is another way to reach a donor and provide them with an opportunity to give to the campaign.

Direct mail solicitations can take many forms. A direct mail solicitation may be a survey that is sent to prospective donors. While gathering information about the individual, the survey's primary purpose is to raise money. Some solicitations may take the form of a long letter written by the candidate or surrogate of the campaign that is designed to create a sense of urgency for the prospective donor to respond immediately. Some direct mail solicitations are tailored to a specific target audience. For instance, veterans may receive a direct mail solicitation from a candidate who is also a veteran and is connecting to veterans on a personal level. Seniors may receive a direct mail solicitation that specifically addresses issues that seniors care about. Sometimes a solicitation may guarantee a t-shirt or yard sign with a nominal donation.

Whatever the form that direct mail solicitations take, a few elements should be present. First, the communication should be personalized. Second, the communication should make a connection with the prospective donor. Whether this connection is a shared interest in making government better or a shared background as a veteran, effective solicitations make the prospective donor feel as though he or she has something in common with the candidate. Third, the message creates an urgency to donate. Whether the communication uses the tactic of asking for money for a specific expenditure, or the letter is part of a campaign to raise a specified amount of money in a certain amount of time, the campaign can be creative as to how the urgency is created. Fourth, the letter must ask for a specific dollar amount, or it must provide options for giving (three of four levels of donation requested) so that the prospective donor understands the expectation. Finally, the communication must have a response vehicle in the form of a self-addressed envelope.

As with e-mail solicitations, direct mail solicitations must make it as easy as possible for the prospective donor to part with their money. E-mails do this by linking to the donation web site in the e-mail. Direct mail solicitations accomplish this by providing a self-addressed envelope. Direct mail should also provide the web address for the campaign's donation site in addition to providing the return envelope.

The elements of a campaign solicitation remain the same regardless of the format. Campaigns must make a connection with the donor, create a sense of urgency, make expectations clear, and make it easy for the donor to reply with a donation. Using those fundamental principles, campaigns should be creative in how they solicit funds. Every donor should always receive a "thank you" note from the candidate as soon as a contribution is received by the campaign. A short note can go a long way.

5.13 How To Lose Donors

There are many candidates who have become adept and talented fundraisers. They understand what it takes to get donations. What is more important than successfully gaining new donors, is keeping those donors. Some candidates have become as adept at losing donors as others are at gaining them. Campaigns can lose donors by making some of the following mistakes:

Forget to thank a donor – Campaign contributions come from the kindness of donors who are willing to part with money that they spent hours of their lives earning. Even if the donation that a campaign receives is as low as $25, many working Americans do not make that much in an hour. A candidate must always show gratitude for the gifts that donors make. If the donor feels as though they have been taken for granted, then they may never make a donation again.

Allow a database to become outdated – Keeping a donor list up-to-date is a constant gardening process. If a campaign sends mail to a donor list that has not been used in four years, a significant portion of the mail sent out will come back to the campaign as undeliverable. Furthermore, if it has been four years since a donor has received anything from a campaign, then the candidate may need to begin the process of connecting with donors anew. A candidate with a good, up-to-date database is a candidate who knows how to keep his donors engaged. A periodic communication keeping donors apprised of what the candidate is doing in office or on the campaign trail may suffice to keep the database in good order, but some minimum level of maintenance is required.

Do not invite a donor to an event – Donors want to feel as though they are important. Even if a donor has given the maximum allowable amount by law to a campaign, the donor should be invited as a complimentary guest to all fundraisers. Chances are, the donor will not attend all of them, but being a good steward of a campaign's donors will help ensure that the donors will give again.

Forget to follow through – Sometimes a candidate makes a phone call to a prospective donor who commits to making a donation. If the campaign team waits a few weeks to follow up with that donor, the donor may feel as though the campaign is disorganized and lose interest. Donors are often professionals who have to follow through with commitments in their own daily lives. If a campaign is unable to follow through on receiving free money, then why should the donor bother helping the campaign?

Campaigns should use common sense when dealing with donors. Thank donors; stay in touch with donors; do not ignore donors, and always make sure that they are quickly contacted once a verbal commitment is made. Campaigns can lose donors in other ways, but the methods above are the most common. Campaigns that use a little common sense and stay on top of their records will make their jobs easier in the future.

Chapter 6
Defining the Candidate and the Opponent

6.1   Building the Image – Setting the Candidate Apart

The image of a candidate does not just reference how the candidate physically appears in public. A candidate's image involves everything from appearance to the campaign message to the personal story that the candidate brings to the race. When voters hear a candidate's name, what impressions does the campaign team want to conjure in their minds? Does the campaign want voters to envision images of a combat veteran or a family person? Does the campaign want a snappy slogan to play in the minds of voters when they think of a candidate? Does the campaign want key words or images to come to the front of voters' minds? Should the campaign logo be the focus of a candidate's image?

In building an image for the candidate, the campaign team must consider four things: 1) the demographics of the jurisdiction of the office sought; 2) the differences between the candidate and any opponent; 3) the issues most important to the voters; 4) the appearance of the candidate.

Knowing the people in the district served by the office the candidate is seeking is important to determining how to present the candidate. People are more likely to vote for those with whom they identify and are comfortable. If the make-up of a district is mostly suburban families, a campaign will wish to utilize images of family whenever possible. If the district is comprised mainly of young professionals, images of a candidate as a successful professional, or scenes with young professionals listening to the candidate, are important. Voters feel more comfortable with candidates whom they feel they share a common bond. They identify with candidates who appear to be more like them and can understand the issues important to them. Appearance is the first impression most voters will have of the candidate, be it on television, direct mail, the Internet or in person. What persona does the campaign want the voters to see?

Highlighting the differences between the candidate and an opponent is what will allow a candidate to rise above the pack in a field race or in a heads-up match. For instance, differences in levels of education, experience, or affiliation can create a stark contrast that allows a candidate to stand out. The key is being the one to use an issue first and use it effectively. If a candidate is the only one with an advanced degree, experience as a prosecutor and a member of the National Rifle Association, and these qualities appeal to voters in the district, then much of a campaign's literature and materials will contain elements that allude to these aspects. In order to run an effective race, the campaign team must build a visible contrast between the candidate and any opponent. The building blocks of this process were gathered in Chapter One when the campaign built the "Strengths" versus "Weaknesses" charts.

Once the campaign identifies the top two or three issues in a district, a candidate should become educated and focus on those subjects. If jobs, taxes and economic development are the most important issues to voters in a campaign, the candidate must speak to those issues instead of education and crime issues. A campaign that deals with the wrong issues will appear out of touch with voters. This "disconnect" will be reflected at the polls on Election Day.

It is also important that the candidate be comfortable with the image that the campaign team has laid out. If the campaign team wants to present the candidate as a family man, but the candidate is not comfortable with this image, then this discomfort will be noticed by voters. If the campaign wants to impress the image of the candidate as a combat veteran, but the candidate is uncomfortable with that part of his or her past, then the campaign should work with other elements of the candidate's persona. A candidate must be genuine and appear comfortable. The candidate must be able to deliver the campaign message naturally and convincingly. If the candidate is unable to easily work with the image and issues of the campaign, then the campaign needs to change gear. Finally, a campaign team should never try to portray a candidate as something that he is not. If a candidate went to ROTC but never finished, then he is not a combat veteran. Voters are able to identify a disingenuous candidate. If they cannot, the candidate's opponent will surely help them out by exposing the candidate's true record.

Pulling the elements of image together in a campaign requires discipline. Many campaigns may begin with a direction, message and image that follow the principles outlined in *The Political Campaign Desk Reference*. Some of those campaigns may gradually deviate from the path they set out upon. Sometimes this deviation is a result of the candidate talking to a voter who is passionate about an issue that few voters in a district find important. Sometimes this deviation occurs because of attacks levied by an opponent. Other times, the deviation can occur because the candidate is not comfortable with the image. An alert campaign manager will maintain discipline. If the campaign changes course, a campaign manager must be able to bring it back on track.

The key to image is simplicity. The campaign has a single underlying message, and the image of the candidate should not be complex. The same goes for the opponent. In defining the candidate or the opponent, a campaign team must focus on the one or two outstanding qualities of each person that resonate with voters. Once these qualities have been identified, then repeating them in the message throughout the campaign is essential.

6.2   Campaign Logo

A campaign logo – the image that is imprinted on signs, literature, television, the web site, social media, and all other materials, is something that some campaigns spend too much time creating. Some candidates will want to incorporate an image of a house if their last name is House, or a hammer if the last name is Hammerstein. Making a campaign sign too "gimmicky" will detract from the message of the campaign.

Simplicity, again, is the rule when creating a logo. The logo should never be cluttered, difficult to make out, nor use fancy fonts. A logo should be straightforward, easy to see, easy to understand and pleasant to look at. The American brain reads left-to-right and top-to-bottom. A sign or shirt with a logo that violates this flow can easily be blocked out by a brain that does not want to deal with a mess. There are thousands of other candidates, products and messages competing for a person's attention that do follow the visual rules, and they will be more likely visible than a cluttered sign or logo.

The best logo is one in which the last name of the candidate is the most visible element. The office the candidate is seeking is next most important, and a campaign slogan is ancillary. Sometimes party affiliation is important and should be added. Lighter letters on a darker background work very well. The use of artsy fonts is discouraged as is the use of too many distracting features such as curvy lines, stars and extraneous wording. In addition, the use of more than two or three colors will also detract from the purpose of the logo and signs. The simpler the design, the better the chance a campaign has of connecting with a voter.

6.3   Wise Expenditures and Unwise Expenditures

The decision to spend money unwisely can reveal a lot about a candidate. It can also impact how a campaign is perceived by its donors.

Invariably, a candidate has an urge to spend money once the war chest begins to swell. Candidates are capable of making decisions about buying trinkets ranging from nail files and flying discs to yard sticks and water bottles. Unfortunately, trinkets have never won a campaign for anyone. Trinkets generally do not communicate a message especially in the repetitive manner that a campaign requires. Trinkets are generally pricey and have little monetary or message value. When a candidate brings up the concept of trinkets, think through very carefully about what the campaign is trying to communicate with trinkets, how widely the message will be distributed and the overall effectiveness of the idea for the campaign.

Once the campaign has thoroughly thought the idea of purchasing trinkets through, it will become apparent that the idea was probably ill conceived because campaign money can be more effectively spent elsewhere to win votes.

Also beware of the temptation to spend large amounts of money on temporary advertising for special events. For instance, a candidate may spend hundreds or thousands of dollars on the idea to fly an airplane with a banner over a big football game. The impact will be small because spectators have to remove their attention from the field or concession stand at the right time to look up and see an object that they may or may not be able to read. It would cost the campaign very little to post large signs near the game that traffic going to and from will see before and after the event. No one gets distracted or annoyed during the event, the saturation is two-fold, and everyone will see them as opposed to just a few spectators. Signs can be taken down and reused. Mission accomplished for little to nothing as opposed to a creating large dent in the campaign treasury.

Wise expenditures include broadcast media such as television and drive-time radio if a campaign can afford it. Signs in a campaign are important for increasing name awareness. Direct mail is important for message delivery and reinforces the broadcast media message. Telephone marketing and Internet based message delivery are also generally good expenditures. Unwise expenditures generally include newspaper advertising, trinkets, and expenditures that do not effectively communicate the campaign message (airplane banners etc.).

When making spending decisions, consider the budget laid out in Chapter 4 as well as how people may view expenditures. Ask the question: Does this item/activity effectively communicate the message of the campaign?

6.4   Importance of Consistency and Repetition

A well thought-out campaign will make certain that the message and look throughout the campaign is consistent. This means that the issues important on television communications should be the same issues in radio ads and direct mail. If there is a slogan on the yard signs, then using a different slogan on television and direct mail diminishes effectiveness of message delivery. If the campaign signs for a candidate are in yellow and blue, but the colors on TV are orange and black and the fonts are different, then the effectiveness of the campaign will be significantly reduced.

In commercial marketing, some of the best product campaigns are ones in which people remember the tag line or slogan decades later. The reason why people remember these catchy advertisements is because the manufacturer paid millions of dollars to make sure that the message was repeated and that it was the same message each time. That is the power of repetition and consistency.

A candidate has to compete against opponents in the same race. What campaigns must understand is that they have to compete against all of the other races during the same cycle in order to be seen and heard. Many messages flood the airwaves, the mailbox and the Internet. The best way to promote a message on a budget is to do what the great marketers do: repeat it and keep it consistent. Voters are busy with many distractions in their lives. If voters only see or hear a campaign message once before an election, then that campaign has been ineffective. In order to penetrate into the minds of voters, a campaign has to be seen and heard many times, and the look and message have to be consistent. If a campaign message is heard on television and received in the mail but the images and messages are different, then the voter may just as well have been contacted by two different campaigns. Keep it simple.

6.5   Important Images for Candidate

Images drive a campaign's air war. If a voter receives a direct mail piece that is nothing but text, then no one will read it. Jumbled images, ill designed signs, and wordy messages all distract from message delivery. If a television spot runs, and the images are not compelling, then it will be less effective than a compelling spot. Much of a campaign is visual, and it is important to use the proper images to promote a candidate. The Internet is the same. Keep it simple, and make it compelling.

Choosing the proper images in a campaign relies on what issues are important to voters as well as what interests the voters. If crime is an important issue in a race, then a candidate needs some strong, pro-law enforcement images. A candidate talking to one or two uniformed men who look like police officers can create the image that the candidate understands crime as an important issue and that law enforcement listens to that candidate. The "officers" in the photo do not have to be police officers. Most police departments do not allow their officers to appear in political literature. However, sheriff deputies are sometimes allowed to be private security guards. The voter does not need to know what the patch on the uniform says. Most voters will not even take the time to inspect the uniform. If they do, a skilled campaign manager will make sure the identifiers are unreadable. The important aspect is to make sure that the voter sees an image of the candidate speaking with someone who provides the impression of law enforcement. Voters will draw their own conclusions and no representation needs to be made about the origin of the uniformed talent in the photo. On the other hand, a campaign should never misidentify a talent, or model in a photo or actor in a video.

If the environment is an important issue in a race, then the candidate can be pictured planting trees somewhere in the district. If the district has many young families, then the picture can have children helping plant a tree with the candidate. If jobs are the number one issue, then the candidate should take images at a small business incubator, in a boardroom, at a construction site, or other location or environment that conjures images of employment, economic growth, and vitality.

In highly agricultural districts, a candidate should have images of being on a farm. It is generally a good idea to have a farmer in the photo as well. If the image is one of a farmer and the candidate talking in front of a tractor, the voter will fill in the blanks and make assumptions that they are discussing issues of agriculture. A candidate should not, however, be shown in a photo doing something that the candidate would not normally do. Talking with a farmer in front of a tractor is one thing, but for a suburban candidate to be seen bailing hay on a farm when that candidate has never bailed hay before may look unnatural, and it will open the door for an attack by the opponent. Worse, it could make a candidate seem ridiculous. One of the most iconic images of a candidate seeming unnatural is the 1988 presidential campaign of Michael Dukakis. The candidate was touring a tank plant in Ohio, and a photo opportunity of Mr. Dukakis presented itself. The candidate boarded a tank and put a helmet on, and the tank made a circuit around a field. Sticking out of the top of the tank was an image of a smiling candidate who looked entirely unnatural in his environment. The image was so striking that his opponent's campaign used the image. George Bush won that election and became America's 41st President.

Appropriate dress in each photo is also important. A picture of the candidate conducting a board meeting would obviously have the candidate wearing a suit. If the candidate is talking to a farmer in front of a tractor, however, it might be wise to have the candidate wearing jeans and a flannel shirt.

Below is a list of suggested photos to obtain of the candidate. Some of them are appropriate for some races and not others. These suggestions are to serve as a guide and to provide ideas. It should not be considered an all-inclusive list.

Suggested photos of the candidate:

- Professional head shot
- Candidate with law enforcement
- Candidate going door-to-door (senior answering door, young couple answering door)
- Candidate hunting with proper attire and following regulations
- Candidate conducting board meeting in suit
- Candidate speaking to elderly couple at "kitchen table"
- Candidate with officeholders (individually and collectively if possible)
- Candidate with farmer
- Candidate planting trees
- Candidate with family (not too formal, and not too casual)
- Candidate with parents (if available)
- Candidate in regional settings (local city halls, county courthouse, etc.)
- Candidate surrounded by many supporters in campaign shirts
- Candidate visiting local business
- Candidate at a gun range

- Candidate speaking at a podium
- Candidate at desk working
- Candidate addressing a jury (if attorney)
- Candidate with veterans
- Candidate in uniform (if appropriate)
- Candidate on a bench in a robe (if a judge)

When taking the pictures, there are a few things to remember. It is important to make sure other distractions are minimized. Too many people in the background might detract from the impact of the image. Too many extraneous objects can also have the same effect. Objects in the background can also be distracting. If a shot is outdoors, the candidate should not be positioned in such a way that it appears as though a tree or plant could be growing from the candidate's head. Pictures with statues in the background should be avoided. For instance a family picture taken at a church may have the unintended addition of a family member in the photo if a statue is behind the family.

Make certain that the expressions are appropriate for the picture. If the person speaking with a candidate looks angry, bored or too amused in a photo, then the impact of the image is diminished. The person in a photo should be engaged. Many shots should be taken of a single image to make certain a usable image is captured. Digital cameras make it very easy to take hundreds of photos and check them before moving on. Make certain all undesirable photos of the candidate are immediately deleted and that no one has access to them that can use them for nefarious purposes.

Environmental factors can also be controlled to make a picture more appealing. For instance, a common picture is of a candidate working at a desk with a pad of paper or a document. By closing the shades in the room, turning on a desk lamp on the desk and dimming the room lights, the picture can now look as though the candidate is burning the midnight oil. Try photos in which the candidate rolls up the sleeves, takes a tie off or changes appearance to go from formal to casual. It is impossible to take too many pictures, and it is important to select just the right one to use.

Whatever pictures the campaign decides to use should be dynamic.

A candidate can look exciting, or dull. Discretion should be used when taking pictures with individuals who may be unpopular or take controversial positions on issues.

If "extras" or volunteers are used to fill in space in photos or videos, such as a make-believe jury or children planting a tree with the candidate, then a Talent Release Form should be signed by the people in the photos. If the talent is a child, then the form should be signed by a parent. The purpose of a Talent Release Form is to document that the campaign has the permission of the person to use the image and/ or audio, and that any compensation has been satisfied. It is generally unnecessary to have someone endorsing a candidate sign a form. The form is to protect the campaign from someone who may want compensation later on or to remind someone that they indeed gave permission in case they forget the details. Whenever the campaign produces an image, the possibility exists that it will appear in print, on television, on the Internet, or in any other medium. The release form also makes this disclosure to the talent.

Whenever a campaign engages in taking pictures or shooting film, it should always hire a professional photographer or videographer. Hiring a professional raises the probability that the pictures will turn out well and that all of the important elements, from lighting to framing, will be considered. Professionals in photo and video are like campaign professionals – they have spent years of their life mastering their craft. They understand what is required to produce the desired end product. Professionals are more dependable than volunteers because their livelihood depends on their performance.

6.6 Defining the Opponent's Image

Earlier in this chapter, the 1988 presidential campaign was used as an example of how an opponent capitalized on an unintended image of a candidate. Not only is it important for a campaign to maintain control of its own candidate's image, it can be beneficial to also define the opponent. If a campaign is able to define its opponent as undesirable, then the opponent must spend valuable resources to counter.

A popular method of candidates attempting to define their opponents involves having a staff member follow an opponent around with a video camera at all events. Small digital video cameras with high definition quality are inexpensive and allow campaigns to upload raw video almost immediately to the Internet. Many cellular telephones also have video camera capabilities that also allow for quick upload to the Internet. The idea of videotaping the opponent is to catch the opponent saying something contradictory or detrimental to his own campaign. This method takes advantage of the fact that the nature of human beings is to make mistakes and that it is not a matter of "if" but a matter of "when". All the campaign has to do is be in the right spot at the right time when an opponent says something they wish they could take back.

Constantly keeping a candidate under surveillance is a two-way street. A prepared candidate should always assume that his actions are being watched and recorded when in public. Although this tactic can be effective, a campaign should not place a majority of its attention or effort into surveillance. It is still important to have a message and deliver it effectively. Creating an atmosphere of "gotcha" politics may make a campaign appear as though it is out of touch with voters.

Other approaches to defining the opponent include communicating the opponent's voting record, or unfavorable quotes, in campaign communications through the Internet, direct mail, television and other means. If a campaign is going to define its opponent, then the materials used should have footnotes that demonstrate to voters that the figures, quotes, or voting record can be found at the source in the public domain. Footnoting lends validity to assertions made by a campaign and strengthens the assertions while also serving to protect the campaign from an elections complaint.

6.7   Common Mistakes

Every campaign makes mistakes. Sometimes these mistakes are so small that they are unnoticeable. Other times, candidate mistakes are so profound that they signal the end of an otherwise spirited race. A candidate should understand that opposing campaigns are always watching for anything that can be used to help define the candidate in a negative way.

Below is a laundry list of tips for campaigns:

1. If a candidate has facial hair, consider shaving – people trust a clean-shaven candidate over one with facial hair.
2. Avoid useless trinkets. Trinkets are a drain on campaign funds and have little impact. They also do little to promote the campaign's message.
3. Prepare for press conferences and public appearances. The more prepared a candidate is, the less likely that inappropriate statements or comments will be made.
4. Always have a fresh perspective from outside the campaign to review all materials. Sometimes campaigns stray from the theme so far that they produce literature and ads that have little to do with the message or may even turn voters off because of inaccuracy, callousness, or irrelevance.
5. Always be concise. Long-winded answers and wordy content on a web site only serve to provide ammunition to an opponent. Brevity is a key to success. Keep it simple.
6. Always have sound bites or "snippets" ready for the press if contacted by a reporter for a story. Reporters generally know what they want their subjects to say, but a prepared interviewee will have the comments ready so that the reporter will be unable to "cherry pick" certain quotes out of context.
7. Be uncomplicated. It is counterproductive for a campaign to create images or literature that are too "busy" or have too much information for a normal person to digest. If an average person's eyes would glaze over looking at something from the campaign, then consider revising it.
8. A candidate should NEVER run his or her own campaign. A member of the candidate's family should also take a supportive position, rather than a management position, on the campaign. A third party, advisably a professional, should run the campaign.

9. Place a disclaimer on EVERYTHING. If in doubt as to whether an item requires a disclaimer, then use one. Everything from the web page, emails, and stickers to phone calls, direct mail and television ads should clearly state who paid for the item.

10. Be mindful of all election laws no matter how small. An elections violation can be a distraction a campaign does not need and can yield unfavorable press coverage.

11. If an opponent violates local, state or federal election law, and it is a "slam dunk" case (failing to display disclaimer, claiming the candidate already holds the office being sought when it is an open seat etc.), file a complaint. Too many campaigns get cold feet on filing complaints because they are afraid the opponent will file a complaint as well. If a candidate has violated an elections rule, assume the opponent will file the complaint anyway. Getting a successful "conviction" on a complaint can force an opponent off message and to spend time, money, and resources to defend the complaint.

12. Place footnotes on all assertions in campaign materials. Footnotes protect a campaign from elections complaints while also validating arguments with a third party source.

Chapter 7

Message Delivery

Every campaign must have a strategy for getting its message out to voters. The various tactics for message delivery are discussed in Chapter 7. A campaign must remember to always be able to clearly document all claims made in campaign materials. Whether they are positive statements about a candidate, a contrast statement, or a negative statement about an opponent, a campaign must back up what it says. In a race in which an opponent is impugned, a complaint may be made. A campaign is hurt if it makes claims that cannot be substantiated, and the last thing a candidate needs is for the campaign to be hit with an elections violation.

Campaigns must also keep in mind that nearly every elections jurisdiction requires a proper disclaimer to be visible on all campaign communications including e-mails, web sites, broadcast media and direct mail. Some free services, such as social media, may also require a disclaimer listing. Campaigns must take responsibility for the items they produce. A disclaimer usually includes the name of the campaign committee, the address of the campaign committee and the name of the campaign chairman or treasurer.

The purpose of Chapter 7 is to provide an overview of message delivery strategies as well as some tactics for those communications. Discussions on direct mail, the Internet, broadcast media, and other portions of campaign strategy and tactics could probably have their own books. The purpose of *The Political Campaign Desk Reference* is to provide a guide for candidates as well as campaign staff. The fundamentals of a solid plan will never change although technology and tactics often do change. Campaigns are encouraged to stay current with changing technology and to continually be creative with message delivery options. Regardless of the method, the important thing to always remember is to follow the plan and stay on message.

7.1 Direct Mail

One of the most effective methods of message delivery is direct mail. Direct mail is not generally viewed as intrusive as phone calls into a person's home or e-mails to a voter's computer. People have a general tolerance for junk mail and, consequently, political mail. The drawback to direct mail is that the lifespan of a piece of direct mail is generally from the mailbox to the trash can. Therefore, in order for direct mail to be effective, it must have visual impact and deliver the campaign message that can be processed by a reader in 30 seconds or less.

Direct mail is most effective when used repetitively in conjunction with a consistent message. This means that the campaign should plan a direct mail campaign so that the target audience receives literature multiple times prior to Election Day, and the mail should be delivered in near-rapid succession. A well thought-out campaign will have direct mail delivered to the target audience every 2 to 4 days prior to the election for as many deliveries as the campaign budget will allow.

For a campaign on a shoestring budget, a recommended series of three direct mail pieces might look like this (Election Day is November 2):

Order	Topic	Date mailed	Date delivered
Piece #1	Introduce Jane Smith	Oct. 20	Oct. 21-24
Piece #2	Jane Smith on Issues	Oct. 24	Oct. 25-28
Piece #3	Contrast with Opponent	Oct. 28	Oct. 29-Nov. 1

Topics for direct mail pieces range from introducing the candidate to attacking the opponent. The first mail piece frequently introduces the candidate and the campaign message. Too many words and too few photos can eliminate the effectiveness of the piece. A piece of direct mail has to compete with other mail in the voter's box for attention. Direct mail must have visual impact. Furthermore, the name of the candidate should be the largest element on the literature. If a person holding the mail sees nothing else, they must see the candidate's name for the piece to have any effect.

The information gathered in chapters 1 through 3 will be utilized in the Direct Mail portion of the campaign. Issues information, strengths and weaknesses, opposition research, as well as microtargeting data all come into focus in the direct mail campaign. Campaigns generally stick to a few typical themes for their direct mail plan:

- Introduction of Candidate
- Candidate on the Issues
- Candidate Endorsements
- Call-to-Action
- Inoculation
- Contrast with Opponent
- Attack on Opponent
- Response to Attack

Introduction of Candidate

The direct mail piece introducing the candidate is the first piece of literature that is mailed in the plan outlined above. The introduction defines the candidate and the message of the campaign. The introduction must be eye-catching, informative, and make the candidate appear exciting to the voter. An introduction uses qualities of the candidate that will appeal to the voters of a district. Also, the candidate's logo should appear somewhere on the introduction piece. Almost all of the literature produced by a campaign will have the campaign logo.

The introductory piece is the chance for the campaign to appeal to the voters' hearts, and it may be the first impression many voters have of the candidate. The introduction does not address issues with much detail. The direct mail pieces that focus on issues will be mailed later in the campaign. Voters should first identify with the candidate before they are presented with the candidate's positions on issues.

In order to appeal to voters in an introductory piece, careful attention should be placed on the images used of the candidate. Family photos are generally excellent images to use as well as a professional head shot of the candidate in appropriate business attire. Other images that can be used include historical photos of the candidate in a past career (law enforcement, military, skilled labor etc.). Images that fit the message in some way and appeal to the voters of the district should be used.

If roots in the community are important to voters, a candidate should emphasize any aspect that establishes them as long-standing members of the community. If the district is a largely white-collar area, emphasize any professional background of the candidate. A story of how a candidate worked his or her way up from having little to living the American Dream generally works well with many audiences. This message helps promote a message of hope while also inferring that the candidate is a hard worker and identifies with others who struggle.

An introductory piece may also list professional and civic affiliations of a candidate in order to identify with members of those organizations and their families. Incorporating the background and images of the candidate that correspond to the community is part of the key to an effective introductory piece. The introductory piece tells a story about the candidate in pictures and uses as few words as possible. The goal is to introduce the candidate in a way that appeals to voters' hearts.

Certain elements should be present in introductory literature. The campaign web site should be listed on the piece of literature. Often, the web site can be listed on the line underneath the return address. If the campaign has a social media presence, then buttons representing the sites on which the campaign has a presence can be listed. A professional head shot is a must. Even if there are action shots of the candidate within the piece, a head shot next to the campaign logo will show voters who they should look at in the action photos. The head shot identifies the candidate. If there is a citation or quote from a publication, a footnote should accompany it. Footnotes lend more validity to a piece of campaign literature because they often represent a third-party, objective source.

Candidate on the Issues

Depending on the budget and the number of issues in a race, the campaign may choose to produce one direct mail piece addressing issues, or it can produce many. A campaign may also create literature for general consumption among the voters in the district, or it can use the microtargeting data collected from earlier chapters in order to tailor a message to specific households. Campaigns on a budget may use targeting data to shrink the mailing universe rather than tailoring specific messages.

In creating "issues" pieces, the campaign has the opportunity to define why an issue is important and to present the argument as to why the candidate is the right choice in the race to handle that issue as an elected officeholder. If handled improperly, the campaign may also alienate voters while also gaining other voters. It is important to avoid polarizing too many voters in a race by addressing topics that are unpopular with many people. A campaign must choose the issues that most of the voters agree upon or that currently resonate with a majority of voters. Intelligent targeting of a controversial piece will help eliminate alienating voters.

An effective issue piece will present the problem the district is facing. Whether it is high taxes, illegal immigration, quality of life, or any other issue, the campaign defines the issue. The campaign must define the issue in such a way that the voter knows that the candidate identifies with him or her. Perhaps using a verbatim quote from an earlier poll that expresses how people view an issue may be effective. This quote, coupled with a prominent picture that exemplifies what is bothering people, may be a compelling way to catch the attention of the voter receiving the literature. Similar to the introductory piece, pictures are as important in communicating the issue as words. The campaign might use images of foreclosed properties, people in line at a soup kitchen, or derelict vehicles in the front lawns of residents to communicate tough economic times.

It is important to articulate the issue on one side of the direct mail piece and to present the candidate as the solution on the other. A campaign does not want to associate its candidate as part of the problem, so it should create the separation by using the opposite side of the direct mail piece. Using 2-sided oversized postcards is the preferred method of direct mail. Using brochures that open up or envelopes with multiple pages of information will more likely get lost in junk mail and thrown away. An issue can be presented on one side, and the solution can be presented on the other in order to tell a complete story. The candidate's logo should also be prominently displayed on the solution side along with pertinent photos. A campaign should make it as easy as possible for voters to receive the information. Each time a card is folded, or each seal that must be opened in order to get to the information, reduces the number of voters who will experience the message.

At times, the issue in the race may be tied to the opponent. If that is the case, then the opponent should appear in some unflattering way on the problem side of the issue piece. Make the opponent "own" the problem while the campaign's candidate "owns" the solution.

Candidate Endorsements

If a candidate has multiple endorsements or even a very strong endorsement from a popular personality in the district, then a direct mail piece dedicated to endorsements may be appropriate. Endorsements that are inappropriate are endorsements from people who are unpopular in the district or endorsements from polarizing figures – people whose endorsements will have both a positive and negative impact.

A compelling image to use is one with the candidate surrounded or flanked by popular figures in the district. The image should be prominent on the side of the direct mail piece where the address appears so that when the voter looks to whom the mail is addressed, the picture and accompanying text is inescapable. Messages such as, "The people we trust, trust Jenny Smith," or "Jenny Smith – Trusted by those we trust" or "ENDORSED – Jenny Smith," or "10 out of 10 people agree – Jenny Smith is the right candidate" can be compelling. Another tactic is to ask the question: "Who do the people we trust support Jenny Smith?" At the very least, the piece has drawn the interest of the reader, and the flip side of the card will most likely get viewed.

The flip side of the card should contain testimonials from the people who endorsed the candidate. Too many testimonials will make the piece too wordy. Again, pictures of the candidate with those making the endorsements, or the candidate in action poses that are descriptive of the testimonials, are effective. Testimonial statements should be short and relevant to the theme of the campaign. Many campaigns will write the statements for the person making the endorsement, and then obtain approval for the quote from the appropriate person.

Endorsements can also be added to mail pieces addressing issues. For instance, a piece whose topic is crime and law enforcement may have an endorsement by the County Sheriff for the candidate prominently displayed. Whenever this occurs, a short quote from the endorser should accompany a photo in order to maximize the visual connect the reader can make.

Call-to-Action

The call-to-action piece is a direct mail vehicle that requests the recipient to respond in some way. A call-to-action is generally accompanied by a self-addressed envelope or postcard. The call-to-action has two components: 1) exposition of candidate and the candidate's request, and 2) response vehicle.

A call-to-action piece is generally delivered in an envelope or as a folded mail piece as opposed to the other types of direct mail discussed in this section. Some calls to action contain a letter informing the recipient of some facts that the campaign wishes to communicate. The call-to-action is then accompanied by a survey or possibly a solicitation for money. Other times, the call-to-action may have a card that merely needs signed, stamped and sent to a pre-addressed destination.

The call-to-action can be used in fundraising as well as microtargeting. The campaign may also be asking recipients to call the opponent's campaign or official office in order to complain about an issue.

If a campaign has identified supporters, or likely supporters, through the use of telemarketing, surveys or other means, then the campaign should make an effort to secure those votes as early as possible. Many states allow for voting by mail or absentee voting. There is generally a period of time, usually between a week and a month, in which voters can vote early. In order to participate in early voting, a voter typically has to request a mail ballot. One type of call-to-action piece may be a brochure that contains information about the candidate but also has one or two tear-off postcards. The post cards are request forms to the local elections office requesting a mail ballot. The voter would ideally remove the card, fill it out, stamp it, send it in and wait for the ballot in the mail. A short tutorial should be part of the direct mail piece so that the voter will fully comprehend what is being asked.

Another type of call-to-action piece might be one in which a challenger wants to inform people in the district about an unpopular vote or action by the incumbent. The campaign can produce a direct mail piece that informs the recipient about the activity of the opponent and has one or two postcards attached. The first postcard is one that requires a stamp and is sent to the opponent. It is a message to the opponent from the voter stating that they did not like their recent action. Information on these cards to the opponent should be minimal so that the opponent must look up addresses and phone numbers in order to respond. The second card is a card that goes back to the candidate's own campaign in order to identify voters who sent the card in. This card requests the voter's name, address, phone and e-mail. When the postcard comes back to the campaign, the information should be added to the campaign database. If the campaign does not want the expense of perforating or folding a direct mail piece, then it can direct voters to call the office of the opponent to tell him how they feel. This type of call-to-action piece can create grief in an opposing campaign and cause the target to spend time and money responding.

Another type of call-to-action card is a slate card that presents a list of candidates for offices on the ballot to the voter. The voter is asked to vote for the people listed in each included race. Slate cards are generally used by local Republican or Democrat parties. Other third-party organizations use slate cards as well. An effective slate card is personalized to each recipient letting them know: 1) the date of the election, 2) the times that polls are open, and 3) the location of the poll for that individual.

The call-to-action is generally more expensive because of the added processes involved in producing the literature. The call-to-action should be clear in the request that it is making to the recipient as well as concise.

Inoculation

One of the reasons a campaign must conduct opposition research on its own candidate, as well as create a list of weaknesses for its candidate, is to understand what information the opponent may use in a campaign. A well-planned campaign will take into account the weaknesses of its own candidate and prepare in advance for an attack. One way to answer an attack before it occurs is to inoculate or address the issue before the opponent does.

An opponent may never choose to launch an offensive portion of the campaign. Therefore, the decision to inoculate should be carefully considered because the campaign runs the risk of exposing the voters to an issue that they otherwise may have never known. It may also be foolish to attempt to inoculate every potential issue. An opponent's campaign also has a budget and a strategy of its own, and it cannot address all of the weaknesses it might consider. So a candidate must consider what weaknesses an opponent will choose to exploit and decide whether or not to address them in some way.

Inoculation serves a few purposes: 1) it allows the candidate to take control of an issue and define it before the opponent does, 2) it can show that the candidate is forthright and honest in choosing to address an issue, and 3) inoculation can become a positive issue for a candidate if addressed properly.

The best way to approach a weakness is to find a way to turn the perceived flaw into a positive issue for the candidate. For instance, a candidate may have a history of making controversial decisions or voting on controversial issues. By being the candidate to bring up the issue first, explain the reasons for the decisions and how they impacted the district, it is possible that voters will gain respect for the candidate even if they disagree with the message. Simply knowing exactly where a candidate stands on an issue is sometimes better than supporting an opponent who has untested positions.

A direct mail piece can address an issue and inoculate it. By using compelling visuals and succinct language, a skilled campaign can take a weakness and possibly convert it to a strength. At the very least, a campaign can answer to a weakness and control the conversation before an opponent has an opportunity to attack.

For instance, if a Bob Smith has been caught for experimenting with marijuana or alcohol much earlier in life, and the likelihood that the opposition has proof either through anecdotal evidence or a citation, a campaign may want to inoculate against it. Bob Smith might create a direct mail piece in which he is candid about what he did as a youth and that he encourages children and young adults to make good decisions today. Adding a picture and a quote from a local police chief or sheriff will also demonstrate that the candidate is now on the right side of the law. Of course, this inoculation tactic works well if the law that was broken was a minor infraction. More serious crimes present tougher challenges for a candidate and can affect the decision about whether to run or not.

Inoculation should be used judiciously when serious or devastating issues face a campaign. If the campaign tests a weakness in a poll and finds that voters do not care about the issue or are apathetic to it, then raising awareness to the issue is an unwise use of resources.

Contrast with Opponents

A contrast piece is one in which the candidate uses the strengths vs. weaknesses charts prepared in Chapter 1. In essence, a contrast piece is one in which the voters will view the candidate's strengths while also seeing the opponent's weaknesses. It is important in contrast pieces that all of the information is true and accurate and can be supported by documentation. A campaign does not want to lose relevance in a race because it used inaccurate information. Footnoting assertions is a good start to protecting against an elections complaint while serving to validate the piece.

Campaign cycles have many candidates for many different positions. Chances are that voters are receiving a lot of mail from a lot of candidates. As is the case with all other direct mail, the contrast piece must be produced so that it has visual impact.

One type of contrast might have two abbreviated resumes side-by-side on one side of the literature. One resume is for the candidate sending the literature. The other resume is for the opponent. Obviously the information on the candidate's resume is flattering while the information selected for the opponent is not. The flip side is a positive statement about the candidate repeating one or two key strengths from the resume on the other side.

Other types of contrast pieces are similar in content but might appear differently. If two people are running for judge, then an appropriate visual may illustrate the scales of justice tipping towards the candidate and away from the opponent. Instead of resumes, the contrast might be depicted on make-believe case files. Whatever device is used to attract the voter's attention to the piece, it should be relevant and not distract from the message.

The contrast piece may set the information up in a matrix in which the first column is a statement such as "Endorsed by the Fraternal Order of Police." The next column would have a picture and caption of the candidate at the top and a blue or green "YES" or check mark in the field next to the statement. The third and last column would have the opponent's picture and caption with a red "NO" or "X" in the field next to the statement. The table should be just a few rows long. Although there may be 20 strong differences between the candidates, a campaign should pick, at most, five or six. More than five or six contrasts can crowd the piece and make it hard to read.

Attack on Opponent

Attack pieces regarding an opponent are similar to the contrast with the exception that the opponent's weaknesses take prominence in the content of the piece, and the candidate issuing the mail may not even be mentioned. The reason a campaign uses attack pieces is to erode the support of an opponent. If an opponent is extremely popular or far ahead in polling, a candidate may not be able to close the gap by winning the remaining undecided voters. Therefore, an attack on the opponent is necessary in order to bring balance to a race in which someone is far ahead of another. The risk that a candidate runs in any negative attack is the loss of one's own support. If an attack is perceived as mean-spirited, unwarranted, or particularly vicious, then the attacker may also lose support.

Making an attack piece seem responsible is a challenge for a campaign. In order for an attack to be effective, the opponent must be identified with an action, issue or condition that is unpopular. For instance, an area may be suffering economically, and the opponent is a county commissioner who makes decisions on local taxes, utility rates and other fees that impact the lives of voters. The challenger to the incumbent may use an attack piece that paints a grim picture of the current state of affairs and pins the responsibility for those conditions on the incumbent.

Another attack may look at the record of an opponent. As the campaign gathered information discussed in chapters 1 through 3, extensive research should have been conducted on the opponent's record including votes, attendance, criminal, and other areas. A campaign may decide to attack any weak point. Nearly every voter understands that if he or she misses work excessively then they will be fired. If an opponent has missed a significant number of meetings over the course of the last year or term in office, then a candidate may decide to paint a picture of an opponent who uses an office as a personal playground and shirks responsibility while the residents of the district are struggling to get by.

An effective way to present an attack is to replace bombastic and hard-hitting statements with leading questions. In the case of the absentee officeholder, the negative statement "Robert Baker missed one out of every five meetings last year while we worked hard," might be replaced with "Is it fair that Robert Baker missed 20% of work last year?" Very few voters would answer the question with a "yes." Even Robert Baker's supporters will be agitated at the question because they know that the only honest answer is "no." An effective piece of literature creates a sense of urgency in the opponent to spend time and money responding to a charge. While Robert Baker is responding to the direct mail piece about how he has missed more work than most working people are allowed in a year, the challenger campaign may be coming out with another attack piece asking another question that will keep Robert Baker on the defense.

A good attack campaign may not directly attack an opponent, and it does not generally make statements as much as it asks questions.

If voters answer a question about a candidate the way in which they unknowingly were directed to, then they feel as though the conclusion they reached is their own. The voters are engaged because they answered the question in their own minds, and the literature that merely posed a question has now planted a seed of discontent. If a campaign has the money for a full scale attack, there will be a total of two or three questions asked of the opponent. Since the questions were asked through the mail, and not in a public debate or other medium, the opponent is forced to spend money answering the attack. Since campaigns are not forced to disclose their direct mail lists, the opponent can only guess as to who has received the attack pieces.

If the campaign has done its job in eliminating the opponent, the opponent's family, and the opponent's known supporters from its database, then it has increased the amount of time between which the message was delivered and the opponent will become aware and respond. If enough time passes between the attack and the response, then the opponent, in answering the attack, is actually resurrecting an issue that may better be left alone. Unless the opponent begins his own series of attacks, then the advantage will likely belong to the candidate waging the original attacks.

Another method of using direct mail for attacks is to present the words of a third party to denigrate an opponent. For instance, if a local union boss, pastor, or other respected leader makes a public statement about an opponent's absenteeism, mismanagement, or other issue, then the quote is fair game for a direct mail piece because it is in the public domain. When third party comments are used in a "What are people saying about Robert Baker" piece, then the campaign waging the attack shifts a portion of the burden of waging an attack to the third party making the statements.

The relationship that the campaign has with the media is important in creating an attack campaign. A skilled campaign manager can craft an issue in such a way that it stands alone without need for the candidate to attack the opponent. Reporters are trained to be investigative, and a campaign that can effectively start an investigation that will lead to the desired results will get a story in the paper or on television. Once a story hits the papers or airwaves, effective quotes for a direct mail piece can be gathered and used, and the source is a third party. In this manner, a candidate never had to take a public stand to go on the attack.

Attacks can also backfire on a campaign. For instance, if a candidate is using a kind-looking, elderly grandmother to make a statement, and the opponent decides to take the image and words of the woman and apply them to his own media, then the opponent has exploited a grandmotherly woman and twisted her words for political gain. This opens up the opponent's campaign to obvious charges of misrepresenting facts and can derail a campaign. This scenario is similar to a situation that occurred in a statewide issue campaign in 2011. The woman, who was described as a "great-grandmother" became a surrogate speaker for her issue and made broadcast media appearances. The news media throughout the state ran with stories about the exploitation of the elderly woman. The campaign that misused the woman's image and words tried to defend its decision but eventually lost the issue by a wide margin on Election Day. Although the defeat may not be fully due to the "great-grandmother" situation, it certainly contributed.

Going on the attack can be a risky proposition that is generally only commenced in circumstances that require it. If an opponent is so far ahead that remaining undecided voters cannot bridge the gap, then going negative may seem like the way to go. The proper way to wage an attack campaign is to engage the voter in such a way that the conclusion a voter reaches seems like his or her own. It is also wise to use third party comments when available so that the burden of the attack is spread around to others. A campaign should always finish strong, so finishing a race with all attacks and no positive messages for a candidate is not wise.

Response to Attack

In close races and campaigns in which a candidate is polling ahead of another, a campaign team can count on an opponent going on the offensive. If the opposing campaign is wisely attacking a candidate, then it is most likely attempting to place a candidate in a permanent defensive position. As a candidate is spending resources answering one attack, the opponent is waging another attack that the candidate must now answer. If a candidate is constantly on the defense, then the message of the campaign is not being effectively communicated. Furthermore, a barrage of attacks that put a candidate in a defense mode will eventually take its toll on valuable campaign resources including time, money and people. A campaign can lose steam and become demoralized if it is not effectively handling attacks.

The best way to respond to an attack is to answer the attack and go on the offensive in the response. For instance, an opponent may choose to attack a candidate for holding numerous elected positions over a short period. In answering the attack, a candidate can talk about how the opponent chooses to talk about the number of positions John Doe has held. "Opponent X is attacking John Doe because John Doe has something Candidate X does not have: Experience." So in one mail piece or ad, the campaign has turned the issue from a negative to a positive and even went on the attack.

A campaign may choose to also ignore an attack. If an opponent chooses a weakness that does not resonate with voters, the best response may be no response. Sometimes responding to a non-issue can lend legitimacy to the issue and create a problem for a campaign. An example would be an opponent attacking a candidate for smoking marijuana decades before. If the issue is tested in a poll and found that voters are generally disinterested, then the candidate would be wise to ignore the charge and continue with the campaign. By addressing the charge and focusing more attention on the issue, a candidate may open the floodgates of questions such as, "how long have you used?" "How much have you used?" "Did you sell marijuana, too?" So the campaign message is derailed as the media and voters now read about the details of a marijuana user instead of the platform of a distinguished candidate for office. If voters are interested in an issue, however, ignoring that issue can work to the campaign's detriment.

The most effective direct mail piece a campaign can produce, in terms of timing, is one that lands in mailboxes the day before the election and is personalized to the recipient household. The piece will inform the voters in that household of when they vote and the address of the polling location. Times that the polls are open should also be printed on the literature. Many of the voters who receive this literature will take it with them to the polls on Election Day.

The more difficult a piece of direct mail is to read, the less likely someone will read it. The use of compelling pictures and brevity is essential for a piece of mail whose lifespan is less than one minute. The design of the direct mail piece is also important. Generally, everything a campaign wishes to communicate should be done on two sides of an oversized postcard. If a voter receives a folded brochure that must be unsealed and opened, the likelihood that the entire piece will be read is decreased. Some issues are too complex to fit on two sides of a card. A folded brochure or pamphlet should only be used if the issue is compelling enough to warrant voters taking the time to open it along with all of the other mail they receive on a daily basis. If the issue is simple, and the message is brief, a double-sided, oversized postcard will effectively communicate the message. Multiple issues on a single piece are not generally advisable unless the direct mail piece is recapping information delivered in previous pieces.

Furthermore, oversized postcards are generally less expensive than a direct mail piece that requires folding and sealing. Campaigns are almost always on a budget, and costs associated with printing and mailing can begin to impact the war chest. Not only are brochures more difficult to access and read, they generally incur higher costs when folded or sealed. Also remember that each campaign is competing with all of the other campaigns to get noticed. It is easy to get lost amidst the other mail from other candidates for other offices. The challenge is to get noticed before being discarded.

Many candidates may be compelled to create a pamphlet or brochure mail piece. Generally, the candidate wants to add statistics, figures, evidence to support a point, or other information that appears relevant. If a campaign chooses to create a direct mail piece that must be opened in order to read, then the outside of the piece must be so compelling that the recipient will take the time to break the seal and open the literature. If the inside is filled with drivel or statistics or charts or organized in such a way that the reader's eyes will glaze over and become numb, then the direct mail piece was ineffective. A small handful of voters may read every piece of mail from cover to cover, but most voters need to have information delivered in easy-to-read pieces that have impact. Good literature will also have additional relevant information such as the campaign web site and reminders to visit the campaign's social media pages.

Most printers can work with campaigns on developing direct mail. Campaigns should use bulk rate postage available to political races in order to save on mail costs. A good printer will have the ability to print bulk rate indicia on the literature or use a bulk rate stamp. When mailing to a database, a campaign should never send literature to the opponent or any known supporters of the opponent. A campaign does not want an opponent to know the content of its literature, when its mail is being sent, how often mail is being sent or to whom. All direct mail should be targeted to voters who have not yet voted and are unknown in their support.

7.2   Broadcast Media

A popular method of mass communication in campaigns is electronic media. Broadcast media includes television and radio advertising. Although television may seem expensive, the results can make it worth it. Television allows candidates to communicate directly to voters who are watching and listening. The three facets most important in dealing with electronic media are 1) ad placement, 2) message, and 3) budget.

Broadcast media is more efficient than a large direct mail campaign in larger districts such as congressional races. Television costs much more than direct mail to reach each voter in small races, but as the size of the universe grows, a campaign will notice more return, in terms of voter response, on each dollar spent from television than it will with direct mail.

Placement

The general strategy is to place ads on television during news programming because many viewers of news programming are concerned voters. During sports season, placing ads during popular games can also be effective. A primary race will have different dynamics than a general election race. Placement of ads on cable programming specifically geared towards a target audience should be strongly considered for primaries. The bulk of the broadcast media campaign budget will be in television rather than radio.

On radio, effective ads are placed during drive time for commuters, on popular stations, and during programming on talk radio. Radio is not as effective as television, but the price per ad is generally much less. Radio should rarely become the dominant expenditure in a campaign. Radio is a medium to which only a select segment of voters listen, and the times that they listen are limited. Local talk radio is generally a good venue for reaching voters. Obstacles to using local radio is the emergence of satellite radio, MP3 ports in vehicles, online music providers, and other competitors to radio that draw the traditional listening audience away. Radio can be targeted, but radio should never be the sole outlet by which a campaign advertises.

Television spots are typically 30 seconds in length. Most ad rates supplied by stations sell time in 30 second increments. Campaigns that find themselves on a budget may be able to purchase television time in 15 or 10 second increments, but shorter increments forces the campaign to communicate a message in a much shorter span of time. If a television station does not allow for a campaign to purchase a shorter increment of time, then a campaign may be able to seek out another candidate in the same election cycle that is also on a budget. If two separate campaigns buy television spots in 30 second increments and split the cost, then they are increasing the frequency that they can appear on television. Experienced media and campaign professionals know how to make these "split" scenarios work well. The candidate that a campaign partners with should be carefully selected in order to avoid conflicts.

Television and cable stations can provide needed demographic information of viewers that will help determine which stations and what times will be most beneficial to a campaign. This information is used in order to target voters. Radio stations should also be able to provide this information about their listeners. A campaign manager or media buyer should check rating points for who is listening or viewing and when. A campaign should hire an experienced media consultant in order to make the best use of their broadcast advertising dollars.

Message

Campaigns usually do not have enough money to produce multiple spots that will each gain enough repetition with voters to have an impact. Therefore, it is important for a campaign to choose one or two messages to promote in a broadcast media campaign. Also, a campaign should budget for a response spot if the campaign anticipates an attack.

A campaign must decide what it wishes to accomplish in 30 seconds. Is it to raise name identification with the candidate? If the campaign is trying to raise name identification, is it because the grassroots, direct mail and other facets of the campaign are failing, or is it because the district is so large that television is the only method of raising name identification? By asking the right questions, a campaign can decide what it wants to accomplish. Each spot should have one message because additional messages create confusion. Time is one of the four primary resources of a campaign, and it is important to use it wisely in conjunction with information when crafting broadcast media messages. Therefore, if a campaign has two messages, then each message should probably be in a different spot. A campaign must also determine if it has the ability to make more than one message penetrate the target audience, meaning that most of the target audience will hear or view the spot enough times for it to be remembered. If the campaign has enough money for only one message to penetrate, then using the campaign's budget for that message would be wiser than attempting to communicate multiple messages.

In the Direct Mail section of this chapter, various types of message delivery were discussed, and each type generally warrants its own direct mail piece. On television a campaign has 30 seconds to communicate whatever it can to the audience. If the campaign tries to accomplish too much, then the ad will be largely ignored. For instance, an ad that tries to introduce a candidate, tell a story about the candidate's life, talk about the candidate's credentials, list one or more endorsements and use images of the candidate as a child then as an adult will have no impact on voters except to send some of them into convulsions trying to understand what they just saw.

A campaign will generally create an introductory ad that raises awareness of the candidate. An introduction should never try to accomplish too much.

A campaign can use 30 seconds to introduce a candidate's credentials for office. A 30 second ad can address a specific issue and how a candidate will handle that issue. The goal of a television ad is to compel the viewer to vote for a candidate. The purpose is not to overload the viewer or provide too much information. A television ad should play to a candidate's strengths or an opponent's weaknesses. And a 30 second ad can tell a story.

Campaigns are generally unable to produce a series of television or radio spots that can tell a story in the same way that direct mail can. In direct mail, a campaign can grab voter's attention and appeal to their hearts. The campaign can address several issues or inoculate an attack. The campaign can go on the attack or list endorsements with direct mail. And direct mail allows a campaign to call on voters to perform an action. Just as each type of direct mail piece is its own production, so should a television ad. Instead of telling a story across multiple ads, a story has to be told in 30 seconds. The message of the story should be clear and simple.

If an opponent attacks a candidate on television, then the response must be made on television. A response should always occur in the same medium that the attack was made. The purpose for responding in the same medium is to reach the exact same voters that the opponent reached when making the attack. If an opponent makes an attack on television, and a campaign responds on the radio, then two things have just happened. First, the television viewers who saw the original attack have most likely not heard the response. Second, the radio listening audience that did not see the original attack ad is now aware of a previously unknown issue.

Candidate endorsements can be incorporated into an ad. A call-to-action can occur on an attack ad or an issues ad. Inoculation seldom occurs on television unless the issue must be addressed as evidenced in poll results. The time on television is valuable and scarce. To spend these resources on addressing an inoculation issue before it is raised means that the campaign has already departed from its message in the most expensive medium. However, if a candidate wishes to control an issue that they see as a weakness, and the campaign has the resources, then television may become the medium of choice.

Budget

A campaign makes many of its decisions based on the campaign budget. Whether or not to place time in television or radio depends on how large the budget is. In order to adequately penetrate, prospective voters need to view or hear an ad repetitively over the course of its run. If a campaign can only run ads for a single day, then it should evaluate if it is spending its money the best possible way. Television and radio spots usually require a significant investment in order to properly deliver a message.

7.3 Phones

If used properly, a campaign plan that incorporates telemarketing can be very effective for a relatively low cost. Telephones can be used effectively in a campaign, but telephones can also be employed in a way that works to a campaign's detriment. A telephone campaign is generally a cost effective way to raise candidate awareness, advocate on behalf of a candidate, conduct virtual town hall meetings, gather information, and microtarget the district.

Some states or jurisdictions may not allow for recorded phone messages to be transmitted en masse. Political calls are generally exempt from such laws, but a campaign should be aware of the laws regarding telemarketing and what is allowed. Even if a candidate feels that a court challenge to a law prohibiting political calls is winnable, the campaign should consider whether the cost and risk associated with such publicity is worth it. Some areas have laws to prohibit calls because the people in those areas simply do not like them. Most jurisdictions also have disclaimer rules that require a short disclaimer at the end or beginning of a call that identifies who paid for the call along with a contact phone number.

When considering adding phones in the campaign plan, the campaign team must consider the goals. What will be gained through the telephone portion of the campaign? How do these calls advance the message of the campaign? Sample phone call scripts are found in Appendix M.

Raising candidate awareness and advocating a candidate

During the final weeks of a campaign leading to Election Day, many campaigns employ a tactic in which voters receive phone messages urging them to vote for a candidate. The calls are recorded messages sent out to voting households usually by a firm that specializes in telecommunications. Sometimes the call is recorded by the candidate, and sometimes the call is recorded by a third party in support of a candidate. The purpose of such a call is generally twofold: to raise name identification of a candidate and to communicate positive information about a candidate.

An effective tactic is to plan on three or four calls to be delivered over the course of the last two weeks of the campaign. Too many calls may become a nuisance. The first three calls are generally successful if recorded by a third party supporter. Popular officeholders that are already elected in the same district are effective as well as other members of the campaign committee that have some stature in the community. An ideal call should be less than thirty seconds including the disclaimer. The call should use the name of the candidate multiple times and speak to the message of the campaign. Rehearsing the call prior to recording is important so that it sounds natural and not forced.

If the first call begins two weeks from Election Day, and the campaign is conducting four messages, they should be spaced three to four days apart from each other. If the calls are placed too closely together, then it may seem like overkill to the voter. The time of day that the calls are placed is equally important. It is generally advisable, when delivering advocacy calls, to reach as many voicemail and answering machines as possible. If someone picks up the phone and listens to an obviously recorded message that is not interactive, the likelihood of them listening to the entire message is low. However, if a voter is listening to voicemail, then he or she is expecting recordings – that is the nature of voicemail. The likelihood of successfully delivering the entire message is increased.

The final call should be delivered on the day prior to Election Day. The final call is recorded by the candidate and is a reminder to vote coupled with a direct appeal for the listener's support.

Virtual Community Forum

Something that some telecommunications firms offer is termed as a virtual community forum similar to a town hall meeting (tele-town hall) on the phone. A virtual community forum is an event in which the candidate is available on a teleconference to speak to people in the district. A virtual forum can be an event that is advertised in which people may call in, or it can be an event that the campaign plans in which it calls targeted voters to provide the instant opportunity to participate in a town hall session.

A virtual forum usually also requires a moderator with a computer who can see which voters are calling in or see which voters are participating through the campaign's solicitation. The moderator can speak to each caller privately to screen their thoughts before being given the chance to speak. The moderator can also join the live town hall to help guide the candidate to stay on message if a rogue caller gets off topic.

A virtual forum is an opportunity to raise candidate awareness, but it also provides other unique benefits. A candidate can express the campaign message or views on issues important to voters. The forum also allows participants to feel as though they have invested something into the campaign of a particular candidate. A forum may be a good time to acquire verbatim responses or feelings of the participants. Forums can also provide access for potential "virtual hecklers" as well. Most systems will allow for monitoring and screening of participants so that the opportunity for hecklers is minimal.

A forum is an expense for campaigns that should only occur if certain other telephone elements have already been used such as information gathering and candidate awareness. A virtual forum will be more effective and garner greater participation if the participants have heard of the candidate.

Gathering Information and Microtargeting

Telephone polls have been around since almost the advent of the telephone. In the past, polling the electorate has been conducted by live operators asking questions from a phone script. Technology now allows for interactive sessions with a recorded operator and a live participant. Such sessions use voice activated software to discern "yes" and "no" replies as well as other basic responses.

The telephone poll is important in a campaign to determine the issues, the impact of the campaign, what demographics support a candidate or position, and what issues will move voters towards or away from supporting a candidate. A poll gathers data so that a campaign can make decisions about how to use different issues or if it needs to inoculate a candidate on an issue. A poll can tell a campaign if it needs to focus on women or men, seniors or young families, whites or Latinos, or any number of demographic breakdowns. Polls also provide benchmarks for a campaign. Is it gaining or losing voters? Are undecided voters moving towards the candidate or the opponent?

Other types of polls can be conducted by live or recorded operators. Recorded interactive polls are generally much less expensive and have the ability to reach everyone in a district affordably. An interactive poll can be used to identify each household that participates in a call as to where it stands on various issues. In order to promote participation, the poll should be recorded in the voice of the candidate and be as short as possible. It may be valuable to identify households that are pro-life or pro-choice, pro-2nd Amendment or pro-gun control, and other so-called social issues. In close races, a campaign team may look to its microtargeting data and decide to send decidedly targeted messages to the micro-targeted households.

Telephones can also be used to secure sign locations, identify potential supporters, and prospect donors. In the past, campaigns would schedule days or weeks of volunteers to make phone calls to voters in order to secure yard sign locations. A smart campaign can now add a question about allowing the use of a yard sign into an interactive poll. After the participant answers the targeting information, he or she is then asked if they support the candidate. "Yes" answers are followed by a solicitation for a yard sign location and/or if they would like to be a donor. Keeping the poll brief is important to maximize the number of participants that complete the entire survey.

The timing of an interactive survey should be during the evening. Since recorded surveys can be broadcast inexpensively, most firms will make three attempts to contact households over two or three days - twice in the evening and once in the morning. The goal of an interactive survey, as opposed to an advocacy message, is to reach as many people at home as possible.

Many candidates overlook the value of using telephones in a campaign. Telephones are like any other medium in which a campaign delivers a message. Finding the right balance between too little and too much when it comes to phone campaigns is important. Phone campaigns through firms can also be used to free up volunteers who would otherwise be on the phone so that they can participate in other volunteer efforts. The information gathered through a telephone campaign can also be used in other facets of the campaign plan such as direct mail, message development, and fundraising.

7.4   Internet

Almost every campaign has a web site regardless of the size of the race. From township trustee and city council to the Presidential races, nearly every campaign has a presence on the Internet. The Internet can be an incredible resource for candidates as well as voters seeking information. As with everything else in the campaign, the web site should be crafted to deliver the message of the campaign and to incorporate the proper images of the campaign.

Certain information should always appear on a campaign web site. Some information is nice to have but unnecessary. There is also information that should never appear on a campaign web site. The important thing to consider about the web site is making it appear seamless with the rest of the campaign. The web site should incorporate the images and captions being used in television and direct mail. The campaign logo should be prominent throughout the web site. The message is the same on the web site as everywhere else in the campaign. The web site links to campaign media as it is produced, and press releases are posted as soon as they are distributed to the media. In essence, the campaign web site is a virtual embodiment of the campaign.

Essential information on a campaign web site includes a professional photo of the candidate, also known as a "head shot", the campaign logo, disclaimer and a short introduction from the candidate expressing why he or she is running for office. Other important links to have from the home page include an endorsements and testimonials page, a press page, a campaign committee page, a donor/volunteer page and an issues page. An "about the candidate" page is also good to have, but some campaigns incorporate this information on the home page.

Secondary information for a campaign web site might include photos from the campaign trail, external links, information about the district, electronic copies of literature, radio and television ads. Information that campaigns should give careful thought to on a campaign web site includes a campaign calendar, a blog from the candidate, personal candidate information, and extraneous campaign information.

The prominent placement of the campaign logo helps connect the web site to the rest of the campaign. A head shot on the web site will help connect the candidate to stories about the candidate in the paper and to show voters the image of the candidate that it has crafted. The head shot should also be on the site as a resource for members of the media who have not received it from the campaign. Placing a high resolution image on the page dedicated to press or media is a good idea. A discussion of earned media occurs later in this chapter. A disclaimer is almost always required by federal or state elections law. The central portion of the home page for the campaign's web site should be a brief statement from the candidate. The statement should answer the question as to why the candidate is running for office and highlight the two or three strengths of the candidate without going into detail.

The campaign web site should also have a link to an "endorsements" or "testimonials" page in which all of the campaign's committee members are listed. Any organizations that have endorsed the candidate should also appear on this page. Pictures of prominent or highly recognizable team members should be present on the page. In addition, quotes from those endorsing the candidate can be placed on the endorsement page. It is one thing to list someone as a committee member, but to have a quote on the web site implies a different level of engagement in the campaign.

A press page should contain press releases from the campaign as well as links to stories about the candidate. A head shot should be available for the press on this page. Reporters covering political races rely on the Internet as a resource, and a campaign should make it as easy as possible for reporters to find the information for which they are looking. A press page may also link to unflattering stories of a campaign's opponent.

An "issues" page should appear on a web site. Any issue about which the candidate has expressed a view should have an explanation on the web page. The description of the candidate's position on each issue should be brief and broad. Becoming too detailed on an issue can create a situation in which an opponent might use a candidate's own words against the campaign. Simply because a candidate has a personal opinion on an issue does not mean that it should be on the site. A campaign should be judicious about what information is included on the web site.

An "about the candidate" page can be a narrative story about the candidate, or it can be a reproduction of the candidate's resume. People want to know about the candidate as a person, and the "about" page is the campaign's chance to humanize the candidate. Pictures should be used on all pages to enhance the appearance and interest of the site, and the "about" page is no exception. Images should have impact, and they should tell a story about the candidate. The campaign created an image for the candidate, and the Internet is the one place that all voters can access this information. A campaign must place careful thought into what is included on the web site.

No web site should be without a page or button that allows a visitor to donate money or time to the campaign. At the very least, a campaign web site should have a way of allowing the visitor to provide e-mail and contact information to the campaign. Volunteers and donors can begin as simple visitors looking for information. Campaigns must make it easy for donors to give, and a web site is a perfect medium for donating.

A campaign should be cautious about printing a calendar of events on its web site. Only campaign staff and pertinent volunteers should know where a candidate will appear. Events can be posted after the fact with pictures to show that the candidate is on the campaign trail. Adding a calendar to the web site may do the opponent's work for him so that he knows what events to attend or where to send a videographer for surveillance. A calendar is also a resource for opponents to organize an embarrassing protest of a candidate because they know where to go and when. It may also have an unintended consequence of missing events in the area and thereby offending people that the campaign does not wish to offend. Campaign calendars on a web site generally are more of a liability than an asset.

Some candidates for office think it is a good idea to post a web log or "blog" on a web site. The problem with a blog is that the people who read blogs are a campaign's opponents. A campaign should assume that its opponent is always looking for a way to embarrass or trip-up a candidate. It is effective to attack a campaign by using his or her own words. Because the nature of a blog is to keep information "fresh," and voters expect a blog to be from the candidate, the volume of text in a blog from which an opponent may find faults becomes enormous. A blog presents opponents with potential ammunition in a campaign. Campaign blogging should be accomplished through third parties and with volunteers who blog. A candidate with a blog creates a potential problem.

Blogs can be effective when reprinting press releases, linking to unflattering stories of the opponent, reprinting some of the campaign's communications, or raising awareness of an issue. Blogs can also be a quick method by which a campaign can respond to an issue or create an issue. The media, along with a campaign's opponents, also look to blogs for tips. If a campaign can help an issue gain prominence through blog activity, then the issue may become a story. When a campaign chooses to blog, it should maintain a high level of discipline, and that discipline should carry through to the use of social media.

Some campaigns have "secret" pages on a web site or utilize web based database management. Anything that a campaign wishes to keep confidential should not be accessed on the web without proper security. Campaign integrity can be compromised by a good hacker, unsecured computer or Internet connection, disgruntled staffer, former employee of the candidate, and other means. It happens, and campaigns that rely on web-based technology to manage a campaign should take every precaution. A campaign database is one of the most useful and valuable assets in a campaign, and placing it on the Internet increases the opportunity for corruption, loss of data, or unintentional data transfer to third parties.

A web site can be an incredible resource for pushing information out to voters. A good web site can also be a fundraising tool as well as a tool to gather volunteer information. Campaigns should always have a web site but also be cautious about what information is placed on that site. The campaign plan should incorporate the Internet costs and tactics into the campaign strategy.

7.5   Letters to the Editor

Letters to the editor of local papers are among the most cost-effective means of using newspapers. Although political newspaper advertising is generally not effective, unless the ad itself becomes a topic for news, letters to the editor are. Letters to the editor are also inexpensive as the only resources they require are time, information and volunteers. Many readers of publications, especially local newspapers, will read the letters written to the publication. Assuming that the letter writers use their own stamps or computers to submit their letters, money is not involved with letters to the editor.

An aggressive letter campaign can be used to communicate the same information that the campaign is communicating through direct mail, phones or electronic media. In a well-run letter writing campaign, the campaign team will assemble a list of local publications pertinent to the district with every possible means of submitting letters listed such as "snail" mail, fax, web form, or e-mail. If a newspaper accepts submissions through a web form or e-mail, then that should be utilized because the paper will not have to transcribe the letter – it will already be in electronic format so that it can be copied and pasted.

Volunteers who write letters should be told to expect a confirmation call or e-mail from the newspaper. Many newspapers will not publish letters unless they can confirm the authenticity of the author. All volunteers should have the list of publications so that they can submit their letters to as many as possible. Letter writers should also be provided with a sheet of campaign talking points. It is important for writers to stay on message, so they need to know the message.

Letter writers are also excellent third parties that can bring up a potentially negative issue for the opponent without it coming directly from the campaign. Readers of the publication who visit the letters section go there to find out what other people are thinking. An aggressive letter campaign can help guide public opinion on certain subjects.

Some volunteers do not feel comfortable articulating issues by themselves. It is not unethical for a campaign to prepare a letter that reflects the views of the volunteer and then to give it to the volunteer for their changes. The volunteer is ultimately the one who submits the letter and takes responsibility for it. Most volunteers take the prewritten example and use it merely as a guideline.

Many newspapers publish their content online as well as in the print edition. A campaign should link from its web site to specific letters that are printed that are in favor of the candidate as well as letters that are unfavorable to the opponent.

A campaign should always aggressively engage in letter writing. It is relatively quick, easy, inexpensive, and usually has fast results. Letter writers can be guided to stay on message, and it is a good way for a campaign to go on the attack through a third party. Opponents will usually have their own letter writing campaign, so it is important to have a large amount of people writing as well as discipline to stay on message.

7.6   Earned Media

Earned media is exactly as it suggests – media exposure that does not cost the campaign financial resources. Earned media refers to news programming and other events that gain some sort of media exposure either on television, radio, print publications, or web sites. Campaigns can gain earned media through many tactics such as press releases, media advisories, press conferences, campaign events, community events attended by the campaign, or interviews on a topic. The next section goes into more detail about successful press releases, media advisories and press conferences.

Campaign events can include rallies in which high profile people will speak to volunteers to promote the candidate and energize the troops. Another type of campaign event might be a big weekend day near the election in which dozens of volunteers will go door-to-door or perform other volunteer activities to reach voters. The two keys to a successful campaign event that generates coverage are volunteers and reporters.

A lackluster event in terms of volunteer turnout, with media present, could turn out to be a poor story for the campaign instead of a positive one. If a campaign stages a rally or has a volunteer blitz and invites the media, then the volunteer coordinator and political director must work together to drive turnout to the event. Members of the media, after witnessing a large group, will then want to see some kind of plan or organization. In essence, they want structure and a point to the event. It might be a good idea to have media shadowing the candidate going door-to-door speaking with voters. At a rally, the media should have access to the candidate as well as the high profile people present that are supporting the candidate. If a reporter obtains a positive quote from a voter or high profile supporter and puts it in the story, then the campaign has scored another victory. The first success was getting a story at all.

If the campaign receives intelligence that a community event is going to be covered by the local media on a specific date and time, then the campaign has a prime opportunity to be seen and gain exposure at the event. For instance, a community picnic or festival is taking place at a local park. Volunteers in campaign t-shirts should arrive well in advance of the media and circulate through the crowd. If the campaign invested in stickers, then festival patrons should be given them to wear on their shirts. A campaign volunteer that is not in campaign clothing should also be available if the media decides to conduct a "man on the street" interview. The interviewee can mention how great it is to see so many people from a certain candidate's campaign supporting the event. If the camera pans the crowd, it will hopefully pick up the many campaign revelers at the festival. If the candidate is attending the festival, the media may take the opportunity for a "spontaneous" interview. Earned media is often the result of being at the right place at the right time.

Some issues are more important to certain areas than others. If a candidate is an expert or authority on a hot-button issue in an area, then the media should be encouraged to use that candidate in an official capacity. Oftentimes this happens as incumbents for office speak about local issues. If an incumbent uses the benefits of the office wisely, he or she can gain media time and exposure that may not be subject to "equal time" rules because of its official nature. Incumbency is a powerful tool that a candidate can use. It usually falls under the "strengths" category. If an issue important to voters can somehow be addressed by the office a candidate currently holds, then every effort should be made to positively address the issue in a way that voters will favor. If a candidate is not a current officeholder or incumbent, being an expert speaker at a high profile conference or civic event might also gain earned media attention.

Earned media can be as powerful as a television spot or publication advertisement. A difference is that people watching the news are more apt to see a news story about a candidate than a television spot paid for by the campaign. A negative difference is that news stories are generally on a short cycle. A story that features a candidate may only play once whereas television spots play numerous times on numerous channels throughout the day over many days. A campaign would much rather have earned media than not, however, and spending resources wisely to gain it is recommended.

7.7   Press Releases, Media Advisories and Press Conferences

Nearly every campaign, at one point or another, will come in contact with the media. An effective campaign builds a relationship with the media that ideally develops into a positive long-term, professional relationship once a candidate takes office. A campaign can meet this goal by keeping the media informed of its activities and events.

Chapter 1 of *The Political Campaign Desk Reference* discussed information gathering and acquiring the contact information for all media that either will cover the race or that is within the jurisdiction of the office being sought. An individual should be identified at each outlet that can be contacted whenever a communication is sent. Also, developing a relationship with reporters is important because they will be more apt to act quickly on a potential story if they have a relationship they value with the campaign. News outlets thrive on information, and the people who provide the most information that is relevant are more valuable than people who provide inane or useless information. Therefore, it is not only important to establish a good relationship with reporters, it is important to also provide relevant news.

Press Releases

The easiest way to push information to reporters is through the use of press releases. Press releases are also most effective when they are written in AP style, which is the same style reporters generally use to write stories. In essence, reporters use a technique commonly referred to as the "inverted pyramid". The pyramid is an abstract representation of how a story should be written. The most important information in a story appears at the beginning and answers the questions of who, what, where, when, why and how. Moving down the pyramid is less important information such as quotes. At the bottom of the pyramid is the least important information such as ancillary background details that are not necessary to the story but enhance it and are still relevant.

Entire college courses and textbooks teach journalism as well as how to write effective campaign communications. It takes some people years to master writing brief, compelling press statements. A campaign does not need to master journalistic style, but it is most helpful to a journalist if the same rules they follow are employed in a press release. For instance, as a journalist writes a story using a press release as a reference, the journalist will most likely write the story according to the style described above. As the journalist writes the story, it is helpful if the progress of the press release matches the natural progression of how the journalist will write the article. In essence, the journalist can follow the press release down and incorporate relevant portions while writing the story. Campaigns that use this style are much more successful in communicating their thoughts directly into print than campaigns that ignore common journalism devices.

Press releases should also be sent via e-mail whenever possible. In an age of mobile communications, reporters are often out of the office or on the road following a story and writing and submitting stories electronically. Furthermore, it is much easier, and leaves less room for error, if a reporter can cut-and-paste a quote from an e-mail press release rather than re-type a quote from a hard-copy release. Therefore, merely sending a fax to a reporter with a press release has become obsolete. Conventional wisdom, however, suggests that a fax copy of the press release should also be sent to the media at the same time it is being e-mailed. If there is an avenue for message delivery to the press, it should be used. Sometimes e-mail goes to a "spam" folder, and the only information a reporter might receive is a fax.

Circumstances in which press releases should be sent include any event that is newsworthy that involves the candidate. From campaign rallies and functions to third party events in which a candidate receives an award, a press release is relevant. If a candidate is releasing a policy statement or taking an opponent to task on an issue, press releases are appropriate. Press releases are excellent for announcing a person's candidacy or filing petitions for office. Press releases can also be used to attack an opponent's weakness on an issue. If a candidate challenges an opponent to debates or responds to a charge, press releases are appropriate. Press releases communicate any information that the campaign wishes voters to have. A press release does not always get printed or reported, but that should not dissuade a campaign from sending releases out with relevant information.

Occasionally a reporter will not view a particular press release as newsworthy. That does not mean that the press release was not worthwhile. A campaign may send out a press release about a similar topic as an earlier press release that a reporter now finds newsworthy. It is possible that the reporter will combine both press releases for a single story, or the reporter uses a quote from the earlier press release in tandem with other information from the more recent release. A reporter may not write a story about every press release from a campaign, but that does not mean the reporter deletes the press releases. Each press release becomes another addition to a greater volume of communications from a campaign.

Press releases should always be brief. Just as news stories in the paper do not go on page after page, a press release should not either. Ideally, a press release is a single page that covers all of the information a campaign wishes to communicate, provides relevant quotes supporting the campaign's story, and supplies the contact information so that a reporter can make a follow-up contact when writing the story. Contact information should usually be that of the campaign manager, communications director, or press secretary so that reporters and their questions can be fully vetted and the candidate prepared before returning the call to the media. Press aides should only handle background information, but quotes should go to the candidate (it is the candidate who is running for office – not the press aide or campaign manager). It is helpful to the candidate to have the questions from a reporter ahead of time. Candidate preparedness also favors a reporter because a call back from the candidate will usually be shorter and on topic so that the reporter can write the story in a more timely manner and have less extraneous information to sift through in order to do so.

Some reporters may insist on speaking directly to a candidate and not wish to supply their questions before the candidate has a chance to call back. Reporters who act in such a manner should be approached with caution because they may not trust that they will get an honest answer if a candidate is prepared; they may want to catch a candidate in an unguarded moment, or they simply may not wish to talk to a press aide because of self-importance. It is important that a candidate becomes well practiced at staying on the topic about which the candidate wishes to speak. Prepared quotes are important, and they should roll off the candidate's tongue as though they are natural responses. A candidate should review the press release and have it nearby when speaking with a reporter.

Often an uncooperative reporter is the result of the campaign not developing the proper relationship at the beginning of the campaign. If the campaign did not take the proper time to introduce itself to the reporter, supply information to the reporter, and maintain communications with the reporter, then should anyone on the campaign be surprised when a reporter is more guarded? The campaign press contact, when making the first introduction to the reporter, should create the understanding that campaign staffers, including the press contact, should never be quoted if possible and that campaign quotes should be attributable to the candidate. Professional campaigns make every effort to keep the candidate in the news rather than allowing the campaign staff to be in the news.

Press releases are an important tool in a campaign, and some thought should be put into them before sending them out. All of the information contained in a release should be correct and everything documented. Hyperbole should be used with caution because a release that is too outrageous may be discarded. Spelling and grammar should be impeccable. Information in a release should also be relevant – a campaign does not want to get a reputation for sending out press releases for inconsequential matters.

Appendix D contains some sample press releases that provide relevant reasons for sending a press release as well as a style that can be effective.

Media Advisories

A media advisory is a type of press release. It is distributed in exactly the same way as a press release, but the amount of information contained in an advisory is limited. A media advisory is generally used as an alert that a newsworthy event is about to occur or that a campaign is going to hold a press conference. A media advisory contains the basic information that the media needs to know in order to be at the right spot at the right time in order to report the newsworthy event.

The format of a media advisory should be easily readable. A media advisory does not require professional journalism style or a narrative format. The ideal advisory has headings with a brief description under each heading. The headings are "Who", "What", "Where" and "When". Sometimes a campaign will add a short quote as a teaser for the event. The description under the "what" heading is the campaign's opportunity to grab the interest of the reporter or news desk assignment editor. Advisories should only contain enough information to convince the press that they should attend an event and where and when to attend.

If the advisory has done a good job of piquing interest in the press, the campaign may receive calls in advance of the event. The campaign can determine how much information it wishes to supply in advance, but allowing one outlet to scoop all of the others may make the event "old news" before it even happens. Some reporters may have demonstrated their willingness to print or air much of what the campaign supplies. It is a general rule to keep the outlets that are most receptive to campaign communications in the "front line" of information.

Media advisories are appropriate to announce press conferences in advance or to let the media know when and where the candidate will be, when the candidate files petitions for office, attends a rally for an issue, or is invited to be with a dignitary who may be visiting the area. Media advisories are also appropriate to inform the media that a candidate is available to comment on an issue thereby allowing access to the candidate for occasions that do not warrant a press conference. Media advisories are inappropriate for communicating complex subjects that a press release can.

Press Conferences

A press conference is an event in itself. A campaign holds a press conference because it wishes to generate a high level of awareness on an important topic for the campaign and to generate exposure of the candidate. Press conferences are driven by both message and image. A skilled campaign will marry the two seamlessly in the press conference. Attention to detail during press conferences is important.

A campaign will generally announce a press conference about 12 to 24 hours prior to the event. Sometimes something occurs that necessitates short notice for press conferences such as events or charges that require a quick response. Whatever the reason for the press conference, a campaign should e-mail an advisory to reporters and assignment editors when appropriate. If a press conference is a planned event that is not necessitated by factors the campaign cannot control, then the campaign should choose to hold it on a day and at a time that news crews will be available. Planning a press conference for days and times in which reporters are generally covering other stories, meetings, or events is a bad idea and a recipe for poor press attendance.

The location for the event should be accessible by the media. The proximity should be near the area where newspaper, radio, and television crews can quickly be present. Being near an interstate or area that is familiar to the press is ideal. Parking should be ample so that reporters do not need to struggle to find parking, pay for parking, or walk far from their vehicle to the conference. Making the press conference accessible does not guarantee success in recruiting participation, but it does help. Sometimes a reporter may be in transit from covering one story to another, and if the location and access is convenient, the reporter may decide to cover the conference.

Sometimes the location of a press conference itself is an illustration of the press conference. If a candidate is running against an incumbent and wishes to announce a jobs package while criticizing the incumbent for a recent loss of jobs, then the campaign may select a location outside a recently closed factory or business. If a candidate wants to talk about crime, holding a press conference outside the county jail might be appropriate. In instances such as these, the campaign should make provisions for any permits required in advance. A candidate does not want to arrive at a press conference about crime and end up getting a ticket or being arrested for failing to acquire proper permits.

Once the initial advisory has been distributed, the campaign should immediately call the members of the press to confirm receipt and to gauge interest. If interest is low, or the time turns out to be bad, then the campaign may need to make a quick adjustment and re-broadcast a new advisory with follow-up calls. If more than a few hours notice was given, the campaign should re-broadcast the media advisory a few hours prior to the press conference. The same assignment editor does not always sit at the newsroom desk every minute of every day. An editor who received a media advisory six hours ago might be a different editor than the one currently covering the newsroom. Therefore, making sure the right people have access to the information at the right time is important. After follow-up calls and re-broadcasts, a campaign should have a good idea as to who is covering the press conference.

The set-up of the press conference is as important as the message of the press conference. The staging of the candidate should be in an area that is camera friendly. If appropriate, campaign banners or signs should be clearly visible behind the candidate regardless of the angle that a camera shot is taken. A podium is generally a good idea so that notes and water can be within reach of the candidate, and a sign with the campaign logo can be placed on the front of the podium. Media microphones can also be placed on a podium. It can be impressive to see a candidate at a podium with multiple media microphones, but the candidate should be situated so that the microphones do not obscure a video or photo shot of the candidate.

If supporters or a group of people will be standing with the candidate, they should be situated so that they complement the candidate but do not distract from the scene. The candidate can be slightly raised above the others by just a few inches, or the supporters can be situated far enough behind the candidate that they are visible but not intrusive or overbearing.

Some campaigns will use visual aids. Any visual aids should be enlarged and placed on boards suitable to be displayed on an easel. Visual aids should help tell a story, but they should not be distracting.

The information on them should also be concealed prior to the beginning of the press conference. Visual aids can be anything from charts and graphs that illustrate a point to pictures or diagrams. Whatever aids are used, they should be relevant. If the candidate can communicate a message without visual aids, then they are not required.

The area of the press conference should be well lit. The candidate should wear colors that are friendly to television and contrast with the background. A slight amount of make-up or powder, even for male candidates, can be appropriate in order to remove blemishes or "shine" from the face. A campaign should reduce the chance that a viewer will be distracted from the message of a press conference because of a shiny spot on a nose or forehead or a dark spot on a cheek.

Refreshments can be served but are not necessary. Journalists do not wish to feel as though they are being coaxed into reporting a good story for a campaign, but at the same time it is important to have a certain level of comfort. Refreshments should be no more complicated than coffee and water and perhaps some cookies or pastries. If the campaign chooses to supply them, refreshments should not be in the same room as the press conference.

Press conferences should begin on time. If an outlet has not arrived within five minutes after the time the conference was scheduled to begin, then the press conference should still occur. If the tardy journalist finally arrives, he or she can catch up at the end or get an "exclusive" interview although the rest of the reporters already have the story. For media outlets that did not participate, the campaign should make every effort to supply them with the information from the press conference. It may be advisable to offer to have the candidate travel to the television station of the local affiliate that did not attend in order to speak with a reporter there and go on camera. Most news outlets do not like to be "scooped" by competitors, so they may make an effort to reciprocate in accommodating the campaign.

A campaign should also record all of its own events. From fundraisers in which a host makes comments to a press conference, the campaign should have a video library of all events. If one news outlet was unable to attend a press conference, then the campaign may be able to supply footage of its own and still get media play from the press conference.

When the media arrives at a press conference, reporters should be greeted and escorted to the appropriate area. Reporters should also receive a press packet with a copy of a press release about the press conference. The press release is the campaign's version of what is said at a press conference and will be a point of reference for the reporter when writing the story. If applicable, visual aids should be included in the press packet. In addition, all contents of the press packet should be e-mailed to the media after the event. A campaign should make it as easy as possible for a reporter to tell a story it wants.

Press conferences are ideally short. Reporters have a lot of area to cover and a finite amount of time. The actual statement portion of a press conference should be no more than 5 to 10 minutes. After the statement portion is over, a question-and-answer session is probably appropriate. If a candidate takes questions, then the campaign team should have prepared well in advance by playing the role of reporters to the candidate and asking the most likely questions. This role play will allow for a more prepared and relaxed candidate.

Once a press conference is completed and the proper follow-up has taken place, the campaign should arrange to have any broadcast stories on television or radio recorded. Footage and still shots from a successful press conference can be a compelling image on television, the Internet, or in direct mail.

7.8   Newspapers

Although more Americans receive more news from the Internet than newspapers, newspapers still play an important role in campaigns. Newspapers provide information that can be cited on campaign communications. Newspapers provide strong visuals especially when a campaign uses a headline that appeared in print. Newspapers are still comprised of professional reporters, and they cover important events that the campaign can link from its web site or social media account.

As long as newspapers exist, they will be relevant to politics and campaigns. Newspapers survive on selling ads, and advertisers depend on high circulation. Many newspapers now rely heavily on their online editions and selling advertising for their web sites.

Placing a print ad in newspapers may be less effective than it has been in the past. Utilizing online advertising on the newspaper's web site may make more sense to a campaign. Smart newspapers will sell print ads with online ads as part of a package.

When a campaign is trying to decide where to spend its limited budget on advertising, it should consider where the people in the district are getting their information. Are the voters in the district visiting the newspaper web site for information? Are voters still reading the newspaper? Is the newspaper a community newspaper or a large newspaper with regional distribution? Answering these questions can help guide a campaign to how much newspaper advertising it will use and what form the advertising will take.

If a weekly newspaper is widely distributed to an entire community, and that community reads the newspaper for its local content, then a print ad may be worthwhile. Letters to the editor are definitely valuable. A campaign should budget for the issue or issues of the newspaper immediately prior to Election Day if it runs ads. If the campaign chooses to run online ads with the newspaper, the budget should include the week before the campaign up to one month before Election Day.

7.9   When the Campaign's Message Is the News

A campaign that is able to create particularly compelling literature or ads may enjoy the unique experience of those ads becoming the subject of the news. For instance, a 2009 race for mayor of a large city pitted an entrenched incumbent against an aggressive and outgoing challenger. The incumbent mayor was traveling to cities throughout the world and being away from the city. The challenger created a direct mail piece that had a map of the world as the background with pictures of some of the cities the mayor had traveled with red lines leading all over the place. The question on the literature read something to the effect of "Where In the World Is the Mayor?"

The direct mail piece was well footnoted, compelling and started a city-wide buzz about why the mayor was traveling all over the world while the city was facing enormous budget deficits. The local media wrote a story on the campaign literature and published copies of the literature. Because the literature was so compelling and had generated a significant amount of conversation throughout the city, the message became the news. Campaigns are fortunate to receive such attention and have that attention be positive.

An example of how the campaign's television spot becoming the news was undesirable occurred in the 2011 elections. Earlier in this chapter, the example of a statewide issue was used in which an issue campaign used an elderly woman to make a point about the issue. The opposing campaign took the same image of the woman and attempted to make its point using the words of the old woman. The news stories that ensued did not portray the opposing campaign favorably, and many voters became incensed at the exploitation of the elderly woman. The campaign, instead of withdrawing the ads, stood its ground and attempted to justify its position, but it had already lost any control it had of the message. Voters do not want to see campaigns taking advantage of the elderly.

From direct mail and television to radio and the Internet, there are many venues for campaigns to broadcast their messages. The fundamental principles remain the same. Keep each communication simple. Use compelling images and language. Backup all assertions with citations and footnotes. Use each medium according to the budget. Finally, use repetition and consistency in appearance and message.

Chapter 8
Grassroots and Internet Campaigning

Before television ads, direct mail, or telephones, grassroots campaigning existed. The term "grassroots" refers to campaigning on a personal basis in which the campaign has direct contact with voters. The grassroots campaign is the "ground war" of the campaign whereas direct mail, Internet, phones and broadcast media constitute the "air war." The Internet is unique in that it is important in the air war as well as the ground war. Because of its interactivity, the Internet is as much of the ground war as it is the air war. As discussed throughout *The Political Campaign Desk Reference*, campaigns use the four TIMP resources – time, information, money and people. The air war uses money and information while the grassroots ground war requires heavy amounts of time and people to make it effective. Chapter 8 will discuss how to utilize these resources effectively.

8.1 Campaigning – As Much About Gathering Information As Delivery

During the entire course of a political race, a campaign team should constantly be gathering information about voters in its target universe. Grassroots campaigning allows individuals on a campaign to work one-on-one with voters. As the campaign team engages the voters, volunteers should be gathering as much information as possible.

Whether it is through door-to-door operations, the Internet, coffees, rallies, forums, or community events, the campaign has constant opportunities to gather information about specific voters and what those voters feel is important. A campaign should always have materials that allow the person on the street to become involved. From using volunteer cards to short survey cards, campaigns can gather important information about voters. Internet surveys can also be effective.

Campaigns are only limited by their resources as to how much information they want to gather.

Information gathering is so important because it will tell the campaign the specific voters that need to be reached and what issues will make them receptive. Information also lets the campaign know exactly where to avoid spending resources. As the campaign progresses, a campaign team will be able to use this information to more finely tune its message as well as its targeting so that resources are spent wisely.

8.2   Door-to-Door

There are few things that a candidate can do in a campaign that are as effective as door-to-door campaigning. Door-to-door campaigning allows the candidate, or a well-trained surrogate, to meet voters one-on-one and appeal directly for their votes. Few candidates have enough personal time to knock on every voting household in a district, so the operation requires targeting in order for the candidate to canvass the most important precincts to winning the campaign.

The candidate should have certain tools when knocking on doors in a precinct. These tools include a walking list of voter addresses, absentee or mail ballot request forms, voter registration forms, campaign handbill, pen, nametag, map, and a bottle of water. With these tools, a candidate will be able to effectively win votes in many of the houses in which contact is made.

The walking list for a precinct should be sorted by street name, then by house number and then by last name. This allows a candidate to travel the precinct and reference the current street. By sorting by house number, the candidate can skip houses in which no relevant voters live. For instance 101 Union Street may have three voters but no one registered as a Democrat. If the candidate is running in a Democratic primary race, then 101 Union Street is an address that should be skipped. Furthermore, a candidate can also see how many people are registered at a single address, their names and how they vote. A campaign team should customize a walking list so that the candidate has room to mark certain notes: whether a voter will allow a yard sign, will vote for the candidate, or other germane remarks.

Absentee or mail ballot request forms are necessary for the people that the candidate identifies as supporters. Anyone who is identified as a supporter should be encouraged to vote early by mail if allowed. A campaign encourages early mail voting to ensure that every possible supporter in fact votes for the candidate. Many races in American history have been decided by a handful of votes or even a single vote. Sometimes this occurs because someone who meant to vote did not either because of forgetfulness, emergency, very recent death, vacation, or any other reason that prevented a voter from going to a polling location on Election Day. A close race cannot afford to allow votes to slip by. Request forms should not be distributed to voters whose support cannot be gauged.

Voter registration forms are important for households with newly eligible voters. If a household has two registered Republicans, and their child recently came of voting age, and the candidate is a Republican, then it may be wise to gauge the politics of the child and register the child to vote. Newly registered voters may also be eligible to fill out absentee request forms. A candidate should make it as easy as possible for supporters to vote especially if those supporters are newly registered.

Campaign handbills are important for door-to-door because they provide the essential information about a candidate that a voter needs. Handbills remind voters that a candidate visited their home, and they serve as a reference for voters. Similar to direct mail, a handbill should be visually appealing and image-driven. An effective handbill communicates the message of the campaign, has compelling pictures of the candidate, and contains some background information as well as a web site address along with any social media sites the candidate uses. The handbill can be something a candidate can use to focus the attention of the voter when canvassing, and the candidate can reference information directly from the handbill.

A pen is necessary for taking notes for the campaign team to transcribe into the database. A nametag is important so that the voter knows who they are about to talk to when peering at the stranger in front of their door through their peephole or curtains. A nametag helps to disarm a reticent voter who might otherwise be unsure about opening the door to a complete stranger. The voter also does not know that the candidate has information about each voter on a walking list. A bottle of water is for the candidate to stay refreshed while walking neighborhoods.

A disagreeable candidate can do more harm than good. For instance, a candidate once went door-to-door in select precincts. One of his opponents was able to track some of the precincts that candidate had gone door-to-door in through phone calls from friends who received a visit. These friends remarked about how disagreeable the candidate had been. After Election Day, the opponent who received information about his disagreeable adversary checked the precinct-by-precinct results. The opponent saw that he received more than 70% of the vote in the precincts where he took the time to walk. On the other hand, the disagreeable candidate received less than 40% of the vote in the precincts where he went door-to-door. The disagreeable candidate had actually done more harm than good to himself.

In making the initial introduction to a voter at their home, the candidate should begin by explaining the reason he or she is running for the office. By the end of the 10-15 second introduction, the voter should have a copy of the handbill in hand. The candidate can follow up with a quick listing of their top two or three strengths and then proceed to the "listening" part of the conversation. A candidate should take notes if a voter is particularly passionate about an issue especially if the issue is one that the candidate can affect once in office. At the end of the conversation, the candidate should ask if they can count on the support of the voter. If the answer is "yes", a note should be taken on the walking list. All "yes" responses should be encouraged to vote early by mail.

Follow up all "yes" or "maybe" responses with a request for a yard sign. Indicate the voter's wish for a yard sign on the walking list. Since the precincts walked by the candidate are the most important targeted precincts, the presence of yard signs will have a greater effect than in other precincts. Ideally, the time spent at each home will be 2-3 minutes. Some voters require more time while others will require less.

Not everyone will be home, and it is good for neighbors to see the yard sign of the candidate in their neighborhood. In the event a voter is not home or does not come to the door, the candidate should have a number of handbills that have a pre-written "Sorry I missed you" note on them. The handbill should be left in an easy-to-find, as well as easy-to-access location so the voter will see it when they return. A candidate should not place a piece of literature somewhere on the door or mailbox that is visible from the street. If the homeowner is on vacation for the next week, a piece of literature might be all a burglar needs to turn a voter into a victim. That type of news will not be good for the campaign.

Some door-to-door campaigns add extra steps to increase effectiveness. About one week prior to walking a precinct, the targeted households receive a post card from the campaign that announces that the candidate will be visiting voters in the neighborhood. These post cards assist in name identification for the candidate but also commit the candidate to going door-to-door there. The pre-walk postcards also help to break the ice with voters in the precinct because they are expecting to see the candidate. Some candidates, to save on costs, may opt for a pre-walk recorded phone message. Phone messages are less effective because not everyone that will be visited has a phone number listed.

Some campaigns will follow up with post-walk cards or phone calls from the campaign as well. The message on the card or call is as simple as a "thank you" and a repeat of the top two or three points the candidate went over during the visit. The pre-walk and post-walk effort also impacts the people that were not home.

The direct, personal contact and appeal for votes made by the candidate in door-to-door operations is one of the most effective appeals in the campaign and is more likely than any other aspect of the campaign to have a high ratio of voters reached to votes gained. A poor door-to-door operation, unprepared candidate, bad message, or unappealing candidate can have a negative effect in door-to-door operations. Candidates should always make an effort to be upbeat, look professional, be prepared and confident in order to "close the deal" when talking to voters.

8.3 Coffees

Campaign coffees are events that the campaign team sets up with volunteers and supporters. Little to no involvement of the candidate is needed in planning and preparing a coffee except to appear when expected at the coffee. Coffees are effective for candidates to gain exposure in neighborhoods in the home of someone who lives in a targeted area. Coffees are host-driven events but require coordination with the campaign.

The traditional coffee event is a gathering of homemakers in a neighborhood on a morning when the candidate can make the best use of time. The host will work with the campaign team to set date and time. The host invites the attendees, and everyone arrives 20-30 minutes before the candidate arrives. The host provides coffee, tea, and whatever other refreshments are appropriate. When the candidate arrives, the host introduces the candidate. The candidate will speak and answer questions for about 20-30 minutes before leaving for the next event.

Once the candidate leaves the event, the host should have sign-up cards for the campaign and envelopes for donations. These cards and envelopes should be distributed to the attendees and collected by the host before everyone leaves. The campaign should follow up with the host quickly in order to obtain any information or donations and to update the campaign database.

Coffees have evolved over time to no longer necessarily be simply coffees. Coffees also are not necessarily women-only events and not required to be mid-morning events. In fact, the only part of the coffee model that necessarily remains the same is that it is host-driven. Coffees can also become neighborhood gatherings, a barbeque, or a reception.

Some candidates will find that certain areas prefer a family oriented event or a backyard gathering to a coffee. The point to the coffee is that it is a good way for the candidate to spend just a little time to meet multiple people and for the campaign to gather information and possibly money. As long as the elements of the event are incorporated (being host-driven takes little of the candidate's time, and helps gather information and supporters), then the format of the "coffee" is up to the host and the campaign. The campaign should be cautious of becoming involved with a large-scale event that requires time and effort to help the host to plan. If the campaign has to spend inordinate amounts of time, money, and people resources into an event, then the purpose of the host-driven event is lost.

A campaign should provide potential coffee hosts with a sheet detailing the purpose of the coffee as well as the expectations of the host. Sometimes a host will invite their neighborhood friends but will also open their home to a wider array of neighbors. In these instances, the campaign may opt to send a post card to all registered voters in the precinct in order to generate more interest and attendance. This type of coffee may make the candidate's job easier because his time can be spent going door-to-door in precincts where there is no coffee scheduled.

8.4 Rallies

Rallies serve many purposes. They generate energy and help build momentum on a campaign. Rallies allow people who do not know much about a candidate to learn a little bit more and meet supporters. Rallies can also be events in which materials and tasks are assigned to campaign volunteers. Rallies can be instructional in nature. They can be open to the public, or they can be by invitation only. The overall purpose of a rally is to generate "buzz" and interest in a candidate and campaign.

A rally is not a fundraising event, so a campaign has to understand what it wishes to accomplish from a rally before choosing a date, time and venue. Time, money and people resources are going to be utilized in executing a rally. Therefore, the campaign should utilize the rally to accomplish as much as possible in a short amount of time spending as little as possible to do it.

Timing of a rally is important as well. With so much time, money and people being expended for a rally, it would be unwise to hold one more than a week or two before Election Day unless the purpose of the rally is to kick off the campaign. The rally must also be held at a time that is convenient for people to attend and at a venue that is easy to access and has plenty of parking. The campaign must choose wisely in order to make it as easy as possible for people to attend the rally.

Unless a race is a presidential campaign or a hotly contested state-wide or congressional contest, a campaign will probably have a small number of rallies and not weekly or regular rallies. Smaller races have to plan what must be accomplished during the event. A rally will not work without one thing: people, and a lot of them. A rally is not a rally without people, and recruiting people to attend a rally is the toughest challenge of a campaign. The best way to recruit people to a rally is to give them a reason to be there.

A campaign may start by creating a purpose for the rally. If the campaign styles the rally as an event that volunteers will receive hand-bills, t-shirts, signs, and poll assignments for poll working on Election Day, then volunteers will be more likely to show. Volunteers alone generally do not make a rally. A campaign will also want to get interested people to attend the rally. By welcoming families and having snacks and drinks available, the campaign may be able to drive turnout to those who may otherwise stay away for lack of child care. The voting households in the precincts surrounding the venue should also receive post card invitations about two weeks out followed up by a phone call placed by a volunteer within a week of the event. All members of the campaign committee should attend.

Another way to create a draw for the event is to invite other elected officeholders or community leaders as "headliners" or guest speakers. Top billing always goes to the candidate, but the addition of popular people to the event makes it more enticing for voters. In addition, other elected officeholders have their own campaign teams and volunteers. If those elected officials are participating in the event, then their organizations should also be invited thereby increasing attendance and creating a bigger event with more momentum and energy.

If a campaign knows that attendance will be good, the media can be invited to attend. Having media attend a rally is a good opportunity for reporters to gain an impression that the campaign is strong and energized. A story that reflects the energy in the crowd is a good thing if the rally is executed properly. If the media is invited to attend, a special zone near the area where people will be speaking should be secured just for media so that they are able to hear, take pictures, shoot footage, and be in the middle of the crowd and its energy.

Voters who decide to attend a rally do not want to show up to an empty hall and be the only people there. If an event looks like a bomb, some people may just pass it up. In order to make the event look as though it is someplace people want to be, the campaign should have the volunteers and campaign committee arrive about 30 to 60 minutes early to cover any required business. People who are early arrivals will already see a crowd and become part of the rally near the beginning.

The rally area should be roomy with very few seats. Standing during a rally helps to promote energy. Campaign signs should be all over the area. Volunteers should have rally signs to hold. The area directly behind the speakers should have campaign banners and signs hung so that they appear in any camera shot.

As people arrive, they should be greeted by a campaign volunteer. If people not previously affiliated with the campaign arrive, they should be given campaign literature, stickers and a card to fill out that captures their contact information as well as social media information. The card should also ask for yard sign locations, volunteers for poll workers, and other tasks for which the campaign needs volunteers. After the event, all of the new information gathered by the campaign should be immediately updated in the database.

Press arriving at the rally should be greeted and escorted to the media area. Reporters will no doubt wish to mingle among the crowd in order to gain information for any story. Reporters should be provided with a program of events that lets them know when the speaking begins and who is going to be speaking. The press thrives on information, so it is important for campaigns to provide the information it wishes reported.

The program of a rally is relatively simple. A rally begins with a period of mingling in which people arrive, fill out cards and get refreshments. A handful of campaign staff will want to work the crowd and engage people who may seem withdrawn, overwhelmed or not participatory. At some point that seems appropriate, when most people have arrived, a short program begins. The program is meant to energize the crowd, so it should be brief and motivational. The master of ceremonies can be a local celebrity, officeholder, or someone selected to get everything started. Whatever speakers are invited to participate should build up to the final speaker, the candidate. Each speaker should only have 2-3 minutes to speak, and there should not be more than 3-5 speakers prior to the candidate. The candidate can speak a little longer than the rest of the crowd.

Volunteers should be directed to respond appropriately to the candidate's comments. If a candidate makes a big point, the volunteers should make sure that the applause is appropriate. If the crowd fails to react properly, the energy from the rally will wane, and the candidate will not appear as effective.

It is a good idea for a campaign to take pictures of the event and possibly record it for Internet distribution if appropriate. The campaign manager or press secretary should also make sure the needs of the press are met. When the event is over, all campaign materials that can be salvaged should be. Reviews of the event should be posted on the web site and social media, and a press release should be distributed with the campaign's review of the event.

8.5   Signs

Some candidates feel as though they have to have more signs than their opponent, or they will lose a race. The attitude that a campaign must have more signs than anyone else in order to "win" a "sign war" is the wrong way to look at a sign campaign. It is also unacceptable for a candidate to feel as though a sign campaign is all he or she needs to do for the race. Signs are merely one tactic in a complete campaign strategy.

A campaign should step back from the traditional method of looking at the sign campaign. Placing hundreds of small signs along a road where a candidate has no permission to place them is not only illegal, but this tactic makes the campaign look bad. Residents do not want to see their landscape littered by unauthorized signs.

Campaigns sometimes also make the mistake of placing most of their money in hundreds or thousands of small yard signs that can only be seen by drivers and passengers just as they are passing. Campaigns should instead approach the sign campaign from a different perspective.

Signs come in all sizes from the small signs that go in the yards of homes to the large signs that can be placed along major thoroughfares. The idea is to raise name identification and awareness rather than flood an area with senseless signs that cannot be seen or read.

In order to begin a sign campaign, a campaign team should study the area of the race. A list of high priority, heavily trafficked roads should be compiled. These roads will be the thoroughfares where the campaign's largest signs will be placed. Then the campaign should look at the precincts that are the most important in terms of targeting. Precincts with high voter participation are important to target as well as precincts in which a candidate may be weaker than others in terms of support. Once the campaign knows where its priority areas are, then it can choose what type of signs it needs and how many.

The highly trafficked areas should have large, corrugated plastic road signs that range in size from 3'x5' to 4'x8'. Signs should be placed as close to the road as the local laws allow and erected as early as local laws allow. It is the major routes that penetration will be greatest. A large sign will cost a campaign between $20 and $50 each including the posts and ties required to root them to the ground. No small yard signs should be placed along major routes because they will be ineffective. Small signs can only be seen from a short distance, and the words on them can only be read from an even shorter distance. Therefore, small signs along routes with fast moving traffic are a waste of resources and should be relocated to more appropriate venues.

Small signs should be placed in the targeted neighborhoods. This is not to say that non-targeted neighborhoods should be skipped, but priority should be placed on the areas where a candidate could use a boost. The objective of small signs is slightly different from that of large signs. Whereas large signs are used to raise candidate awareness, small signs in a neighborhood make more of a statement. They should look exactly like the large signs. The difference is that people driving into their own neighborhood will see the signs of the candidate and understand that the neighbors feel like this candidate is a good choice for them. It helps to inspire confidence in a candidate and build momentum and energy for a campaign, while also doing its part to raise awareness.

Campaigns should rarely invest in billboards. Billboards are very expensive and amount to nothing more than a large sign location. A well placed large sign that costs the campaign $25 can accomplish nearly the same job as a $500 to $5,000 billboard. Campaigns should carefully consider spending resources on billboards when a large sign can do the same job. Sometimes a campaign will secure a billboard location so that an opponent does not have a chance to rent it. There are many outdoor advertising vendors who own billboard locations throughout the country for campaigns that wish to invest in these large signs.

The easiest way to procure a sign location is to call or visit the homes of people along the major thoroughfares and target precincts. Volunteers can introduce themselves, deliver a 15-20 second advocacy message supporting the candidate, explain that the campaign is requesting yard sign locations, and respectfully request permission to place a yard sign that will be removed by the campaign after the election. Most people will say "no", but some will approve the sign. Once the phone or home visit operation to procure sign locations is complete, the campaign should have a healthy database of sign locations. The campaign now knows how many signs it will need and how many it should order for the locations. In order to arrive at a good number for ordering, the campaign should order 10% more large signs than it has locations in order to replace lost and damaged signs and to fill in areas that need them. In addition, a campaign should place a large sign at the highest priority polling locations if permitted.

As discussed in Chapter 6, the sign logo should be easily readable from a distance. The sign should not have distracting shapes or too many words. A proper sign does not mix dark colored words on a dark colored background. A good campaign sign emphasizes the candidate's last name above all else and then details the office being sought. Other information for signs is extraneous and should generally be avoided. Mixing multiple fonts on signs can also be distracting. As with many items in *The Political Campaign Desk Reference*, keep it simple.

It is important for a campaign to follow-through on a sign campaign even after the election. Signs should be removed as quickly as possible. Win or lose, there will always be another campaign, and a candidate does not want to lose supporters for failure to retrieve a campaign asset.

8.6 Increasing Importance Of the Internet

The Internet is becoming the primary method by which people obtain their news and information. As the ways in which people get their information change, campaigns must be able to change with them. If voters in a Congressional district receive their information on their tablet computers or their smart phones, and a campaign is spending the majority of its resources on newspapers, radio and other forms of communication, then the campaign is missing large portions of voters when it comes to message delivery.

Although the fundamentals of strategy and planning remain the same, and the four primary resources are unchanged, the methods by which campaigns communicate do change. In recent years, many social media sites have gained a critical mass of users that includes active voters. Not only should campaigns seize the opportunity to engage in social media, there are also opportunities to advertise on these sites.

The Internet can be used in many ways. From the campaign web site and email communications the campaign creates, to social media, blogs, Internet ads, and search engine results, the Internet has become important to campaigns at all levels. Many campaigns have begun hiring consultants who do nothing but monitor and create Internet material for the campaign. The following sections will discuss some of the ways in which campaigns may utilize the Internet. The tactics described in *The Political Campaign Desk Reference* should not be considered complete. The Internet changes quickly, and a campaign must plan for innovations and changes, and that means campaigns should be creative and innovative. The campaign plan should account for an Internet component. Be creative, but always remember to keep campaign communications simple no matter what method of communication is used.

Most campaigns have web sites. Sometimes a campaign will decide to be creative and create a "parody" web site or blog site of an opponent, also referred to as a microsite. If a campaign chooses this path, it should consider whether its actions will be viewed as ethical. The campaign should also consider whether visitors to the parody web site will understand its intent and that it is not meant to steal the identity of the opponent. A campaign should also consider whether the parody site will seem mean spirited to voters. Many campaigns refrain from such tactics because using parody in such a way takes skill in order to carry it off effectively without appearing juvenile. Campaigns should consider the image of the candidate that it has spent resources building before engaging in activities that could damage that image.

8.7   E-mail Campaign

If a campaign has a web site, and it should, then it has the ability to acquire supporter and voter information and e-mail them. The challenge to having an effective e-mail operation in a campaign is to send out just the right number of e-mails and to make the e-mails relevant, interesting and short. As the campaign's database grows, so should the people that the campaign e-mails. Campaign staff should make it a habit to update the campaign database with e-mail information whenever someone comes in contact with the campaign.

Some officeholders and candidates are about as interesting to listen to as watching grass grow. Those politicians somehow become just as unexciting and droll in their e-mails. When a campaign sends out an e-mail, it should be relevant and interesting. The e-mail can link to an article or articles in the paper, but it should not reprint an entire article. A campaign e-mail is the campaign's opportunity to tell supporters what an article said. Once the campaign links the article, then it is up to the supporter to read it if so desired. The campaign should not care if the recipient actually reads the article as long as the important information of what the article said is communicated. Many campaigns can eliminate scrolling down through an e-mail for its supporters by simply supplying a brief synopsis and links. In an on-demand society, this style is a plus.

E-mails, like direct mail and television, should be visually appealing. The campaign should use compelling graphics and pictures in such a way that they enhance the interest in the e-mail without distracting from the e-mail. Each e-mail should also incorporate the campaign logo. The text should be large enough to read without squinting.

Some campaigns feel like they need to e-mail supporters every day. Campaigns that frequently e-mail supporters with inconsequential information will find nearly all of its e-mail ending up in spam folders or deleted without ever being opened. A campaign that chooses to send e-mails only when it has a purpose is a campaign that understands and respects the time of its supporters.

Valid reasons for e-mailing supporters include announcing a new television spot with a link to it, reporting a campaign's press conference immediately after the conference, thereby granting exclusive access to the campaign before news outlets have an ability to report it, or reminding people of upcoming events or rallies. Some emails can be fundraising challenges, but sending too many of these out also has the same effect of killing an e-mail campaign. Every e-mail should have a prominent link that allows supporters to contribute as well as a link that allows the supporter to apply for a mail ballot. An opt-out link might also be required by local or state laws. An opt-out also is a good idea because a campaign does not want to e-mail people that do not wish to have the e-mails.

Because of the speed at which information can be distributed through e-mail, it is a powerful tool, and a campaign will want to control information distributed over the Internet. E-mail also has the potential to become "viral" meaning the people who receive the initial e-mail can forward it to other people and so on. If a campaign sends an e-mail out at noon on Monday to 1,000 supporters, it could possibly spread to an exponential number of people by noon on Tuesday. Not every e-mail is viral-worthy. If a campaign is selective about how it distributes e-mail and makes an effort to avoid inundating supporters with information overload, then the few e-mails a campaign sends will be more effective than the daily e-mails others might send.

8.8   Social Media

As more people use the Internet at home, at work and on their phones, social media has exploded. There are many social media sites from professional networking sites to more mainstream sites. LinkedIn is a professional networking site that many campaigns and candidates will use. Facebook tends to attract more mainstream users and has wide appeal. Another social networking site that campaigns may use is Twitter that allows campaigns to blog updates in 140 characters or less. Google now has its own social network. By the time a reader reads this edition of *The Political Campaign Desk Reference*, various social media outlets may enter the Internet while others may make their exit due to irrelevance or lack of users.

Social media is an inexpensive method to gain an Internet presence on a campaign. Social media should not replace a campaign web site, but it should be used in conjunction with a web site. Social media allows a campaign web site to link to the site and vice versa. If a campaign posts a press release or new information on its web site, then the social media sites can update and link to the new web content.

Social media sites also allow the use of tags that will make certain posts stand out to specific people or people who subscribe or follow a certain topic or group. Knowing how to navigate through social media and use it effectively takes time, and campaigns should consider having a member of the campaign staff that will monitor and update the campaign's social media presence.

Social media is dynamic and interactive. It allows for a campaign to comment on posts from other sources. This also means that others can comment on posts by the campaign. A campaign should monitor social media activity so it knows what others are saying. Sometimes an opposing campaign will use social media to exploit a weakness of the candidate that the mainstream press has not exposed. Sometimes the Internet and social media becomes a venue for spreading misinformation. A campaign should stay apprised of the information that is spread through the Internet and social media in order to respond if necessary.

By having a presence on various social media web sites, and building a base of followers, a campaign can help spread its message while also protecting itself from imposter sites. Parody is a form of speech that the United States Supreme Court has ruled in favor of protecting in the past. A campaign should always act ethically and never cross the line of making visitors to a page wonder if they are looking at the actual candidate's page on social media or an imposter site. A social media site may also have policies against the practice of using another's identity without permission.

Social media sites also allow the campaign to harvest e-mail addresses, phone numbers, addresses and other information from supporters. This information should be added to the campaign database. In addition, the campaign can monitor social media to see if a shift occurs in what concerns voters most. If people are posting about jobs and the economy at the beginning of a race and shift to illegal immigration or another issue by the end of the race, then a campaign team may want to adjust its strategy or gather more information to verify that a shift in attitudes has occurred.

The same principles apply for social media as for all other methods of campaign communication. Keep the communications simple. Use compelling graphics whenever able. Stick to the campaign message. Act ethically. Keep the information fresh.

8.9   Blogs

As information technology evolves, so do the many ways that people talk about politics. In any given area, there may be dozens of political blogs, or web logs, run by individuals or organizations that comment on local officeholders, candidates and government.

Although blogs are not widely read by the general public at large, even if a blog is one of the more nationally known blogs, the people who do read the blogs can be influential. Many examples exist in which news stories began in the "blogosphere" because information that is not yet suitable for print, or unsubstantiated information, can circulate on the Web. As time progresses, blogs develop their own sources.

Television and newspaper reporters, always on the lookout for a story, sift through the blogs. Blogs are a good place for tips or to understand how people might feel about a subject. A campaign may want to have volunteers scouring the blogs and to make favorable comments about a candidate in posts. Blogs can be used to see how less-than-flattering information about an opponent will resonate. Very few rules govern the content of the Internet although information posted should still be true and valid if posted by someone from the campaign.

Too much time spent on blogs is not wise. A small handful of volunteers can skim them daily and make appropriate comments. Remember the four resources of a campaign. Is it wise to spend too much of them on blogging? If a campaign chooses to engage in using a blog, it should consider carefully what it wishes to gain. What does a blog offer that social media, the web page and e-mail updates do not? How often does the campaign need to update the blog to keep it "fresh?" Do enough voters visit blogs to make it worthwhile? By creating a greater volume of words from the campaign, is there greater exposure for attacks?

Benefits of a blog include the ability for the blog to link to the web site, link to the official social media sites and to become part of the overall apparatus of the campaign. A campaign that uses blogs also has protected itself against parody sites since the "official" blog will be widely known. Other blogs may reference the campaign's blog if the information is relevant and fresh.

8.10 Internet Ads

Most Internet sites allow for promotional opportunities. These ads can be purchased on sites for various news media. Ads can also be purchased from search engines to appear when certain terms are searched.

Promotional space can be purchased on various social media or web sites. Wherever there is an outlet that voters view on the Internet, there may be an opportunity for an ad from the campaign.

Most news sites are able to provide campaigns with demographic information about the users on its site. The news outlet may be able to help the campaign target its ads to show only when users from specific zip codes view pages, users of a certain age, sex, or other demographic.

Some social media sites also allow for ads to be posted on their site. Whenever possible, the campaign should target to users within the district and to the targeted demographics that any polls may have indicated. Campaigns may be able to target to users who have specific key words in their user profiles.

The 2008 campaign for president is an example of how a campaign can be innovative in its use of Internet Ads. Some campaigns for President had ads in creative places on the Internet and even video games. Because of the ever changing nature of the Internet and advertising, campaigns would be wise to remain educated about emerging technologies and channels of communication. Internet ads also are limited in space, so it is important for campaigns to use the most compelling images and language possible while still keeping the message simple.

8.11   Internet Search Engines – Own the Message

A candidate recently became upset when he conducted a search for his own campaign web site and the Internet search engine did not provide a result for his campaign's web site. Instead, he found that one of his detractors, possibly someone who worked for his opponent or was a friend of his opponent, paid for the search engine to find sites for remedial education instead of results for the candidate. The candidate was right to be upset, but he should be upset with his own campaign team instead of his opponent.

It is the campaign's responsibility to make certain that its web site, and associated blogs, social media, and positive news stories, appear in search engine results high on the list of relevance. Since many voters use the Internet as their primary source of information, being on top of Internet searches is important for an effective campaign.

The best way that a campaign can make certain that its web site appears appropriately high in Internet searches is to contain relevant information. This means that tags inside the coding of the web site should be appropriate and relevant. The text content of the site should also contain the candidate's name, information and positive information. If a campaign attempts to increase its relevance by inserting tags or content that has no relevance to the race, the candidate, the opponent, the jurisdiction of the race, or other methods, then search engines may opt to drop a site from searches due to irrelevant content. A search engine is only as successful as the results it returns to its users. If a web site attempts to undermine or outsmart a search engine's ability to produce relevant results, then it should drop the site's relevance or prevent it from appearing on searches.

Another way for a campaign to enhance its presence when a search is conducted on a search engine is to pay to appear when key words are entered. Paying a premium can help put a candidate's page at the top of a search before the unpaid results are shown. By doing this, a campaign can also enhance its own relevance in Internet searches as more people click on the link.

Relevant links within a web site, as well as links from third parties, help enhance the relevance of a campaigns site. A campaign should link to relevant sites and news stories from its site. The campaign should also link to its entire social media force from the campaign site and any blogs that are relevant and friendly. A reciprocal link should be placed on each of the campaign's social media pages to the campaign's web site as well as the campaign's donation site. The campaign should also link from social media to positive news stories about the candidate. These reciprocal and relevant links help the search engines determine when a page should appear in search results.

The earlier a campaign can launch its web site and begin building relevant content and linking to appropriate sites, the sooner in the race that the campaign web site will show up in searches.

8.12   Smart Phones and Smarter Voters

As telecommunications become more advanced, the options on phones also become more advanced. Many voters are now carrying around Smart Phones that allow them to access their e-mail, social media, web sites, texting, as well as a host of applications. Phones have cameras that take still shots as well as video. In addition to all of these functions, voters can also use their phones to send and receive phone calls. The possibilities for campaigns are becoming limitless when it comes to using Smart Phones.

As more voters began using e-mail, campaigns wanted to harvest e-mail addresses for their databases. Telephone numbers were still important, but e-mail became the new grail for campaigns. E-mailing is cheap, nearly everyone has it, and nearly everyone can read it. Now that a critical mass of voters is carrying around phones, campaigns want those mobile phone numbers. One way to harvest mobile phone information is to have voters give the campaign their numbers. By persuading potential supporters to text a message to the campaign, voters with phones willingly supply their numbers. Sometimes the campaign may give away campaign buttons, t-shirts or yard signs for a short text. In return, the campaign now has a means by which it can contact its supporters through text message or phone. If additional information is supplied, then the campaign has a more complete database.

Smart phones also help with keeping candidates accountable. If a candidate uses incorrect statistics in a speech or makes a wild claim, voters can get on the Internet and check the facts in seconds without leaving their seats. If a candidate makes a false claim in a speech, it is possible that dozens of voters are taping the speech for posterity. Smart phones make for smarter voters. Although a campaign should always act ethically, this new method of immediate accountability is an incentive for campaigns to double-check their facts and to footnote all claims.

Voters also have a growing arsenal of devices that they use in their daily lives that will help them make decisions. Tablet computers have also become popular. Because information is literally at voters' fingertips, campaigns have a responsibility to stay current with technological changes. It is important to have a relevant web site that appears first in searches. It is important to engage in social media. Use of Internet ads is important, and upcoming elections will take advantage of placing ads in smart phone "apps" or even creating their own applications.

8.13   Community Events

As summer approaches, many communities will have picnics or festivals. Churches have carnivals and fundraisers. In the fall, some areas will have harvest festivals or an Oktoberfest. Whatever the event, it will most likely draw large crowds. Many voters will probably be among those in the crowds, which make these community events good places for campaign exposure. During a campaign, the candidate's primary tasks are to meet people and raise money. Community events are a good way for a candidate to meet potential voters.

A good way for a campaign to properly work an event is to have volunteers canvassing door-to-door in campaign t-shirts in the neighborhood where the event is on the day of the event. Instead of knocking on doors, volunteers can cover more ground by simply delivering or "dropping" literature at homes in the neighborhood. This type of operation is referred to as a "literature drop" or "lit drop."

After conducting a lit drop for 1-2 hours, the volunteers then attend the event wearing their campaign t-shirts. Volunteers may even distribute campaign literature at the event unless event organizers do not want it distributed. The campaign t-shirts are walking billboards for the candidate at the event, and it is good for the attendees to see that a candidate supports their festival.

Since community events draw large numbers of people, having campaign signs posted near the venue, or along routes that terminate the venue, are good ideas. Placing signs where people can see them will assist in raising awareness of the candidate.

The best way to maximize the candidate's effectiveness when attending an event is to meet and greet people. The candidate should walk among any dining areas with 2-3 volunteers. As the candidate greets people, makes an introduction, and gives a short spiel about the campaign, volunteers can hand literature or other campaign materials to the potential voters. Community events provide an opportunity for a candidate to meet a large amount of people in a short amount of time. The drawback is that there is no efficient way to identify whether a person attending the event is a voter.

Some events will allow candidates or local Party organizations to have a booth. Booths are good for storing materials, but they do not actively greet voters like a candidate does by mingling in a crowd. If a cost is associated with a booth, it may be an unwise investment unless volunteers are able to staff the booth for the duration of the event. It is generally a good idea to team with a local Party organization in order to split costs and staffing responsibilities. Booths sitting by themselves do not gain votes or deliver message. It takes a candidate or a campaign team to engage potential voters at an event.

If the campaign has a supporter who is working a booth at a festival or event, the worker should wear a campaign t-shirt. When a volunteer that is working in a food, beverage, or game booth is wearing a shirt for a candidate, then the endorsement becomes more personal to the potential voters that see the shirt.

Community events may also be a good place to obtain volunteers, e-mail addresses and other information. Campaign staff assigned to the event should have sign-up forms or volunteer cards in order to gather as much information as possible. Some people may give the candidate or staffer a business card. All contacts should be entered into the campaign database after each event.

A candidate's time at an event is more productive with a few volunteers. Visibility of the campaign is also increased with additional volunteers. A candidate may attend numerous events in a single day. Each event should have a different set of volunteers in order to "work" the event when the candidate is not present. Staffing levels are dependent upon whether a campaign has enough available volunteers at any given time.

8.14 Town Hall Forums

Some campaigns do not generate much interest. Races for President, Congress or statewide office have a greater potential of drawing crowds for a campaign event than do races for city council, township trustee, or other down ballot competitions. In races that have high interest, or that have the ability to affect a volatile issue, town hall forums may be a good way to reach voters. A town hall forum is essentially a one-sided debate in which the opponent is not invited.

Town hall forums are generally in the evening at a venue that is easily accessible with ample parking. Attendees are greeted at the door and handed a sheet that asks for their input as well as contact information. Attendees are also given a pen as well as a campaign handbill. Light refreshments should also be available. The comment sheets of the attendees should be collected at the end of the forum, and the information should be added to the campaign database.

A town hall forum should be advertised through earned media as well as e-mail and direct mail to known supporters. For a town hall to be effective, a campaign must drive turnout of people, and it is important to get as many undecided voters into the audience as possible. The campaign volunteers and supporters can be present to provide support, begin applause at appropriate moments, and to listen to what the undecided voters around them are saying.

Other methods of driving turnout include sending a direct mail postcard to targeted precincts and neighborhoods or voters of a certain age depending on the issue. The campaign can also make phone calls into homes of targeted voters to attend the event. A town hall is a voter's chance to have a say in the policies of a candidate. High school and local college students can also be invited. If word of the event is spread through a high school civics department or college political science department, then students may be given an incentive to attend the event.

Town hall forum formats are controlled by the campaign. The topics the campaign talks about are dictated by the campaign message. Other topics may arise from a question and answer session that follows a presentation by the candidate. The candidate should be knowledgeable and articulate on the issues that will come up in the forum. The same rules of preparation that would apply to a debate would also apply to a town hall forum.

Town hall forums should have a moderator that takes questions from the audience or brings a microphone around to attendees that wish to ask questions. The presence of a moderator that controls a microphone also allows the campaign to control the duration and direction of the event. Sometimes a campaign has to help get a discussion started in a shy crowd. Having volunteers ready with a question for the candidate is a good way to break the ice with attendees who are anxious about asking a question in a public forum.

As the town hall forum winds down, attendees should be encouraged to fill out their comment forms and to write their areas of concern on their cards. The campaign can use these forms to identify any issues that a poll or other research did not. Priorities of issues can change during a campaign, and a skilled team will always be alert to these trends. Town Hall forums should only last an hour or slightly more so that the candidate can make the best use of time. Meeting as many people as possible on the campaign trail is one of the candidate's primary goals, and a Town Hall can help achieve this objective.

8.15 Handling the Hecklers

Sometimes a campaign will encounter an opponent that engages hecklers or has people that show up at campaign events or community events to make a scene or gain attention or distract the campaign. It is important that the campaign proceed with its plans as though any hecklers do not exist while also preparing in advance for the appearance of potential hecklers.

For all campaign events, it is important to control the venue and its surroundings. Because an event is put on by a campaign, and a fee is paid for a venue, and attendance is by invitation, the campaign can use security and facility personnel to help handle hecklers and escort them off premises. It is always wise for third parties to handle hecklers instead of campaign personnel. Hecklers generally have video cameras because they are trying to incite the opposing campaign into doing something embarrassing or unseemly. It does not provide hecklers, or the opponent's campaign, any usable material if a police officer or facility manager is escorting them off premises for making a scene.

Sometimes a heckler may show up at a community event and hound the candidate. It is important that event personnel are made aware of any nuisance. At no time should the candidate address a heckler directly. Attention is what a heckler wishes to have. The more attention a heckler receives, the greater the scene that will be created. If a campaign staff member can place distance between the candidate and any hecklers without using physical contact, then the candidate can still meet voters and gain support.

It is important that a campaign is trained to identify people who are potential hecklers. Observe people near the candidate, and if someone becomes boisterous or tries to incite the candidate, then campaign staff should step in. Handing a heckler a business card and telling him to call the office to set up an appointment will generally suffice to diffuse a situation. Meanwhile the candidate has moved away and moved on. Hecklers will make themselves look bad if they are interrupting other people who wish to talk to a candidate. Unfortunately at community events, people at the facility will generally ask the heckler, and the object of his heckling, to leave the premises. In such instances, the campaign should comply and seek another time to attend the event when no hecklers are present.

Some hecklers will follow a candidate around as he or she goes about their personal, daily routine. They will pretend to be journalists asking a question. They try to get the candidate when he or she is alone so that they can try to incite the candidate or to back them in a corner in which they feel compelled to answer inane questions. This type of heckler is looking to make the candidate lose their "cool." When a candidate is in situations such as these, the candidate should smile and inform the cameraman and/or heckler that they are welcome to set up a meeting with campaign staff or office staff if their question is of an official nature. The candidate should hand the heckler a card and inform them that they are welcome to contact him the same way any other member of the civilized public would. The candidate should then smile and walk away.

Whenever possible, a campaign should take photos and video of hecklers. This will allow the campaign to lay out to the public, and possibly the authorities, a pattern of harassment. No campaign will want to spend valuable resources on defending a lawsuit, campaign complaint, or criminal charges of harassment. If a campaign can learn how to handle "screwballs" with finesse and professionalism while also documenting all disturbances, then it will come out ahead. Voters understand that although a candidate is a public figure that is accessible to voters, harassment crosses a line of civility.

Sometimes a campaign will have a heckler that is paid for by an opponent's campaign show up in costume to gain media attention or to disrupt proceedings. This type of heckler engages in street theater and attempts to steal the show in order to make a point. Perhaps a candidate refuses to debate an opponent, so the opponent sends a staffer around in a chicken suit. Rather than becoming rattled or unhinged by the heckler, which is part of the goal of a heckler, the candidate can make a joke. "This proves my opponent has gone to the birds!" is a great retort if a guy in a chicken suit shows up. A candidate that is hounded by this type of heckler may decide to capitalize on the attention by getting one of his own campaign staff to show up in a hawk outfit as he talks about being a budget hawk. There are many ways to handle hecklers, but allowing a candidate or campaign staffer to lose their cool because of a little heckling is the wrong way to do it.

Campaigns should count on the eventuality of dealing with hecklers. The key is to place distance between them and the candidate and to have third parties, whenever possible, escort them from a venue. Never get into a fight or verbal altercation with hecklers. Always assume someone is recording the heckler and the candidate.

8.16 Internet Video

Digital video is cheap to shoot and easy to upload to the Internet. With sites such as YouTube and Facebook that allow for video uploads and quick distribution to audiences, a campaign must always be on guard. Smart campaigns are also watching the opponent and recording the opponent.

Video is important because campaigns are in the public domain. Campaigns should always be aware of when they are being taped and by whom. Some opponents are unethical and may send volunteers to a press conference or event that pretend to be someone they are not. A campaign is under no obligation to make its opponent's job easier, but a campaign should also be prepared to allow for its candidate to be recorded. Smart campaigns will simply record the images of the people who are at an event so that they can be identified later if they claim to be someone they are not. Exposing an opponent as unethical can help to derail that campaign's message.

A campaign should always be up front in recording its opponent. A volunteer or staffer should not feel compelled to volunteer information or answer unasked questions. However, if a volunteer or staffer is asked a direct question, the question should be answered with the truth. The opponent may even allow the campaign to tape the candidate anyway.

If a campaign can catch an opponent in a contradiction, then that is a prime opportunity for using Internet video channels. Showing a candidates' answer to a question in a forum from a few months before and a contradictory answer to the same question later, the campaign can establish a record of the candidate waffling on issues. However, if a campaign takes an opponent's answer out of context in order to make an inaccurate video, then the campaign's own credibility can come into question. Remember that the opponent also should be recording their own video. Taking an opponent out of context and treating the recording unethically can turn the media and voters against a candidate.

Other items that campaigns want to catch on video would be an opponent stumbling over an answer to a question, contradictory statements, evasion, inarticulate or uneducated answers, and comments that are unbecoming of an officeholder.

Chapter 9

Nuts and Bolts

*T*he *Political Campaign Desk Reference* has covered everything from starting the campaign, conducting initial research, developing message, waging an air war, to conducting a ground war and discussing the importance of the Internet and some tactics for its use. Readers should understand the difference between strategy and tactics and the significance of each. Someone reading *The Political Campaign Desk Reference* should know how to create a campaign plan, budget for a campaign, prioritize expenditures, and schedule a timeline. *The Political Campaign Desk Reference* should guide a reader as to what basic background information they need to start a campaign, to find out about opponents as well as where to go to get information. A reader of *The Political Campaign Desk Reference* knows the four resources of a campaign (time, information, money and people) and how to use them. In essence, *The Political Campaign Desk Reference* is an excellent orientation on the basics of organizing and running a campaign.

Most manuals do not get into the finer points of how to manage effectively. Entire college courses and majors are designed to teach management skills. Others courses might deal specifically with the significance of the Internet, its history, and its practical use on campaigns. Sometimes campaign operatives take years to build good management skills. This chapter will provide some useful techniques and thoughts regarding effective management and decision making. It is not a complete guide. However, this chapter will deal with common situations that arise in campaigns and how to approach them.

9.1 Monitoring the Opponent

Every campaign should monitor opponents. Some campaign managers will argue that a campaign should simply focus on its plan without regard to the opposition. However, a professional campaign should always be cognizant of what is happening with the opponent. Does the opponent have a campaign calendar on their web site? If the opponent has a calendar, then the campaign will know where and when an opponent will appear. A campaign should monitor the opponent's "issues" pages and print them out often in case of changes.

Does the opponent's web page biography pass the "sniff" test? If an opponent is untruthful, or if the opponent embellishes, then the campaign may be able to poke holes in the opponent's credibility. Does the opponent have a proper disclaimer that is required by law? If the disclaimer is missing, then a campaign should file a complaint immediately before changes to the web site are made. There is no down side in catching the opponent in an elections complaint.

Early in the race is when most campaigns will make mistakes. An opponent's web site may have glaring errors or even false statements. Anything worth filing a complaint about should be exploited. If an opponent can be sidetracked or derailed early in the race, then a campaign can save a lot of money.

Once the campaign is in full monitoring mode, a volunteer, staffer or team of volunteers should be recruited to record all public appearances of an opponent. A campaign should record an opponent for multiple reasons. If a campaign can gain intelligence on what the opponent is saying, how the opponent is saying it and if the opponent is going on the attack, then all of this information is valuable. There will probably be multiple instances in which a candidate and the opponent will be in public together. If a candidate knows in advance the arguments and attacks of the opponent, then preparation will be effective. The opponent will be the one in a debate or forum caught off guard if they are not monitoring.

Recording the opponent's public appearances may also expose inconsistencies. Perhaps the opponent speaks a little more "loose" with a crowd he or she thinks is "friendly." The opponent may be more apt to say untrue things about the candidate. The opponent may feel comfortable embellishing their own record to the point worthy of a campaign complaint. An opponent may fumble a question, say something unpopular, or the opponent may appear as though he is inept.

Situations such as these described here are usable on the Internet and may even help a reporter with a story.

Finally, a good reason to follow an opponent to record their public appearances is to keep them honest. Once they begin to recognize the videographers for a campaign, they may become more timid, embellish less, or skip certain issues. The best result is to make sure the opponent does not misrepresent the candidate recording him.

There are multiple opportunities for a campaign to monitor its opponent. Whether it is the Internet, public events, or gathering direct mail from people on the campaign who received it in the mail, the campaign must be vigilant. A campaign should also monitor the opponent's television spots for the same reason it monitors the Internet, direct mail, and public appearances. Monitoring the opponent should always be an integral part of the campaign.

9.2   Viral Marketing

Viral marketing is a phenomenon that relies on the networks that a campaign has built in order to spread its message far and wide. Chapter 5 discussed the importance of the campaign's database in terms of fundraising. During the discussion on targeting in Chapter 3, *The Political Campaign Desk Reference* discusses how to use the voter database to develop the universe of voters to which the campaign will appeal. Viral marketing relies on the e-mail and social network database of the campaign in order to spread its message.

Although viral marketing is effective on statewide and national campaigns, it can be very useful in local races. The spread of a message through viral marketing may take many forms. For instance, a campaign may post an item of significance on its social media site. Followers of the campaign on that site may link to that posting (video, photo, document etc.) and share it with their friends. In essence, a single message can be spread exponentially if the conditions are right.

The proper conditions to achieve a viral result are simplicity of the message, effective illustration of the message, and relevance of the message. *The Political Campaign Desk Reference* stresses the need to keep messages simple. This does not mean that a message must be "dumbed down", but the message must be able to be absorbed in the midst of all of the other media "noise" that voters encounter through television, radio, print, Internet, and personal interaction. A message that requires too much explanation will have little chance of gaining a viral status. Effective illustration of the message is important because the message must be able to grab the attention of the voter and hold it until the message is complete. A message that brings an emotional reaction out of the voter is ideal for viral marketing. Emotions can be a very powerful tool in viral marketing. Laughter and anger are often used.

What is more important is that the message must also incite the voter to pass it along to his or her friends. If the message is relevant, then it has met the final condition necessary for becoming a viral marketing piece. Simple, effective, and relevant messages win the day in the viral universe. These themes are repeated throughout *The Political Campaign Desk Reference.*

Viral marketing has itself become an art form. From "flash mobs" to Internet videos, countless people engage in viral marketing every day. Many people, when they view a video or forward an e-mail do not realize their role in viral marketing. They do not think about their necessary role in making the message viral because they have been impacted in some way by it.

Along with the conditions of the message, a viral marketing campaign needs a method of message delivery. That is where the campaign database and social networks enter the scene. A campaign can broadcast its message to its database through e-mail with the hopes that people will then forward the message to others not in the database. Those recipients would then send it to their friends. Soon, a message that was originally sent to only a few people may have been seen by hundreds or thousands. In a national campaign, the magnitude of response may be even greater.

So what qualifies for an effective viral message? Perhaps the campaign produced a poignant video that has the ability to make voters angry at the opponent. Instead of creating the ad for television, the campaign may have decided to release the ad exclusively on the

Internet and e-mailed the link to the video to its supporters. If the ad is simple, effective, and relevant, then it has the potential to become viral. Sometimes an ad will contain something "off the wall" or "over the top" in order to invoke a feeling that the person must pass the message along if only to show people the one component of the message that they feel is outrageous. If that is the case, then the mission has been accomplished.

Under the right circumstances, direct mail can become a viral phenomenon. In a race for a mayor of a major city, the challenger attacked the incumbent for literally traveling all over the world during his first term in office. The challenger developed a piece of direct mail that asked the question in large letters "Where in the World is 'Bob Smith?'" "Bob Smith" is the name used for illustrative purposes. The background of the piece was an antique map of the world with pictures of the cities the mayor had visited. Red lines connected all of the cities, and the presentation was comical even to the supporters of the mayor. The direct mail piece then described the costs associated with all of the travel. The reaction of voters who received the direct mail was overwhelming, and the newspaper ran a story about the direct mail piece. More people were exposed to the issue and the direct mail piece than the campaign had originally hoped. Scanned copies of it were e-mailed around the Internet, and what was supposed to be a simple direct mail piece became a campaign's unintentional, albeit successful, experience with viral marketing.

Because it is difficult to predict if something will become viral or not, a campaign should not plan on having any portion of its message "go viral" in order to win. However, a campaign should attempt to be creative and appropriately edgy, in order to help spread its message.

9.3   Effective vs. Ineffective Meetings

Something that can drag a campaign down is the need to have too many meetings. Sometimes the candidate will want to have meetings for reasons ranging from insecurity about the campaign to attempts to micromanage aspects of the plan. There are very few campaign meetings in which the candidate will need to be present. The nuts and bolts of the campaign should be taken care of by the team. By having the candidate at campaign meetings, the campaign team opens itself up to constant scrutiny, tangential conversations, and a complete derailing of a normal meeting. A candidate should rarely attend campaign team meetings. If a candidate does attend a meeting, the duration of his or her presence should be minimal.

It is the campaign team's responsibility, and the campaign manager's duty, to effectively manage the candidate. If the candidate is being managed professionally then the candidate should have neither the time nor inclination to attend meetings. A candidate who feels as though he or she is being managed effectively will tend not to meddle. That means that the campaign manager must be the liaison between the candidate and the rest of the team, and the campaign manager briefs the candidate about meetings. The campaign meeting is directed by one person this way, and not two.

An effective meeting will have an agenda that will generally start by considering the schedule for the coming weeks. Each member of the campaign team will take their assignments based on the campaign schedule. Any questions about how to approach certain people or tackle a specific problem can be easily answered while discussing the schedule and who will be responsible for each coming task. Careful note should be taken regarding who is responsible for each task in order for the proper follow-up to occur. Meetings are excellent for making sure everyone on the team is on the same page. With everyone aware of all of the assignments, completion of tasks is more likely because team members will hold each other accountable.

After the scheduling discussion, each member of the campaign team should report on how the past week/days have gone. Team members should bring up issues that they have had or explain how they handled certain situations. This meeting time is to work out any bugs from past events so that future events are smoother.

After individual reports, the campaign manager can communicate anything that the candidate wanted to pass along. The campaign manager should also set the tone and pace for the coming week and what to expect. It is not appropriate to admonish any team member during a meeting. Individual one-on-one meetings are appropriate for such things. Campaign meetings are designed to get everyone on the team on the same page without the presence of the candidate. The candidate does not need to see, nor should the candidate have the desire, to see how the proverbial sausage is made.

Campaign meetings are also not good times to "brainstorm" for the campaign. If a team member has an idea, then the conversation should occur with the appropriate member of management in the chain of command. Raising ideas in campaign meetings when a direction is already set can undermine the authority of the campaign manager. A good campaign manager or director will seek advice and counsel from less experienced campaign staffers. Not only does this engage staffers and make them feel as though they have a role in management, but the campaign manager may also learn something in the process.

After each campaign meeting, team members should receive a summary along with tasks and assignments so that there will never be a question as to who will be responsible for each aspect of the campaign for the coming week or weeks. If these basic steps to an effective meeting are followed, campaign meetings will be relatively short and generally effective. If tasks are not clearly assigned or the candidate is involved with managing the campaign, then meetings will not be effective, and team members will leave without a clear direction or understanding as to the power structure of the campaign.

9.4   Weak Link in the Team

Effective campaigns require team members with "can do" attitudes and people who are able to seek answers to things they do not know about. A campaign cannot suffer team members who need to be hand-held through everything they have been assigned. Campaign teams also need to be confident that when a task is assigned it will be done, and if there is a problem, the person assigned will not wait until it is too late or an emergency to fix it. A campaign cannot handle team members who "don't do windows" meaning they will not do whatever it takes to win. Volunteers have more ability to name their own tasks and jobs, but senior staff, paid staff, or team members with titles do not have that luxury.

Weak team members sap the vitality of a campaign. Other team members immediately identify "slackers", "whiners" and "drama queens." These types of personalities suck the morale out of a campaign team, and can severely impact the effectiveness of a campaign. Political campaigns, based on their temporary existence and fast-paced environment, have a lower threshold of tolerance for bad personalities. The best way to deal with such team members is to either re-task them or terminate their involvement on the campaign. The sooner action can be taken, the better. Damage is done each minute such a person is on the team.

The campaign manager should handle all personnel issues discreetly and amicably. Discretion is important in order to allow the team member a level of dignity. If a situation is handled with privacy and discretion, other team members will know that their own personal issues will be handled with such professionalism. Proper handling of situations builds trust among the team.

If a team member is not working out in a position for any of the aforementioned reasons, an option may be to re-task the offender. A good manager will be able to identify specific situations in which the team member has not responded appropriately or fulfilled duties. Options should exist to retain a person who earnestly wishes to help the campaign. A manager should never create a situation in which the team member becomes bitter and attempts to sabotage the campaign in some way. If the team member is not amenable to re-tasking, then termination remains as an option to a manager. Perhaps the team member will be satisfied as a volunteer.

Any time a team member leaves a campaign, for any reason, it is essential that any passwords or locks are changed. A team member who knows the procedures of a campaign and has passwords and keys to the campaign office is a disaster waiting to happen. It protects both the campaign and the former team member to take necessary precautions in order to safeguard information and material assets.

Myriad scenarios can occur, but a campaign manager has to be able to make swift and just decisions. A campaign manager has the responsibility to maintain a well-oiled campaign machine and to keep morale high. Campaign issues should never become issues with which a candidate should deal. A candidate should be aware of all issues and have faith that the campaign team is equipped to handle all situations.

9.5 Security

Team members should always be in the habit of undertaking certain asks that protect the resources of the campaign. Although espionage, computer hackers, and people sifting through trash may sound like the makings of a spy novel, a campaign must always guard its resources. Espionage occurs in the spy world, the corporate world, and the world of political campaigns. The most important resource to protect is the information resource. Opposing campaigns would like to have access to the other's database, campaign plan, budget, strategy, e-mails, and paper waste that allows them to see what is going on.

Campaign computers should never be left running overnight unless they are being used. Whenever a team member leaves a computer, all programs should be logged off. If the campaign computer network has a wireless router, then it should be encrypted. Computers should be individually protected.

A campaign should always have a good confetti shredding machine. All e-mail communications have potentially sensitive information. If they are printed, they should be shredded before discarding. All campaign documents should be shredded before they leave the campaign office.

The campaign manager often has information and documentation that is sensitive and only available to a select few. If the campaign manager does not have an office that can be independently locked, then all sensitive information should be stored in a lockable cabinet. The cabinet or office should remain locked when not directly under the campaign manager's supervision.

The campaign office should be secured whenever it is empty. Stepping out for lunch and leaving the office for five minutes to bring something back creates an opportunity for someone claiming to be a potential "volunteer" to step in and have access to sensitive information. Only trusted members of the campaign team should have keys. Volunteers and junior staff members should rely on senior staff to grant access to the campaign office. An improperly supervised office can be a costly information leak for a campaign.

Many basic security measures are a matter of common sense. However, it is easy to become comfortable with the people in an office, and procedures designed to protect the information, as well as the people in the office, can easily slacken. Discipline in maintaining proper security will grant peace of mind to a campaign as well as the candidate.

9.6   Preparing for Debates

Debates are events that challengers usually want to join while incumbents generally try to avoid them. Sometimes incumbents cannot avoid a debate and therefore must prepare just as thoroughly as the challenger.

A debate offers a challenger the opportunity to point out problems with the incumbent. A debate also grants a challenger a certain level of legitimacy that an incumbent will want to discourage. Chapter 8 discussed town hall forums. If an incumbent wants to get in front of the debate issue and avoid the confrontation, then town hall forums are a good way to fill a void. An incumbent can answer a challenge to debate by replying that the town hall forums are a much better way for voters to interact with their current officeholder, ask questions, and have an impact while a debate will only serve to deprive voters of such an environment.

If a debate is unavoidable, then the campaign and candidate should prepare adequately. In preparation, the campaign team should revisit the information gathered in Chapter 1 as well as the opposition research gathered in Chapter 3. In particular, the strengths vs. weaknesses charts become important. These rules apply to challengers as well as incumbents.

Campaigns should confer on various aspects of the debate. Civil campaigns will be able to agree on the points governing campaigns. Campaigns should agree on moderator, venue, date, time, and how questions will be asked. Negotiations regarding debates can be cumbersome if one of the parties involved tries to bully the others or make outrageous demands. Sometimes a candidate will make outrageous demands in order to kill the debate. Incumbents generally do not want debates for the reasons mentioned above. A challenger may acquiesce to certain demands just to get the incumbent in the same room with the media watching. Debates have been part of political discourse since politics have been around. A campaign that tries to quash a debate or refuse to participate in a debate runs a risk of offending the electorate.

Prior to the debate, the campaign should adequately brief the candidate on all issues pertinent to the office. Issue briefs can be a single page with bullet points covering the issue as well as the candidate's solution to any problems. In addition to issues, the candidate should be briefed on the strengths and weaknesses of the opponent. A skilled debater will be able to use an opponent's weaknesses to stay on the offensive. It is in the best interest of a candidate to keep the opponent on the defensive while showcasing his or her own strengths. A candidate should also be aware of his own shortcomings in order to properly prepare for any attack.

If a campaign has done its job in monitoring the opponent, then the team will know how the opponent is framing his arguments. Watching video of the opponent's public appearances will help in preparing for a debate or forum. A campaign will be able to better understand the opponent and how he responds to questions. Video of the opponent may also provide revelations about what makes the opponent uneasy.

Once a candidate has had a chance to review all of the materials, a role playing session is a good idea. The campaign should have a well prepared stand-in to play the opponent in such a session so that the candidate can respond to potential attacks. Good research is required to anticipate the opponent's attacks. A handful of campaign team members should act as moderators asking questions. The candidate's responses should be evaluated and fine-tuned. The questions should be asked until the candidate's answers come across as thoughtful, genuine and polished. It is helpful to have a video recorder and monitor available for playback. Sometimes the candidate can adapt to a question through self-evaluation along with the input of others.

9.7   When Is It OK To "Go Negative"?

One of the toughest decisions a campaign may make is whether to "go negative" or not. Going negative refers to a strategy in which one campaign spends resources to highlight the weaknesses of an opponent. Going negative takes many forms including overt attack ads to issuing a mild comparison direct mail piece. Going negative does not necessarily mean that a campaign is "slinging mud" or taking a low road to win a campaign. A campaign can go negative in a responsible manner that does not erode the integrity of a campaign as long as the issues in the negative advertising are truthful, relevant to the race, and documented.

It is generally unacceptable to go negative on a candidate because of an issue that is not related to the campaign. For instance, an opponent's child may be caught in the middle of an illegal act, or an opponent's brother has financial problems resulting in bankruptcy. A campaign that chooses to draw a parallel between the shortcomings of a relative and a candidate runs a high risk of a negative backlash. Voters generally do not respect a campaign that will attack someone who is not running for office if the candidate under attack had nothing to do with the relative's misfortune. A campaign should avoid attacking a family member of an opponent.

Business associates, mentors, and close acquaintances can become an issue in a campaign if the opponent's association with a person affects the opponent's beliefs or actions. Whether it is fair or not, people are often judged by those with whom they associate. For instance, a contributor to a candidate may be convicted of committing a crime. The candidate with whom this person is associated may also become tainted by the crime regardless of the candidate's involvement or lack thereof. A candidate can overcome such association with the passage of time if the candidate had nothing to do with the crime, but it will require campaign resources of to mitigate this type of association.

If a campaign is calculating about when it wishes to release damaging negative information, it will want to do so at a time that allows the opponent little chance to respond before the election. Releasing information too close to Election Day, however, may diminish the impact of the information. If a campaign had information for months that was only released days before a vote, voters may view the information as suspect and disregard it. On the other hand, releasing information early in a race can be advantageous if the issues help derail the opponent's message. A candidate may more easily achieve victory and conserve resources if the opponent is on the defense from the outset of the race.

A popular way to go negative without appearing negative is to create a comparison between the candidate and the opponent. A campaign can use any of the tactics described in previous chapters such as press releases, Internet, direct mail, or broadcast media in order to create the comparison. It is wise to stick to issues and avoid personal characteristics in making distinctions. What candidates believe about social issues such as 2nd Amendment rights, abortion, and many other topics can be valid comparison issues if voters are concerned about them. The past actions of candidates in regard to raising taxes, meeting attendance, or votes on key issues may also be valid issues. The campaign message will determine what issues are the most important. Remember that it is important for third parties, rather than a candidate, to make an attack whenever possible.

Attacks should be easy to make and difficult for the opponent to explain. The question of ethics always applies when going negative. Footnoting all claims will both protect the campaign making them as well as validate the claims thereby substantiating them in the minds of voters. A tactic discussed in earlier chapters includes making the attack in the form of a question followed by evidence that leads the viewer or reader to the conclusion that the campaign wishes. For instance, "Is John Smith fit for office?" is a question that a direct mail piece or television spot might ask. The question can then be followed by a small handful of footnoted points that help the voter reach the conclusion of "no." When a campaign is able to help voters achieve a self-realization in such a way, then the advertising has been more effective than simply making a declaration that John Smith is not fit for office.

9.8   The Campaign Kickoff

The first opportunity that many campaigns will have to employ many of the tactics in *The Political Campaign Desk Reference* will occur at the campaign kickoff. The campaign kickoff is where the campaign team introduces the candidate to the public, begins creating the image, presents the campaign message, works with the media, distributes press releases, and utilizes the web page, social media and other methods of communication.

If a candidate is running for mayor of a major city, and jobs have been on the decline, then the challenger campaign team may choose to kick off the race in a part of town hit by economic decline to illustrate the shortcomings of the opponent. With jobs as the key issue, the campaign team will recruit local business owners to stand behind the candidate as he or she makes her initial speech.

A campaign only gets one opportunity to kick off its race. Everything related to the event should be meticulously planned. The campaign should recruit business owners that represent a cross-section of the community. Participants should be young and old, male and female and representative of various ethnicities. Although the candidate is the focus of the press conference, a campaign should attempt to send a subtle message of inclusion to voters. By being inclusive, voters will understand that the candidate will attempt to be representative of all groups.

The campaign should also have determined its logo that will appear on signs and communications. The logo should be on a large vinyl or plastic sign behind group at the announcement. A podium should be placed in front with a campaign sign attached to the front of the podium. The presence of a podium will also serve as a platform for the media to set microphones. The supporters behind the candidate should be wearing campaign t-shirts and stickers. The image should be one of organization and strong support.

There should also be a small spectator crowd of about 10 supporters who will stand near the media. These supporters can provide ambient applause and show signs of approval. The crowd of supporters can also help to mitigate any supporters of the opponent who show up as well as hecklers. Also among the crowd, the campaign should be recording its own kickoff event.

The campaign should make every attempt to accommodate the media. By distributing a media advisory prior to the kickoff, building a rapport with the media in advance, and confirming that the media will attend will help make the campaign kickoff successful. The campaign should work with local law enforcement or businesses to make certain that space is set aside for media vehicles to park. The venue should also be easily accessible to the media.

If there is a specific spot that the campaign wishes the media to set up, then that area should be roped off. If a platform is available, then it may be appropriate to set it up so that the media has an unobstructed view of the candidate and the backdrop. By roping off a media area, the campaign also is able to control the framing of the kickoff. Although the campaign will encourage the media to participate from the roped off area, if a reporter or videographer wishes to move around, they should be permitted.

As supporters arrive, a staff member should be assigned to greet them and make sure they know where they are to stand and what they are to do. All participants should have received a set of talking points ahead of time. The talking points help the supporter to stay on message if questioned by reporters. Supporters should be offered refreshments so that they are comfortable, and they should know what is expected of them.

As media arrives, the communications director, press secretary or campaign manager should personally greet them. The campaign should have press packets assembled for the press. The press packets will include a press release from the campaign detailing what the theme of the kickoff is as well as the message of the campaign. A professional head shot of the candidate should be included with the packet. Any relevant news clips, materials or supporting documentation should be included in the press packet. In addition to the paper materials, a digital copy of the contents should also be included so that the media can work with the press release as well as the photo of the candidate without transcribing or scanning.

The kickoff should be short so that media has time for questions. Once the kickoff has ended, various members of the media may wish to have a one-on-one with the candidate. These individual interviews should still occur with the campaign backdrop behind the candidate. The campaign team should have conducted a role play session with the candidate the night before the press conference in order to practice answers t the most likely asked questions. By the time the candidate is working with the press, he or she should seem comfortable, polished, and articulate.

After the kickoff has ended, the campaign should e-mail the entire media list with the press packet contents so that news directors and those who did not attend know what happened. In addition, support-ers should receive an email, and the video and press release should be uploaded to the campaign web site, blog, social media, and any other outlet available.

The campaign kickoff marks the beginning of the public portion of a campaign. By the time the campaign holds its kickoff, the cam-paign plan should be established, and the tactics following the kickoff should be laid out. The kickoff can lead to a fundraising push from supporters. The resulting media response can also be used to help the campaign gain momentum. The campaign should link to the stories about the kickoff from all Internet venues, and media coverage links can be e-mailed out to supporters with a fundraising request.

The campaign kickoff can be one of the most powerful events of a campaign. If a campaign pays close attention to detail, then it will be effective. Once the campaign kicks off, however, voters and the media will be paying attention, so the need for attention to detail becomes more important.

9.9   What To Do If the Media Does Not Show

There will be times when a campaign has done everything it can to bring media to an event, whether it is a campaign kickoff, press conference, rally, or other event. The problem with news is that there are a limited number of reporters, and a campaign cannot control external factors such as breaking news elsewhere or inclement weather preventing news crews from traveling. In politics, as in show business, the event must go on.

A campaign team has its own capabilities for video recording. Digital recorders with high definition are inexpensive. The campaign should proceed as though the media is present and record its own press conference or event. The campaign can even interview some of the attendees with questions that the media would typically ask. The campaign can also conduct its own breakaway video with the candidate.

If the media did not show, then each outlet has no idea that their competitors did not show. The campaign should still push the press packet information out to stations and call the news directors to see if they will entertain an interview at the news station or over the phone. The campaign can also deliver digital copies of the press conference and interviews to the news outlets either by courier or by upload if available. The campaign should make it as easy as possible to help the media report the news.

The video can also be posted on the Internet, and the campaign team can still be e-mailed with the update. If the campaign puts the right effort into getting the footage, press release and information into the hands of the media, then the stories may still run. What makes this process easier is if the campaign has fostered a good relationship with reporters and news directors.

9.10 Adapting To Changing Technology

Campaigns that can adapt to changing technology will be the campaigns that ultimately have an edge. As technology changes, so do the ways by which voters receive information. Since the first edition of *The Political Campaign Desk Reference* was published, social media, smart phones, and tablet computers are innovations that campaigns are commonly using.

A smart campaign will not lose sight of the fundamentals of a strong campaign. The campaign plan is something that will always be integral to a campaign regardless of the technology available. Planning was the key to success thousands of years ago when Sun Tsu counseled military leaders, and planning is the key now. A good campaign plan will integrate new methods of communication and message delivery. A good campaign manager will understand his own limitations and hire the right person to assist with emerging technologies, new channels of communication and new media.

Time, information, money, and people will also remain the four fundamental resources on a campaign. Changing technology may affect the way in which we utilize these resources.

As technology changes, campaigns should also stay focused on other principles. Information may flow more freely as technology changes, but ethics remain important. Simply because information shows up somewhere in the Internet or elsewhere does not mean that it is true or that a campaign should even use it. A campaign remains responsible for what it distributes regardless if the source is incorrect. Campaign communications should always stick to the message. Campaign communications should also be simple regardless of the channel. If a campaign remembers the fundamentals, and acquires personnel that can assist with innovations, then changing technology is not a challenge but an advantage.

9.11   Attention to Detail

When a United States President or governor of a state has an event, they make sure that they have hired people capable of paying close attention to every detail. Why should this be any different for a local race? If something is good enough for the President or the Governor, then it should be good for the local campaign.

If a student of politics watches the President speak on television, they will notice that nearly everything has been planned. The clothes and jewelry that the President is wearing has been planned. The people surrounding the President are selected. The placement of the flags and signs around the President has been discussed and debated until the perfect places have been found. The place where media will stand has been planned. Every detail, including timeline down to the very creases in the flags, has been purposely situated. Nothing is left to chance.

A campaign should take great care in how it words all campaign communications. This includes blogs, social media posts, press releases, candidate biography, e-mail blasts, web pages, and anything that the campaign distributes including direct mail or broadcast media. The campaign should use proper grammar and punctuation. Whenever the campaign makes a claim, it should back it up with a relevant citation.

Whenever the candidate appears in public, his attire should be appropriate, and his remarks, if any, should be tailored to the event. Events should be coordinated well in advance so that the details can be worked out. A campaign staff member should always ask themselves what the candidate would want to know or how the candidate would want to be perceived in order to help guide attention to detail. Doing the minimum when it comes to campaigns does not get the job done.

Attention to detail is something that should pervade every aspect of the campaign. The campaign plan should pay attention to details. When conducting opposition research, the campaign should use detail oriented people because it is in the details where some of the best information is gathered. In developing the strengths and weaknesses, campaigns must look at details. Always assume the opponent is paying attention to details. If a campaign hopes that it can gloss over a detail in hopes that the opponent will miss it, then the campaign is not preparing the way it should.

There are some things that only experience can teach. Working on campaigns will help an operative understand where the details are and how to handle them. Experience running for office will educate a candidate on what details are important to watch as well. A campaign team must work together and be deliberate when executing any portion of the campaign plan.

Appendix A –
Sample Campaign Plan

Keep Helen Troy, Cook County Solicitor
Campaign Overview

Background

The position being sought by incumbent Helen Troy and former State Representative Howard Johnson is Cook County Solicitor.

Helen Troy is the current Cook County Solicitor. Her strengths include the fact that she has held the position since January 2001, her gender, the awards her office has won, her business experience and her legal experience. Troy has a small amount of money on hand and should be prepared to raise at least $160,000 for the Solicitor's race. Since becoming Solicitor, Troy has improved customer service, increased efficiency and returned money to the county's General Fund – all positive issues for the campaign. Potential weaknesses for Troy include a potential issue from office document migration (implementing technology), which may also become a strength if marketed properly. An obstacle all Republican candidates must overcome is the trend that Cook County is experiencing in which countywide Republican candidates receive fewer votes in each successive election – a trend that is evident since at least 2000.

Troy's opponent for the Solicitor's office is Howard Johnson. Johnson is a former State Representative from Ohio's 100th District and former mayor of Happy Valley. He was defeated in 2002 by Barry Wilkes in a closely watched rematch after Ohio's redistricting. Johnson will use his experience as a real estate broker to explain why he is the most qualified for the position. He will also use the fact that he has been an elected officeholder before and possibly use images of him with Columbus officials, swearing-in images, and statewide endorsements.

Johnson will also likely attempt to re-create his image in the form of a conservative (despite his Democratic party affiliation) taking note of some of the Republican legislation he supported in Columbus. Johnson's time in such organizations as Cook County Municipal League and the Cook County Community Action Association, among others, has provided him an opportunity for countywide networking. Between the years 2000-2004, Ohio Secretary of State's web site shows that Johnson was able to raise $180,523. This figure does not account for what he raised during his years on Happy Valley Council or as Mayor. He has experience and training in raising funds from his time in Columbus, and Troy's campaign must assume that he will raise enough to run a strong campaign.

Howard Johnson has also kicked off what he terms as an "exploratory tour" akin to the Hillary Clinton tour that launched her 2008 Presidential campaign. The tour idea is a gimmick but demonstrates that Johnson is thinking hard about what to do with his campaign. He will most likely have some sort of conclusion event (press conference, press release or rally) that will be the platform from which he will make criticisms of the current office. A key weakness to Johnson is that he took at least $1,300 from pro-abortion groups in three different donations from his time in Columbus.

Troy's campaign must use the power of incumbency to her benefit. A "makeover" should occur in the office so that Troy is referred to as Cook County's "Award-Winning" Solicitor. The addition of the "Award Winning" mantle sends a message to people that not only will Helen Troy tell you she's a good Solicitor, but third party entities have evaluated her performance and agree. Troy must also place more emphasis on her background as a small business owner thereby making her a contributor of the economy and an elected officeholder sensitive to the economy. The economy will be a large issue in the 2012 elections. Johnson can be painted as being part of the problem, and he was subsequently a one-term State Representative. He will blame his loss of his seat on redistricting. That argument will not hold water against the counter argument that voters would have returned him to office if he had done a good job – "how dare he suggest that the voters in Cook County cannot make informed decisions!"

A well thought-out campaign will evaluate Troy's past performance since 2000 and list geographic areas of the county where she is very strong, neutral and weak. The precincts of the county in which Troy has both won and lost elections will be highly targeted. A strong campaign will also shore up support in strong areas. Attention given to weak areas of support will be limited to improving name identification and spreading the "award-winning" message.

Results for the 2004 and 2008 elections for Solicitor:

2004	Votes Cast	% of Heads-on	% of total cast
Troy	180,125	54%	47%
Masur	156,193	46%	41%
Total Cast	384,336		
Won by	23,932		
Didn't Vote	48,018		

2008	Votes Cast	% of Heads-on	% of total cast
Troy	198,696	52%	46%
Maxwell	182,149	48%	42%
Total Cast	433,058		
Won by	16,547		
Didn't Vote	52,213		

Looking at historic numbers from 2004 and 2008, one can see a trend in the Solicitor's race. The most notable trend is apparent erosion between 2004 and 2008 of the percentage that Troy won by in a heads-up match. Troy also experienced erosion in the percentage of votes to total ballots cast in the election. The most disturbing figure is the raw margin of votes that separate Troy from her opponent in 2008 versus 2004.

If 1/3 of the voters who skipped the Solicitor's race in 2004 decided to vote for Jim Maxwell, Helen Troy would not be Solicitor today. This is a figure that astute Democrats will not ignore. Furthermore, Troy's race is a snapshot of a larger trend in which Republicans in Cook County have to spend more and work harder for the votes they earn. Finally, we see that the larger the voter turnout, the less Troy wins by. 2012 promises to be the most energized election in over a decade. That fact, along with the changes in absentee voting law that have gone into effect since 2004, will drive turnout in the election higher. Democrats will be particularly energized because they ant to keep the White House, and Ohio will be seen as a key state this year – especially since the statewide Democratic sweep in 2006 and the sweep back to Republicans in 2010. Ohio is the quintessential swing state.

Budget

A strong countywide race will require the use of direct mail, TV and a grassroots campaign. The budget outlined below is an estimate of anticipated costs. The pages following will give a brief description of each of these costs.

TV Network	$150,000
TV Cable	$60,000
Signs	$20,000
Direct Mail 1(pre-absentee)	$20,000
Direct Mail 2 (pre-absentee #2)	$20,000
Direct Mail 3 (lands 8-10 days out)	$20,000
Direct Mail 4 (lands Wednesday/Thursday before Election Day)	$20,000
Direct Mail 5 (lands weekend before Election Day)	$20,000
Phones	$20,000
T-shirts, stickers, letterhead, etc.	$4,000
Web Site	$5,000
Social Media ads	$2,500
General Consulting	$15,000
Absentee Chase	$19,500
Total	**$396,000**

TV

In a down-ballot race that will not drive voters to the polls, such as the Solicitor race, name identification is the primary factor determining success. Message and image will set the candidates apart once high name identification is achieved. Therefore, an aggressive television campaign is essential in securing a victory for Helen Troy.

In an election that has the potential of being drowned out by a heated race for President on both sides of the aisle, it is important to reach as many Republican and independent voting eyeballs as possible. A network and cable plan will present message and raise name identification. Traditional Republican channels and programming (Fox News, Golf Channel) will be targeted to shore up the base on cable, and network will deliver the message to a broader audience during news hour programming.

In order to maintain continuity of message, a single message should be crafted for television that will reflect the message of the campaign. The spot will highlight Helen Troy as an award winning Solicitor, subtly reinforce her gender and speak to her business background.

Signs

The Troy campaign will use large signs and yard signs to boost name identification throughout the county. The emphasis of effort should be focused on acquiring large sign locations along major thoroughfares in Cook County. The budget reserves $10,000 for signs.

Sign location acquisition will occur through the use of some volunteer lists. In addition, the Troy campaign should use a phone calling firm to acquire sign locations in areas where coverage is weak or name identification needs help. An advocacy message will be delivered along with an "ask" for sign locations.

Signs should go out 4-6 weeks from Election Day as local ordinances allow.

Direct Mail

The direct mail campaign will be the most effective portion of the campaign. This is where the Troy campaign delivers the message to targeted voters on award-winning Solicitor, business background and incumbency (past performance). Direct mail is also where the voter receives the image of the candidate, and the campaign solely controls it. The message in the direct mail mirrors that of the other media ads. There will be 5 targeted mailings (based in swing areas and areas of support):

Mailing 1) *Introduction* – Helen Troy is "Our Award Winning Solicitor"

Mailing 2) *Business Experience* – Speak to Helen's paralegal experience as well as her former business.

Mailing 3) *Endorsements* – Rundown of party and local endorsements with a final tag of the most important endorsement of all – experience.

Mailing 4) *Comparison* – "Helen Troy is the only candidate for Solicitor who…"

Mailing 5) GOTV – Slate card and instructional for recipients on their voting location. We create slate card, or other group creates slate card for us (but we pay for).

Direct mail will be delivered in the areas targeted by the campaign. Due to the size of Cook County, it is unrealistic to mail all voters throughout the county. A discussion of targeting is detailed in another section.

Phones

Telephones will be used heavily by the Republican and Democrat

214

candidates for President. Targeting phone calls to weaker areas as well as strong areas will help to reinforce support from traditional sources and to move voters towards Troy. Democratic voters will be eliminated from the lists. Messages can be from Helen as well as some surrogates:

Call 1) Advocacy call requesting sign locations – this is the most expensive set of calls. It is countywide and recorded in Helen's voice. The system used is voice-activated. The respondent hears Helen's voice on the phone asking questions and providing information about herself. The last question is an ask for yard sign locations. Occurs in mid-late August.
Call 2) Helen Troy call with introduction – 1-2 days prior to absentees beginning
Call 3) Surrogate call on behalf of Helen – 4-5 days prior to Election Day
Call 4) Helen call – 1-2 days prior to Election Day

Advocacy Call Overview

The advocacy call also serves as a microtargeting call. If the Troy campaign utilizes the technology that allows for caller interaction, it can identify voters who are more likely to vote for an award winning Solicitor, a female Solicitor, a Solicitor who takes a tough stand on illegal immigrants or a Solicitor who has strict policies protecting personal information.

Grass Roots

A strong grassroots campaign will be essential to victory in the 2008 General Election. A timeline will be developed to include dates and times of targeted festivals and celebrations where members of the general public will be.

Precincts will also be targeted for weekend "lit drops" in which volunteers in Troy shirts will deliver literature to households that are likely to vote. Lit drops will begin in late Spring and should be coordinated in precincts where large community festivals will be that weekend. Volunteers can go to festivals after dropping in neighborhoods, and festival attendees will see the Troy team at the festival and find its literature at their home.

Volunteers will also send in letters to the editors of the local community newspapers. These letters should reflect the themes of the campaign and therefore be written from talking points developed by the campaign, but letters should be in writers' own words.

Door to Door

Beginning in summer 2012, Helen Troy and the team will begin going door to door in targeted precincts at the homes of likely voters. The precincts she visits will coincide with areas where festivals are occurring or where large voter turnout is expected – particularly in the "swing" areas. Walking times include evenings after work and late morning through the afternoon on weekends.

Troy will have literature, walking lists, voter registration forms and absentee ballot forms for door-to-door. All pro-Troy voters that the campaign identifies should be provided with an absentee ballot application.

Internet Campaign

An aggressive Internet presence and campaign will complement the air war. The Internet campaign will consist of:

- Web site
- E-mail acquisition of likely voters
- Presence in the blogosphere

- Donations from the web
- LinkedIn Presence
- Facebook Page
- YouTube Content
- Twitter Account

Every campaign has a web site, but a web site does not do anything for voters if they do not look at it. By pushing the web site content to voters through an aggressive e-mail campaign, we can increase web traffic to the campaign site. The Web address for the campaign site should go on all literature and campaign materials as possible. In addition, an e-mail push during the final legs of the campaign will bump traffic exponentially.

The Troy campaign was one of the first races in the county ever to have a web site. Troy launched her site in 1999 in preparation for the 2000 elections. Since then, social media has exploded, and we will be taking advantage of it.

Beginning 45 days out, the Troy campaign will begin running Facebook ads. These ads will raise name awareness and be targeted to users of voting age within a five mile radius of each municipality in Cook County.

We will also push web content and link to YouTube videos through Twitter, Facebook and LinkedIn. The web site will link to all of the campaign's profile. Through the use of relevant content, strategic linking, use of social media, and properly using our e-mail lists, our Internet presence will be strong.

Incumbency

Helen Troy has the unique power of incumbency to promote the good deeds of her office and to speak publicly on issues that affect voters. As a current officeholder, Troy should be submitting monthly or bimonthly columns to the local Community Press newspapers – especially those in targeted areas. Topics can range from identity theft and how government officials in any capacity can protect against it, how government officials in any capacity can help fight illegal immigration, predatory lending and other hot button issues.

Furthermore, the message of the office must reflect the numerous awards that have been won.

Troy can also testify on various bills in Columbus thereby getting press for her trips. As such she will be able to claim that "she has had more of an effect on current legislation than Howard Johnson has had, and perhaps that is why voters sent him packing six years ago."

Troy should also conduct two or three town hall forums throughout the county during the campaign. These forums should be tailored to issues that voters will be concerned about when voting.

Targeting

In reviewing the 2008 results of candidates, a comparison of John McCain's performance to that of Helen Troy will be helpful in determining where Troy can improve her vote totals in 2008. Areas that stick out as needing improvement include:

- McKinley Township
- McKinley City
- Taft City
- Harding Township
- Hayes Township
- Garfield City
- Grant Village

In particular, John McCain outperformed Troy by more than 8.5% in the 102nd Ohio House District – the district now represented by William

Hackforth. McCain received more than 9,000 more votes than Troy, and this area accounts for the largest disparity in performance between McCain and Troy in 2008. As a graduate of Maple Hills, this should not be a difficult task to reconnect with the West Side.

Other areas that Helen Troy received between 47%and 53% of the vote (areas that can be improved) include:

- Lochland
- Mt. Joy
- North Freemont
- Columbus Twp.
- Fieldspring Twp.
- 25th Ward – Taft City
- 4th Ward – Taft City
- Autumndale

Geographically, the Troy campaign should focus attention on natural coalitions to bolster support. Republican clubs, women's organizations, conservative groups, pro-life, pro-2nd Amendment and other organizations are ones in which the Troy campaign should spend some time.

Images

Images requested for campaign:

- Old campaign signs or logos
- Any swearing in photos from the past
- Photos with parents
- Family Photo (if possible)
- Photo with any parents
- Photo with Sheriff
- Photo with Clerk
- Photo with Congressman

- Photo with State Legislator
- Photo going door-to-door
- Photo with sea of supporters in "Troy" shirts

Opposition Research

Having been an elected officeholder for many years, Howard Johnson has a history of votes that are part of the public record. Also, it is important to obtain information from past ethics reports as well as contributions. Information to be gathered should include:

- All votes on Council
- All votes and initiatives as Mayor
- All votes as a state legislator
- Any "silly" programs
- All proposed legislation
- Any intelligence from other legislators
- Attendance to meetings – did Johnson have a high rate of absenteeism?
- Personnel files from past employers
- ethics disclosure reports
- Past contributors from State of Ohio
- Past contributors locally
- Property records
- Records of real estate dealings he has participated in or his employees
- Any record of money or advantage gained on property or otherwise in areas he had influence as elected officeholder
- Any delinquent taxes
- Liens/Judgments
- Tickets/criminal
- Past campaign expenditures
- Voting record from BOE

Appendix B –
Sample Prospect Letter

Keep Helen Troy, Cook County Solicitor

A prospect letter is a fundraising letter that is sent to prospective donors. Prospective donors can be identified from past donor lists of other candidates, voter database files, phone call identification, members of friendly organizations and other methods.

The point of a prospect letter is to personalize it to the individual being asked to contribute, and to create a need and urgency for the donor to want to give. It is also helpful if a candidate can supply a specific purpose for the particular donation being sought.

September 6, 2012

John Doe
555 Ohio Drive
Taft City, Ohio

Dear John, ❶

Two months from today is Election Day, and I need your help. ❷

Labor Day has now come and gone, and this summer flew by. The Troy campaign was out in force at the various community festivals, and we are looking forward to the Oktoberfest season!

The Democrats have targeted my race, and Howard Johnson has been raising money to defeat me. Although we have been raising money as well, we have to compete and educate voters about our success in office over the past four years. ❸

We need to tell people how we have won awards for customer service, our web site, our computer system and the efficiency our office has improved since you last voted for me four years ago.

We have a great staff of people who work hard to serve the public and bring incredible service to those who need us.

Unfortunately, Howard Johnson doesn't want our story out there and is spreading misinformation. He doesn't tell people about the many awards we have won or how we are spending less now than four years ago. Howard Johnson will say whatever he has to in order to get this job.

Under the Helen Troy administration, **we have raised our service to a level never before seen, and we have cut costs doing it.**

The Troy campaign needs to tell its success story on television, and we desperately need your help to do this.

Enclosed is a self-addressed envelope. I ask you to take a few moments of your time to fill it out. I also ask that you consider sending along a donation to help the Troy campaign tell its story on television.

Your generous contribution of $100 will be helpful in our television effort. $100 allows us to play one spot on the local network morning show or one spot on cable news in the evening. If you are unable to give $100 but still wish to contribute, then I ask you to consider a smaller gift of $50 or $25.

Every little bit helps, and your donation will immediately go to our television campaign.

If you would allow us to place a yard sign in your yard, please indicate so on the enclosed envelope as well, or you can sign up to volunteer.

John, your help is greatly appreciated, and I cannot win without you.

Please send the enclosed envelope to my campaign at your earliest convenience.

Thank you for your support, and I look forward to seeing you on the campaign trail!

Sincerely,

Helen Troy
Cook County Solicitor

Elements that help make a fundraising letter work:

❶ Personalize the letter – This immediately helps connect directly to the prospective donor. Generic salutations have a much lower rate of success, and the chances that the recipient will read past the salutation are much less.

❷ It is usually a good idea to get right to the point in the first few sentences. Readers do not want to guess at why they received a letter, and the campaign does not want prospective donors to wonder why they are reading a letter.

❸ Create a need - Prospective donors must understand why the campaign needs money. Donors do not give for the sake of giving.

❹ Create urgency. The readers' attention will also be drawn to the bolded sections. The urgency will help with getting a prospective donor to act sooner.

❺ If a campaign can specify exactly how a prospective donor's money will be spent, then the donor will be more likely to give. Every campaign wants money, but people who are parting with their money like to understand exactly where there investment is going.

Appendix C –
Sample Remittance Envelope
Keep Helen Troy, Cook County Solicitor

When sending a solicitation in the mail, it is important to make it as easy as possible for people to send back their money and information. On this page and the next page is an example of a remittance envelope. Notice that the flap is nearly as long as the envelope so that the responder can print their information in the spaces provided.

Yes, Helen, you can count on me. We need good leaders to keep us safe. I'll support you by:

- ☐ Placing a sign in my yard
- ☐ Volunteering in the campaign office
- ☐ Distributing literature to my neighbors
- ☐ Writing letters to editors and/or writing on blogs
- ☐ Providing sign locations
- ☐ Making phone calls
- ☐ Working at a poll on Election Day

Helen, I know it takes money to run a campaign. Please accept my donation of:

☐ $1,000   ☐ $500   ☐ $100   ☐ $50   ☐ Other $_____

---

fold

Name

Address

City, ST ZIP

Phone   Email

Employer   Occupation

I also participate with the following:

☐ Professional linking sites   ☐ Blogging   ☐ forward emails to friends
☐ Internet video   ☐ Face pages

Other information can be gathered on these envelopes such as key issues for this particular voter. Information is one of the four resources of a campaign.

A disclaimer stating who paid for the mailing and the address of the campaign committee can go here.

Seal Line

Inside Self-Addressed Return Envelope Foldover

fold

Keep Troy Solicitor
555 Main Ave.
Taft City, OH

Outside Self-Addressed Return Envelope Foldover

Appendix D –
Sample Press Releases
Keep Helen Troy, Cook County Solicitor

The following pages contain sample press releases from the Helen Troy Campaign. Although the Troy campaign is a fictitious campaign in a fictitious county, the elements are the same. Successful press releases have the date of the release as well as the name and phone number of the campaign press contact clearly visible. The style of the press release is also an "inverted pyramid" meaning that the important information is in the first paragraph, and less important information is placed in subsequent paragraphs. The three "pound" symbols at the end of the release signal the reporter that there is no further text forthcoming.

MEDIA RELEASE

FOR IMMEDIATE RELEASE
January 9, 2012
Contact: Helen Troy, cell: 555-555-1212 ❶

Troy Makes it Official

Republican Solicitor Troy Files to Keep Seat ❷

(Taft City, OH) Cook County Solicitor Helen Troy has filed her petitions to keep the seat to which she was elected four years ago after unseating long-time Solicitor F. Gilbert Quinlan. ❸

"In the time that I have been Solicitor, I am pleased with the work we have done," said Troy. "I am particularly proud of the effort we have made to protect consumer information in Cook County. The advances we have made in our computer system and office efficiency serve the people of Cook County well." ❹

Troy will run her campaign highlighting her experience as a small business owner and employer for over 20 years as well as her extensive legal background and experience as an assistant prosecutor and County Solicitor. ❺

Issues that Troy has placed at the top of her priorities include consumer protection, efficiency in government, and customer service. ❻

"One of the biggest problems Ohio faces is protecting consumers from fraud," Troy said. "We must make our records accessible but safe so that the public is served best." ❼

Troy is partner in the law firm of Troy and Roma providing legal services to Taft City and surrounding townships. She is a lifelong Cook County resident living in Taft City with her husband Perry. They have three children William, Laura and Anthony. ❽

❾

Elements of this press release:

❶ Always have contact information. If not the candidate, then the appropriate campaign professional associated with the campaign should be listed.
❷ Use the candidate's name in the headline. Headline should be relevant and short. Keep it simple.
❸ Get to the point. The first paragraph in a press release, as well as a news story, will always tell the reader what the story is about. The following paragraphs add details to the opening paragraph. The first paragraph is the exposition.
❹ Quote the candidate early in the release. The quote should be something that reporters will find "quotable." This means that

the quote should be relevant and contain some level of interesting fact or assertion. The more interesting the quote is to readers, the more likely it will be used.

❺ Listing strengths of the candidate is good – readers should be acquainted with the candidate's strengths.

❻ List the issues that voters care about. By the time a campaign makes an announcement, it should have completed the footwork to know what issues "move" voters.

❼ A second quote allows the candidate to say something more specific. In this instance, the candidate is addressing an issue that the campaign identified as important to voters.

❽ Background information allows reporters to fill column inches if they need to. Always provide pertinent background information or the reporter may choose to use their own notes, and a campaign is never sure what notes a reporter may have made.

❾ The end of a press release, media release, or other transmission traditionally ends with some sort of signal that no further pages are forthcoming. The reporter understands that once they have reached a "# # #" or "- 30 -" symbol, they have reached the end of the release.

MEDIA RELEASE

FOR IMMEDIATE RELEASE

March 18, 2012
Contact: Helen Troy, work: 555-555-1212

*Troy Unanimously Endorsed By Bar Association*❶

(Taft City, OH) Republican Solicitor Helen Troy's support from the Cook County Bar Association was reaffirmed this evening in a vote by the Bar's full membership. The vote for Troy's endorsement was unanimous. ❷

"I am honored by, and thankful for, the confidence the Cook County Bar has placed in me," said Troy. "I am working hard to serve Cook County, and I am working just as hard to run a campaign."

Over 300 members of the Cook County Bar Association were in attendance to vote on the endorsement. Members included many from the 100th District that Troy's opponent, Howard Johnson represented for a single term in the Ohio legislature six years ago before being ousted in an election. ❸

"The Bar Association is an excellent cross section of the County, and they know me and my opponent well. I look forward to keeping this seat in firm conservative, Republican hands for many years to come," Troy said. ❹

Troy is a Taft City attorney and has operated a successful law practice for over 25 years with her law partner Frank Roma. Troy is the former Law Director of Taft City where she was elected for three terms. Helen and her husband Perry live in Taft City and have three children, William, Laura and Anthony.

Elements of this press release:
   ❶ The headline is powerful – the candidate received a unanimous endorsement.
   ❷ Make sure that the first paragraph helps support the validity of the headline.
   ❸ The information in this statement helps diminish any "shine" that Troy's opponent may have. If the opponent is not well known, it is best to leave his or her name out of the press release.
   ❹ This statement explains the relevance of the endorsement.

Appendix E –
Sample Media Advisory
Keep Helen Troy, Cook County Solicitor

Below is a media advisory. A media advisory alerts the press that a newsworthy event is going to happen. Media advisories usually go out to announce press conferences or the appearance of a candidate at a newsworthy event. This advisory is teasing a press conference for the following day.

MEDIA ADVISORY AND PHOTO OP
Aril 10, 2012
CONTACT: Helen Troy
555-555-1212 ❶

QUESTIONABLE TRAVEL EXPENSES DISCOVERED AT HOWARD JOHNSON'S OFFICE ❷

Troy blasts former State Rep. for excessive staff travel ❸

In response to questions about having the highest absentee rate while a State Representative, Howard Johnson suggested that the reason he missed nearly one out of every five meetings in 2002 is because he was traveling. The Troy campaign has learned that Johnson's staff racked up quite a travel bill on the taxpayer's dime. ❹

WHAT: **Find out exactly how much of your tax money was wasted on**

travel expenses for State Representative Howard Johnson and his staff . . . and find out what you can do to stop further abuses! ❺

WHEN: **TOMORROW! – THURSDAY, APRIL 11 1:00 P.M. ❻**

WHERE: **CONFERENCE ROOM OF ZZZ TRAVEL CENTER DOWNTOWN ❼**

# # #

Elements of this media advisory:

❶ Date and contact information are important if the press is going to call.

❷ Although it is just a media advisory, this teaser may make mention on the news ahead of time if an outlet chooses to report on it.

❸ This is an extension of the teaser. This makes certain that the media knows it will obtain something worth airing.

❹ Do not provide too much information, but give enough to let people know there is a legitimate issue..

❺ Sometimes the media is aware that there is an issue out there, but unless someone is willing to make it news, they may not run with it. If the media already has this issue on its radar, then they know they will have newsworthy information.

❻ Be specific about time and location. If parking might be an issue for media trucks, then make special arrangements and let the media know in the advisory.

❼ The venue helps the press understand that there will be an illustration – by holding a press conference about travel in a travel agency, the media will be able to play on the irony that the campaign has introduced.

Appendix F –
Sample Talent Release Form
Keep Helen Troy, Cook County Solicitor

Everyone who appears in any sort of campaign ad including direct mail, television, radio, newsprint, web site or any other medium should have a consent or release form on file with the campaign. These forms are important so that the campaign knows who has given explicit consent for use in the campaign. If the campaign uses talent without explicit consent, then it may end up in a legal battle, and the opponent's campaign may have a campaign issue where it did not before.

TALENT RELEASE FORM

I hereby consent to the use of the photographs, portraits, motion pictures, voice recording, electronic images, video, slides or prints described below by the Keep Helen Troy Solicitor campaign and the candidate Helen Troy. I consent to the use in full or in part, in any manner in which they seem fit, including use in any and all direct mail, television ads, radio ads, newspaper ads or any other medium the aforementioned candidate or campaign sees fit.

I release the Keep Helen Troy Solicitor campaign, the candidate, representatives, vendors, volunteers, and affiliates from all liability in connection with the use, reproduction, and publication of any of the photographs, portraits, motion pictures, videos, voice recordings, electronic images, slide films, prints, and/or statement or testimonial.

DESCRIPTION OF PHOTOGRAPHS, PORTRAITS, PICTURES, MOTION PICTURES, VIDEO, VOICE RECORDINGS, ELECTRONIC

IMAGES, SLIDE FILMS OR PRINTS

_____

_____

_____

_____

NAME   **SIGNATURE***   **DATE**   **++WITNESS++**

_____

_____

_____

_____

* Parent or guardian should sign if talent is under 18.

Appendix G –
Sample Television Scripts
Keep Helen Troy, Cook County Solicitor

The following pages provide examples of television scripts for the Keep Helen Troy Solicitor campaign. The key is to communicate a single message effectively in the 30 seconds allowed. Campaigns using the Internet for video distribution are not confined to the 30 second rule. Internet spots can run longer, but brevity and simplicity are still important. Campaigns on a budget may be able to purchase air time in 15 second or 10 second increments.

AD COPY DRAFT

Television: _X__   Radio: ____ Internet: ____
Date: 6/15/12   Duration :30
Producer: Strategic Political Consulting

Candidate: Helen Troy

TITLE: Award Winner

CODE: HT0001

VIDEO:	AUDIO:
Pictures of Helen dissolve among courtroom shots of her prosecuting criminals ❶ CG: Helen Troy – Our Award Winning Solicitor	**Male Announcer**: Helen Troy has fought some of the toughest criminals in Cook County – and won. ❷

Dissolve to video of Troy with family CG: Helen Troy - Streets are Safer ❸	**Male Announcer**: And because of Helen Troy's efforts as a former prosecutor and law director for Taft City, our streets are safer. ❹
Dissolve to video of Troy with elected officeholders CG: Helen Troy – Trusted by the People We Trust ❺	**Male Announcer**: That's why Helen Troy is trusted by the people we trust. ❺
Dissolve to video of Helen Troy working at desk writing. Camera slowly tightens on Troy, and she looks up. ❻ CG: Helen Troy – Our Award Winning Solicitor	**Male Announcer (as camera is tightening)**: And Helen Troy is working to protect us as our Award Winning Solicitor. ❻ **Helen**: I'm your County Solicitor, Helen Troy, and I have been working hard to keep your records safe.
Dissolve to yard sign with disclaimer ❼	**Helen**: I'm Helen Troy, your award winning Solicitor, and I ask for your vote November 6th. ❼

Elements of "Award Winner":

❶ If the photos are shot properly, it will be evident that Helen Troy is the tough prosecutor putting a scary looking criminal in his place.

❷ The corresponding language of the audio should match the video.

❸ If much of the district where the candidate is running is made up of families, then the candidate should make an attempt to identify with them. By looking like the voters, the candidate makes a connection.

❹ The audio message lists some of the strengths of the candidate.

❺ Images of people that the voters already know are powerful, especially if those people are popular and well-liked.

❻ An image of the candidate hard at work makes it appear that the candidate belongs in the position. The audio also slips in the "Award Winning" mantra at the same time that the words "Award Winning" appear on the screen.

❼ The campaign logo is now present. Sometimes a candidate may have the logo in the bottom corner of the entire spot. Also, the audio at the end is the candidate making an appeal in her own voice. Voters like to hear candidates as well as see them. If the candidate does not knock on the voter's door, then the television spot may be the one way the candidate can talk to the voter in the home.

AD COPY DRAFT

Television: _X__   Radio: _____   Internet: _____
Date: 6/25/12   Duration :30
Producer: Strategic Political Consulting

Candidate: Helen Troy
TITLE: Response
CODE: HT0002

VIDEO:	AUDIO:
Video of Helen in courtroom speaking to camera. Shot starts very wide to take in State seal, judge's bench, witness stand and jury box. No other talent in courtroom. ❶ CG: Helen Troy – Our Award Winning Solicitor	**Helen**: You have been hearing a lot of things about my campaign. ❶
Tighten fast to Helen's torso as she walks to the rail in front of jury box. CG: Helen Troy – Our Award Winning Solicitor	**Helen**: Over the years as an assistant prosecutor and law director, my life has been threatened by the most vile criminals in this county. ❷
Tighten to head shot of Troy with State Seal visible in background – seal does not need to be in focus. ❸ NO CG.	**Helen**: But until now, no one has ever lied about me, my family, or my record. I am proud of my record serving you and protecting this county. ❸
Switch camera angle with only Helen and jury box in field of view. CG: Helen Troy – Our Award Winning Solicitor ❹	**Helen**: Just as guilty criminal defendants will say anything to avoid justice, my opponent will say anything to get a job – a job that requires trust. ❹

Dissolve to yard sign with disclaimer ❺	**Helen**: I'm Helen Troy, your award winning Solicitor, and I ask for your vote November 6th. ❺

Elements of the "Response" ad:

❶ The setting is the courtroom where the voter perceives that the candidate will be in the job. By shooting the spot in the courtroom, the candidate is showing comfort in the setting. What the candidate is saying is the "hook" that draws the viewer in.

❷ This is an interesting comment. If a viewer was not watching before, he or she is now.

❸ Official seal in the background.provides an "air of authority." Until now what? The viewer wants to hear what's next.

❹ The tight shot of the candidate eliminates distraction so the viewer pays attention to what is being said. In the audio, the candidate is comparing the opponent to the worst criminals in history, but she does not say he is a criminal.

❺ Same ending as the other TV spot helps connect the message of the campaign.

Appendix H – Sample Radio Scripts

Keep Helen Troy, Cook County Solicitor

Radio scripts can be 30 or 60 seconds long. Some stations will have restrictions on radio time. Since there is no visual impact in radio, political radio ads must be crafted with special care. The listener must fully grasp the message without the benefit of images. The first spot is nearly an exact copy of the television spot audio. The second spot is an extended 60 second version. Ads cut for radio can also be uploaded to the Internet.

AD COPY DRAFT

Television: ___   Radio: __X__   Internet: ____
Date: 6/15/12   Duration :30
Producer: Strategic Advantage Consulting

Candidate: Helen Troy
TITLE: Award Winner
CODE: HT0001-R

Music-Auxiliary Sound:	VOICE:
TV spot begins with a second of ambient courtroom sound. Mail Announcer begins after gavel strike is heard with a voice that says "guilty!" Light music track begins and fades in – music with strong beat and baseline. ❶	**Male Announcer**: Helen Troy has fought some of the toughest criminals in Cook County – and won. ❶

Ambient courtroom sound dissolves away, music track volume rises but not overpowering announcer. ❷	**Male Announcer**: And because of Helen Troy's efforts as a former prosecutor and law director for Taft City, our streets are safer ❸
Music continues	**Male Announcer**: That's why Helen Troy is trusted by the people we trust. ❹
Music continues	**Male Announcer**: And Helen Troy is working to protect us as our Award Winning Solicitor. ❺ **Helen**: I'm your County Solicitor, Helen Troy, and I have been working hard to keep your records safe. ❻
Music ends	**Helen**: I'm Helen Troy, your award winning Solicitor, and I ask for your vote November 6th.

❶ The opening helps the listener understand the setting and also provides a "hook."

❷ The voice talent begins talking, so the ambient courtroom noise should go away. Appropriate music is also a way to help the listener feel certain ways about the candidate or what is being said.

❸ The announcer, representing a third party, identifies with the listener and refers to Helen Troy as "our" Solicitor. By saying "our," the announcer identifies with the listeners as being one of them.

❹ If time allows, these "people we trust" should be identified

❺ By slipping in the "Award Winning," the spot reminds the listener that Helen is not the typical Solicitor – she has won awards.

❻ The spot ends with a personal appeal.

AD COPY DRAFT

Television: ___   Radio: __X__   Internet: ____
Date: 6/15/08   Duration - :60
Producer: Strategic Advantage Consulting

Candidate: Helen Troy
TITLE: Award Winner
CODE: HT0001-R

Music-Auxiliary Sound: VOICE:

Music-Auxiliary Sound:	VOICE:
TV spot begins with a second of ambient courtroom sound. Mail Announcer begins after gavel strike is heard with a voice that says "guilty!" Light music track begins and fades in – music with strong beat and baseline.	**Male Announcer**: She's known as the iron hammer. <pause> Helen Troy has fought some of the toughest criminals in Cook County – and won.
Ambient courtroom sound dissolves away, music track volume rises but not overpowering announcer.	**Male Announcer**: And because of Helen Troy's efforts as a former prosecutor and law director for Taft City, our streets are safer. In prosecuting our worst criminals, Helen Troy has put her own safety at risk for our families.
Music continues	**Male Announcer**: That's why Helen Troy is trusted by the people we trust like Governor Cox, and Cook County Sheriff Hugh Gamble.

Music continues	**Male Announcer**: And Helen Troy is working to protect us as our Award Winning Solicitor. Helen Troy saved millions in cost cutting measures last year, and Helen Troy stood up to those who wanted to put your social security numbers on the Internet. **Helen**: I'm your County Solicitor, Helen Troy, and I have been working hard to keep your records safe. Criminals should not be able to steal your identity from the comfort of their homes or the prison computer, and I successfully fought them.
Music ends	**Helen**: I'm Helen Troy, your award winning Solicitor, and I ask for your vote November 4th.

This spot is basically the same as the first spot except that it embellishes the wording more. The beginning starts with giving Helen a tough-sounding nickname. The ad allows for naming some of the people that support Helen. The ad also has more time to list accomplishments that voters will care about. Helen's personal appeal in this ad is also longer.

Appendix I –
Effective and Ineffective
Campaign Literature

Keep Helen Troy, Cook County Solicitor

Campaign literature is the informative "handbill" that campaigns distribute in door-to-door operations and literature drops. The following example shows a good piece of literature in which the key elements are highlighted:

- Candidate's name is large
- Message is clear and simple
- Campaign "brand" or yard sign is visible
- Content is more picture oriented with relatively little wording
- Add web site address to literature as well as social media icons when appropriate

Keep Helen Troy

Our Cook County Solicitor

- Effective literature will use the campaign brand or logo
- Effective literature uses bullets instead of long narrative
- Effective literature utilizes a message consistent with all other campaign materials

Many state laws require a disclaimer stating who paid for the literature. This is a good spot for a disclaimer.

Head shot of candidate

Effective campaign literature Side 1

Helen Troy - Trusted...

Photo of endorsing supporter

Photo of endorsing supporter

Photo of endorsing supporter

Quotes from supporters should be message-based

Quotes from supporters should be brief

Quotes from supporters should be relevant

...by Those WE Trust

Web site can go here

Keep Helen **Troy** Solicitor

Effective campaign literature Side 2

Ineffective campaign literature Side 1

Time for a Change!

This side of the campaign literature has been wasted. Instead of compelling photos and bullet points to communicate information, this side is comprised of a long narrative that busy voters will not take the time to read.

This piece also fails to incorporate the campaign brand that appears on yard signs. The campaign brand should be consistently appearing on literature, social media, television and other campaign materials.

Examples of ineffective literature, such as this one, are taken from actual designs used in campaigns.

Information in this format is less likely to be read by a voter receiving multiple campaign pieces in the mail or at an event. Literature that fails to be compelling is likely to be ignored over better designed pieces.

In politics, candidates must compete with campaigns and hundreds of other messages that voters receive while reading, watching TV, listening to the radio, or surfing the Internet. Keep it simple to make the literature effective.

Effective literature must be visually compelling. Pictures are more effective than merely words on a page.

Ineffective campaign literature Side 2

Appendix J –
Effective and Ineffective
Direct Mail

Keep Helen Troy, Cook County Solicitor

Direct mail follows many of the same rules that campaign literature does except that a campaign may produce many pieces of direct mail to speak to different issues. The same components remain:

- Candidate's name is large
- Message is clear and simple
- Campaign "brand" or yard sign is visible
- Content is more picture oriented with relatively little wording
- Add web site address to literature as well as social media icons when appropriate

Helen Troy keeps us safe!

- As with handouts, direct mail should have bulleted information.

- Newspaper headlines are excellent illustrations because they lend an objective point of view that supports a point.

- The most important information should appear on the address label side because that is what the recipient will look at first.

Troy prosecutes gangs
Taft City Gazette, May 1, 2012

The return address is a good place to place the disclaimer. This allows the rest of the card to be used for message.

Head shot of candidate

Keep Helen
Troy
Solicitor

Effective Direct Mail Side 1

Why won't these people vote for Helen Troy?

Photo of convict	Photo of convict	Photo of convict	Photo of convict
Convict #	Convict #	Convict #	Convict #
Photo of convict	Photo of convict	Photo of convict	Photo of convict
Convict #	Convict #	Convict #	Convict #

Because Helen Troy put them behind bars!

Keep Helen
Troy
Solicitor

Effective Direct Mail Side 2

- Asking questions is a good way to help voters reach a conclusion that you want.
- The photos of convicts will draw attention and set the direct mail apart.
- Remember to use the candidate's name repetitively as well as the brand.

Who can keep us safe?

Helen Troy

- Comparison pieces provide concrete reasons why one candidate is better than the other.

- Remember that asking a question and providing the information allows voters to reach self-realization to the desired answer.

- Illustrating a point with a headline provides third-party support for a point.

vs.
The Opponent

- Use the opponent's weaknesses on comparisons.

- Choose relevant points that resonate with voters.

- Make it simple - do not use information that requires much explanation.

Troy prosecutes gangs
Taft City Gazette, May 1, 2012

The return address is a good place to place the disclaimer. This allows the rest of the card to be used for message.

Effective Direct Mail Side 1

Why is Troy the only choice for solicitor?

	Troy	Opponent
Experience as Solicitor with a conviction rate of 97%	YES!	No
Certified by the state to prosecute capital murder cases	YES!	No
Convicted 11 prisoners sitting on death row	YES!	No
Endorsed by the Fraternal Order of Police	YES!	No

The choice is simple:
Keep Helen Troy Solicitor

Effective Direct Mail Side 2

- Comparison pieces can be more effective than pieces dedicated strictly to being "negative" because they provide side-by-side reasons to vote for one candidate over another.

- If the direct mail asks a question, and the reader draws the desired conclusion on their own by using the facts that were presented, then the conclusion of the voter is more ingrained than a declarative statement.

- If possible, back up assertions with footnotes in order to validate assertions.

Time to set the record straight

Helen Troy's claims are overblown!

If a candidate is spending time trying to downplay the opponent's strengths, then he is losing.

It is also difficult to determine what this piece of literature is about. Both candidates' names are being used which can confuse voters.

This literature fails to be compelling because it uses few pictures. The various fonts are also confusing.

HOWARD
Johnson
for Cook County Solicitor

Paid for by Friends of Howard Johnson
123 Taft Road
Taft City, Ohio

Ineffective Direct Mail Side 1

I am endorsed by Bob Smith

Endorsements can be compelling and effective, but it depends on how they are used. If a campaign's only strength, or reason for running, is a powerful endorsement, then it may not be compelling enough to win a race.

Endorsements should be used in materials when an issue is promoted by the candidate, and the endorsement that is showcased is relevant to that issue.

Bob Smith trusts me - so should you

Ineffective Direct Mail Side 2

Appendix K – Sample Letter Requesting Public Information

Keep Helen Troy, Cook County Solicitor

Public information is generally accessible through the Internet or by phone. A person conducting campaign research should identify the authority from whom certain public information is available. After exhausting resources on the Internet, the researcher should then attempt to gather the information with a phone call. If those steps fail to yield the information requested, a letter is generally the next step. Professional government agencies should not withhold public information, and it is generally considered improper for a government employee to ask why the information is being requested. Some government employees may be nosy and may tell a researcher that by knowing why they want the information, they can better serve them. Either the information exists, or it does not exist, and the government employee does not need to know why the information is being requested.

The request should come from someone not closely tied to the campaign. Although there is nothing wrong with requesting public information, by having a top campaign volunteer or official request information, the likelihood of the opposition discovering the request increases. This type of mistake generally allows the opponent to know what a candidate is seeking and what the candidate will find. Consequently, the value of the information gathered will decrease. Information is one of the four main resources of a campaign, and it should be guarded closely.

July 8, 2012

Public Information Officer
Ohio Ethics Commission
555 Broad Boulevard
Columbus, Ohio

To whom it may concern,

This is a public information request is for any and all Ohio Ethics filings, reports, disclosure forms and any document considered public record that relates to former State Representative Howard Johnson. Years that Howard Johnson was required to file reports include 2000, 2001 and 2002. This request should include those years but not be limited to that time.

Please send all information gathered to:
Greg Gilmore
123 Main Street, Apt. 5
Taft City, Ohio

If you have any questions or require more information to complete this request, please contact me immediately by phone at 555-555-1212

If you are unable to fill this request, please respond in writing with the reason for which this request is denied.

Thank you.

Sincerely,

Greg Gilmore

Appendix L –
Sample Fundraising Script
Keep Helen Troy, Cook County Solicitor

Chapter 5 discusses how the candidate is the campaign's best fundraiser. Donors will more likely respond to a direct appeal from a candidate than most other people. Therefore, a candidate must become comfortable in asking for money.

Below is a sample script of how a conversation may go between a candidate and a donor. Conversations will vary greatly from candidate to candidate and donor to donor. The important elements for a candidate to remember are:

- Short small talk – donors like to know that the candidate has taken a personal interest in them – a good candidate will have notes from which to work that include names and ages of spouses and family members, employment information, and any interests gathered from past conversations
- Acknowledging any past contributions the donor has made
- Creating a need – why the candidate needs the money
- The specific request
- Obtaining a commitment (record and follow-up)

SCRIPT

Helen: Hi, Bob, this is Helen Troy, how are you doing?

Donor: Helen, it's good to hear from you! How is the office doing?

Helen: We're doing great. Did you see in the newspaper where we won an award last month for taxpayer protection by refusing to put personal information on the Internet?

Donor: I did. That's great news. You've made us all proud that we supported you.

Helen: Thanks, Bob. How's Marcy and your boy, William?

Donor: Marcy's fine. I'll tell her you asked about her. She'd love to get together for lunch with you sometime. William is in his sophomore year at Ohio, and I think he wants to be a lawyer like his father. I'm really proud of him.

Helen: Bob, that's great. If he needs a reference, I would be honored to be on his resume. I know how hard of a worker he is.

Donor: Thanks, Helen. ❶

Helen: Bob, I really appreciate the support that you and your partners gave me when I ran last time. I couldn't have done it without you, and you gave me the boost that I needed to win. ❷

Donor: Helen, we need you in that position. Your predecessor was a disaster. All of my people tell me now that your customer service is through the roof, and you respond to requests quickly.

Helen: Thank you for letting me know that. It will encourage my staff to know that people notice their hard work.

Bob, you know that I'm coming up on my reelection, and I have tough opposition from Howard Johnson. He's going to get a lot of money from the unions. ❸

Donor:	I saw that, Helen. We need to make sure he doesn't win. He has no experience, and he doesn't understand the office. That's why he lost his legislative seat after only one term.
Helen:	I understand. That's why I am in full fundraising mode right now. I am calling all of my friends and a lot of people I don't know. I just found out that Howard is going to spend $100,000 on television during the last week of the campaign. I don't have the funds to compete with his big donors yet. Bob, I need your help. Can I count on your support this time?
Donor:	Helen, you can always count on my support. You talked about $100,000. I can't do that much, but what are you looking for?
Helen:	I'd like to know if you would host an event where you would be the main host for $15,000 and invite your associates and friends for $1,000 each. I'd like to raise $50,000 in one night. That would send a strong message that we're going to be tough. ❹
Donor:	Wow. I can probably host an event for you. In fact, I'd love to host an event for you. That's a lot to raise in one night, though.
Helen:	I know it is, but it's not too much more than what you did for me last time. Please know that I am grateful for the help you have already given me.

Can I ask for a home hosted event where you commit to $10,000, and I'll add my own people into the invitations to help get to $50,000? |
| **Donor**: | How close will $50,000 get you to your goal? |

Helen: Bob, your event could make my race. $50,000 makes us competitive on television, and I'm planning on another fundraiser to give us an advantage. I'm going to throw some of my own money into this if I have to. ❺

Donor: Alright, Helen, I admire your tenacity. Count on me and Marcy for $10,000. We'll host the event, and I'll ask my associates to contribute as well. I might need your people to make some calls to your lists to get us to $50,000.

Helen: That's great! Thank you for your support. Should I have my finance chairman call your secretary to set up the particulars?

Donor: That would be fine. Give me about 6 weeks to work on it. ❻

Helen: Thank you, Bob. You don't know how much this means to me.

Donor: I'm glad to help. Thanks for doing a good job as Solicitor.

Elements of this conversation:

❶ Always start with some small talk. The candidate should show some personal interest in their friend, and it makes the conversation much more pleasant. The candidate may even learn some important details by engaging in a short personal conversation before delving into the meat of the solicitation. Most donors have limited time, so it is important not to dwell too long on chit chat.

❷ You can never thank a donor too much for their support. Always acknowledge previous assistance and let the donor know they are appreciated and remembered.

❸ Create a need. Not only is there a campaign coming up, but this candidate has opposition, and she is telling the donor what she is up against thereby communicating a stronger need.

❹ Set a goal to reach. Sometimes the donor will exceed the goal, but most donors will try to meet a realistic goal.

❺ Let the donor know exactly where the money will be spent. When a donor can specifically place a finger on something that a campaign is producing and fund it, then the donor knows exactly what impact he or she is having.

❻ Obtain a commitment, record the commitment and set someone up to follow-up with the donor.

Appendix M –
Sample Phone Scripts –
Advocacy

Keep Helen Troy, Cook County Solicitor

A common tactic that campaigns use is the recorded telephone message. The idea of the recorded telephone message is to deliver an advocacy message on behalf of the candidate in 30 seconds or less. The message can come directly from the candidate or a trusted third party such as a popular elected official.

Successful recorded messages are generally delivered to phones at times when people are not typically at home. The idea is to get the message on the recipient's voicemail so that when they check their messages, they will listen to the whole spiel. Whereas many people get perturbed by recorded calls talking to them when they answer their phone, the nature of voicemail is such that they expect the messages to which they are listening to be recorded. Therefore, an advocacy telephone message is best delivered on voicemail.

Below are a few sample scripts that contain some key elements:

- Message is short
- Candidate's name is mentioned multiple times
- There single theme to each call – Each call should be focused
- Disclaimer informing who paid for the call

SCRIPT 1 – Candidate Call

Hi, this is Helen Troy calling, your award winning county solicitor. I'm sorry that I missed you. I wanted to let you know that I am running for reelection, and I would greatly appreciate your vote. The Troy administration has brought customer service to a new level, and that's why we've been given awards by national organizations. The Troy administration also works to protect your personal information. I'm Helen Troy, and I ask for your vote November 6th. This call was paid for by Keep Troy Solicitor 555-1212.

Script 2 – Trusted Elected Official

Hello, this is your County Sheriff Hugh Gamble. I've known our award winning solicitor Helen Troy for many years. When Helen Troy was a prosecutor, we helped put the bad guys behind bars. As our award winning solicitor, Helen Troy has taken a tough stand to protect your private information. I support Helen Troy, and I ask that you join me in voting for her November 6th. This call was paid for by Keep Troy Solicitor 555-1212.

Script 3 – Spouse

Hi, I'm calling you today to tell you a little about Helen Troy, our award winning county solicitor. There's a side to Helen that you may not know about. Not only is Helen Troy our award winning solicitor and a career crime fighter, she's a loving mother and devoted wife. She takes all of her responsibilities to heart and knows that when she protects you – she protects her own family. How do I know this? Because I'm Helen Troy's husband. Please vote to keep Helen Troy our Solicitor November 6th. This call was paid for by Keep Troy Solicitor 555-1212.